Helen and Alex

Thank you for having me.

Have a wonderful year in australia

Love, Lindsay x

pies and tarts

← oops sorry. That was my wet inky finger!

HOMESTYLE

pies and tarts

MURDOCH BOOKS

contents

Perfect pies and tarts

Crisp and piping hot from the oven, pies, tarts and quiches come in an array of shapes, flavours and uses. They are also a versatile choice for a range of occasions, ideal for picnics, dinner or as a light snack to accompany drinks. A wide variety of ingredients can be used as fillings—from cheese and seasonal vegetables to seafood or any type of meat. These combinations may include familiar favourites such as steak and kidney or more exotic pairings of Tandoori, lamb or the Tunisian classic, brik a l'oeuf.

When it comes to pastry, some of the ready-made varieties can be a convenient option, (and a necessary one in the case of filo, as it is too difficult for the majority of cooks to make), however results are far better if you make your own. From buttery puff to rich short crust, pastry is not technically difficult to make but it does require both a light hand and some patience.

Always allow yourself plenty of time when making pastry as most types needs to rest in the refrigerator at various stages of preparation. Also ensure you have all the ingredients at hand before starting. Unless otherwise recommended in a particular recipe, use butter, not margarine, as pastry made with butter tastes so much better. Take care not to 'work' the pastry too much once wet ingredients have been added to the dry ones as this will strengthen the gluten networks in the flour and make your pastry tough. When rolling pastry out and fitting into a tin, avoid stretching it as this will cause it to shrink in the oven. By paying attention to these few rules, your pastry-making success will be assured and all that's left is to decide which pie, pastry, tart or quiche to create from this fabulous compilation!

Savoury pies

Picnic chicken pies

PREPARATION TIME: 20 MINUTES | TOTAL COOKING TIME: 1 HOUR 15 MINUTES | MAKES 6

400 g (14 oz) minced (ground) chicken

35 g (1¼ oz/¼ cup) shelled pistachios, chopped

½ apple, finely chopped

1 teaspoon finely chopped sage

280 g (10 oz/2¼ cups) plain (all-purpose) flour

80 g (2¾ oz) butter

1 egg, lightly beaten

1 egg yolk

125 ml (4 fl oz/½ cup) vegetable stock

125 ml (4 fl oz/½ cup) unsweetened apple juice

1½ teaspoons gelatine

1   Preheat the oven to 200°C (400°F/Gas 6). Combine the chicken, pistachios, apple and sage in a bowl and season well. Fry a teaspoon of the filling and adjust the seasoning if necessary. Cover and refrigerate until needed.

2   Put the flour and ½ teaspoon salt in a large bowl and make a well in the centre. Put the butter in a small saucepan with 80 ml (2½ fl oz/ ⅓ cup) of water and bring to the boil. Pour into the centre of the well, add the beaten egg and mix to form a smooth dough.

3   Grease a six-hole 80 ml (2½ fl oz/⅓ cup) muffin tin. Set aside one-third of the dough and divide the rest into six portions. Roll each portion into a small circle and line the muffin holes with the dough, leaving a little dough hanging over the side of each cup. Divide the filling among the pastry-lined cups, packing the filling down and making a small dome shape in the centre—the filling will shrink as it cooks. Divide the remaining dough into six portions and roll each into a small circle to make the lids. Brush the edges with water and lay one on top of each pie. Fold up the pastry hanging over the edge and roll or crimp it. Cut a small hole in the top of each pie. Brush with the egg yolk mixed with a tablespoon of water.

4   Put the muffin tin on a baking tray and bake for 30 minutes; then check the pastry tops. If they are still pale, bake for another 5–10 minutes. Leave to rest for 5 minutes, then lift the pies out of the muffin tray, put them on the baking tray and bake for 15 minutes, or until the sides of the pies are golden brown (be careful not to break the pies when you move them).

5   Bring the stock and half the apple juice to the boil in a small saucepan. Sprinkle the gelatine over the surface of the remaining apple juice and leave to go spongy, then pour on the boiling stock and mix until the gelatine dissolves. Place a small funnel (a piping nozzle works well) in the hole of each pie and pour in a little of the gelatine mixture. Leave to settle, then pour in a little more until the pies are full. It is important to fill the pies completely to make sure there are no gaps when the gelatine mixture sets. You may need more or less liquid, depending on how much the meat shrinks. Allow to cool completely before serving.

NUTRITION PER PIE
Protein 25 g; Fat 17 g; Carbohydrate 32 g; Dietary Fibre 3 g; Cholesterol 25 mg; 1565 kJ (375 Cal)

Line the muffin holes, leaving a little pastry hanging over the sides.

Put the pastry lids on top, then fold up the pastry hanging over the side and roll it.

Put a funnel in the hole of the pie and pour in some of the gelatine mixture

Bacon and whole egg filo pies

PREPARATION TIME: 30 MINUTES I TOTAL COOKING TIME: 30 MINUTES I MAKES 6

1 teaspoon oil
4 spring onions (scallions), chopped
6 lean bacon slices, chopped
125 ml (4 fl oz/½ cup) milk
60 ml (2 fl oz/¼ cup) cream
2 tablespoons chopped parsley
pinch of ground nutmeg
7 eggs
10 sheets filo pastry
melted butter, for brushing

1   Heat the oil in a frying pan and cook the spring onion and bacon for 2–3 minutes, then set aside to cool. Mix together the milk, cream, parsley, nutmeg and 1 egg and season with salt and cracked pepper.

2   Brush 1 sheet of filo pastry with the melted butter, then brush another sheet and lay it on top. Repeat until you have a stack of 5 sheets. Cut into 6 squares. Repeat with the remaining 5 sheets of pastry. Place 2 squares together at an angle to form a rough 8-pointed star and fit into a 250 ml (8 fl oz/1 cup) muffin tin. Repeat with the remaining squares.

3   Preheat the oven to 200°C (400°F/Gas 6). Divide the spring onion and bacon mixture evenly between the filo pastry cups. Pour over the cream mixture and carefully break an egg on the top of each pie. Bake for 10 minutes, then reduce the oven to 180°C (350°F/Gas 4) and bake for a further 10–15 minutes, or until the pastry is lightly crisp and golden and the egg is just set. Serve the pies immediately.

Make an 8-pointed star from two pastry squares and place in the muffin tin.

Carefully break an egg over the filling inside the pastry shell.

NUTRITION PER PIE
Protein 15 g; Fat 15 g; Carbohydrate 10 g; Dietary Fibre 1 g; Cholesterol 245 mg; 1130 kJ (270 Cal)

Mini spinach pies

PREPARATION TIME: 45 MINUTES + 30 MINUTES COOLING | TOTAL COOKING TIME: 35 MINUTES | MAKES 24

80 ml (2½ fl oz/⅓ cup) olive oil
2 onions, finely chopped
2 garlic cloves, chopped
150 g (5½ oz) small button mushrooms,
    roughly chopped
200 g (7 oz) English spinach, chopped
½ teaspoon chopped thyme
100 g (3½ oz) crumbled feta cheese
750 g (1 lb 10 oz) shortcrust pastry
milk, to glaze

1   Heat 2 tablespoons of the oil in a frying pan over medium heat and cook the onion and garlic for 5 minutes, or until soft and lightly coloured. Add the mushrooms and cook for another 4 minutes, or until softened. Transfer to a bowl.

2   Heat 1 tablespoon of the oil in the same pan over medium heat, add half the spinach and cook, stirring well, for 2–3 minutes, until softened. Add to the bowl. Repeat with the remaining oil and spinach. Add the thyme and feta to the bowl and mix. Season well and leave to cool.

3   Preheat the oven to 200°C (400°F/Gas 6) and grease two 12-hole round-based patty pans or mini muffin tins. Roll out half the pastry between two sheets of baking paper and cut out 24 rounds with a 7.5 cm (3 inch) cutter. Use these to line the patty tins, then add the spinach filling. Roll out the remaining pastry and cut rounds of 7 cm (2¾ inches) to fit the tops of the pies. Press the edges with a fork to seal.

4   Prick the pie tops once with a fork, brush with milk and bake for 15–20 minutes, or until golden. Serve immediately or leave to cool on a wire rack.

Spoon the spinach filling into the pastry-lined patty tins.

Seal the edges of the pies with a fork, then prick the tops once.

NUTRITION PER PIE
Protein 3 g; Fat 12 g; Carbohydrate 14 g; Dietary Fibre 1 g; Cholesterol 12 mg; 725 kJ (175 Cal)

Little chicken and vegetable pot pies

PREPARATION TIME: 45 MINUTES + 20 MINUTES REFRIGERATION | TOTAL COOKING TIME: 1 HOUR 20 MINUTES | MAKES 6

150 g (5½ oz/1¼ cups) plain (all-purpose) flour
90 g (3¼ oz) butter, chilled and cubed
1 tablespoon finely chopped thyme
1 tablespoon finely chopped flat-leaf (Italian) parsley
3–4 tablespoons iced water

FILLING
750 g (1 lb 10 oz) chicken breast fillets
1 lemon, quartered
5 spring onions (scallions)
2 bay leaves
375 ml (13 fl oz/1½ cups) chicken stock
60 ml (2 fl oz/¼ cup) dry white wine
60 g (2 oz) butter
1 large onion, thinly sliced
1 tablespoon finely chopped tarragon
100 g (3½ oz) button mushrooms, thinly sliced
90 g (3¼ oz/¾ cup) plain (all-purpose) flour
2 large carrots, cut into small cubes
1 celery stalk, cut into small cubes
90 g (3¼ oz) peas
1 egg, lightly beaten, to glaze

1   To make the pastry, sift the flour and ¼ teaspoon salt into a large bowl. Add the butter and rub it into the flour until the mixture resembles fine breadcrumbs. Stir in the chopped herbs. Make a well in the centre of the mixture, add almost all the water and mix with a flat-bladed knife, using a cutting action, until the mixture comes together in beads. Add a little more water if necessary.

2   Gently gather the dough together and lift it out onto a lightly floured work surface. Press together into a ball. Flatten slightly into a disc, wrap in plastic wrap and refrigerate for at least 20 minutes to let the dough relax.

3   Preheat the oven to 180°C (350°F/ Gas 4). Place the chicken, lemon, 4 of the spring onions, bay leaves, chicken stock, white wine, 375 ml (13 fl oz/1½ cups) water and ½ teaspoon of salt in a large saucepan. Bring to the boil over high heat. Reduce the heat and simmer for 20 minutes, until the chicken is cooked through. Remove the chicken from the liquid with a slotted spoon and set aside. Boil the liquid for 10 minutes, or until it has reduced to 500 ml (17 fl oz/2 cups). Strain into a bowl and set aside. Roughly cut the chicken into small pieces.

4   Melt the butter in a large saucepan over medium heat. When it is sizzling, add the onion and cook for 2–3 minutes, or until soft. Add the tarragon and mushrooms and cook, stirring occasionally, for 3–4 minutes, or until the mushrooms are soft. Add the flour and cook, stirring constantly, for 3 minutes. Pour in the reserved poaching liquid, bring to the boil and cook, stirring often, for 2 minutes, or until slightly thickened. Remove from the heat, then stir in the carrot, celery, peas and chicken. Divide the filling evenly among six 375 ml (13 fl oz/1½ cup) ramekins or dariole moulds.

5   Divide the dough into six even portions. Roll out each portion into a flat disc, 12 cm (4½ inches) in diameter (or use a cutter). Moisten the ramekin rims and cover with pastry rounds, pressing down firmly to seal the edges. Re-roll any pastry trimmings to make decorations. Prick the pie tops with a fork, then brush with the egg. Bake for about 30 minutes, or until the pies are golden.

NUTRITION PER PIE
Protein 28 g; Fat 25 g; Carbohydrate 36 g; Dietary Fibre 4 g; Cholesterol 154 mg; 1990 kJ (475 Cal)

Stir the carrot, celery, peas and chicken into the thickened mixture.

Roll out each portion of dough to a circle or use a cutter for neat edges.

Cover the filling with the pastry tops, pressing down firmly to seal the edges.

Sweet potato, pumpkin and coconut lattice pies

PREPARATION TIME: 45 MINUTES + 20 MINUTES REFRIGERATION | TOTAL COOKING TIME: 55 MINUTES | MAKES 8

2 tablespoons oil
1 onion, finely chopped
2 garlic cloves, crushed
1 teaspoon grated ginger
1 small red chilli, chopped
250 g (9 oz) orange sweet potato, peeled and cubed
250 g (9 oz) pumpkin, peeled and cubed
½ teaspoon each of fennel seeds, mustard seeds, ground turmeric and ground cumin
150 ml (5 fl oz) tinned coconut milk
15 g (½ oz/¼ cup) chopped coriander (cilantro) leaves
4 sheets puff pastry
1 egg yolk, to glaze

1   Heat the oil in a pan and cook the onion, garlic, ginger and chilli for 5 minutes, stirring continuously, until the onion is cooked. Add the sweet potato, pumpkin, fennel and mustard seeds, turmeric and cumin. Stir for 2 minutes, then add the coconut milk and 2 tablespoons of water. Cook over low heat for 20 minutes, stirring frequently, or until the vegetables are tender. Stir through the coriander and let cool.

2   Preheat the oven to 190°C (375°F/Gas 5) and grease a baking tray. Cut out eight 9 cm (3½ inch) circles from two sheets of the pastry. Place them on the tray and divide the filling between them, spreading it to within 1 cm (½ inch) of the edge. Mound the filling slightly. Brush the edges of the pastry with a little water.

3   Use a lattice cutter or sharp knife to cut out eight 10 cm (4 inch) circles from the remaining pastry. Carefully open out the lattices and fit them over the mixture. Press the edges together firmly to seal. Using the back of a knife, press the outside edge lightly at 1 cm (½ inch) intervals. Refrigerate for at least 20 minutes.

4   Mix the egg yolk with a little water. Brush the pastry. Bake for 20–25 minutes, until golden.

Mark the remaining two sheets of puff pastry with a lattice cutter.

Open out the lattices, fit them over the filling and press the edges to seal.

NUTRITION PER PIE
Protein 7 g; Fat 30 g; Carbohydrate 40 g; Dietary Fibre 3 g; Cholesterol 45 mg; 1800 kJ (430 Cal)

Mini oyster pies

PREPARATION TIME: 30 MINUTES + 20 MINUTES COOLING | TOTAL COOKING TIME: 45 MINUTES | MAKES 30

500 ml (17 fl oz/2 cups) fish stock
1 tablespoon olive oil
2 leeks, chopped
30 g (1 oz) butter
1 tablespoon plain (all-purpose) flour
1 teaspoon lemon juice
1 teaspoon chopped chives
8 sheets puff pastry
30 fresh oysters
1 egg, lightly beaten, to glaze

1 Pour the stock into a saucepan and simmer over medium heat for 15 minutes, or until reduced by half, to 250 ml (9 fl oz/1 cup).

2 Heat the oil in a saucepan over medium heat. Add the leek and cook, stirring well, for 5 minutes, or until soft and lightly coloured. Transfer to a small bowl to cool slightly.

3 Melt the butter in a small saucepan over low heat. Add the flour and cook, stirring well, for 2 minutes, or until the flour is golden. Remove from the heat and gradually add the stock, stirring well. Return to the heat and bring to the boil, stirring constantly for 2 minutes, or until thickened. Add the lemon juice, chives and leek and season well. Set aside to cool for 20 minutes. Preheat the oven to 200°C (400°F/Gas 6) and grease two baking trays.

4 Using a 6 cm (2½ inch) round cutter, cut out 30 circles of pastry and put one oyster and a heaped teaspoon of the filling on top of each, leaving a narrow border. Lightly brush the edges with beaten egg.

5 Cut thirty 8 cm (3 inch) circles from the remaining pastry. Cover the filling with these rounds and press the edges with a fork to seal. Brush the tops with the remaining beaten egg, put on the trays and bake for 15–20 minutes, or until golden and well puffed.

NUTRITION PER PIE
Protein 3.5 g; Fat 12 g; Carbohydrate 17 g; Dietary Fibre 1 g; Cholesterol 24 mg; 785 kJ (190 Cal)

Gradually add the stock and boil, stirring constantly, until thickened.

Place an oyster and a heaped teaspoon of filling on each pastry round.

Creamy mushroom pie

PREPARATION TIME: 45 MINUTES + 35 MINUTES SOAKING AND CHILLING | TOTAL COOKING TIME: 1 HOUR | SERVES 4–6

250 g (9 oz/2 cups) plain (all-purpose) flour
75 g (2½ oz/½ cup) fine polenta
125 g (4½ oz) butter, chilled and cubed
60 ml (2 fl oz/¼ cup) cream
2–3 tablespoons iced water

FILLING
10 g (¼ oz) dried porcini mushrooms
150 g (5½ oz) oyster mushrooms
1 large leek
150 g (5½ oz) butter
2 large garlic cloves, crushed
200 g (7 oz) shiitake mushrooms, thickly sliced
200 g (7 oz) Swiss brown mushrooms, thickly sliced
350 g (12 oz) field mushrooms, sliced
100 g (3½ oz) enoki mushrooms
2 tablespoons plain (all-purpose) flour
125 ml (4 fl oz/½ cup) dry white wine
125 ml (4 fl oz/½ cup) vegetable or chicken stock
60 ml (2 fl oz/¼ cup) cream
2 tablespoons chopped thyme
1 egg, lightly beaten, to glaze

1   To make the pastry, sift the flour into a large bowl, then stir in the polenta and ½ teaspoon salt. Add the butter and rub into the dry ingredients until the mixture resembles fine breadcrumbs. Make a well in the centre, pour in the cream and mix with a flat-bladed knife, using a cutting action, until the mixture comes together in beads. Add a little iced water if the mixture is too dry.

2   Gently gather the dough together and lift out onto a lightly floured work surface. Press together into a ball and then flatten slightly into a disc. Wrap in plastic wrap and refrigerate for 20 minutes.

3   Soak the porcini mushrooms in 3 tablespoons boiling water for about 15 minutes. Cut any large oyster mushrooms into halves. Thoroughly wash the leek and thinly slice it.

4   Preheat the oven to 210°C (415°F/ Gas 6–7). Heat a baking tray in the oven. Lightly grease an 18 cm (7 inch) pie dish.

5   Drain the porcini mushrooms, reserving the soaking liquid, then coarsely chop them. Heat the butter in a large, deep frying pan over medium heat and cook the leek and garlic for 7–8 minutes, or until the leek is soft and golden. Add all the mushrooms to the pan and cook, stirring, for 5–6 minutes, or until soft.

6   Add the flour to the pan and stir for 1 minute. Pour in the wine and reserved mushroom soaking liquid and bring to the boil for 1 minute. Pour in the stock and cook for 4–5 minutes, or until the liquid has reduced. Stir in the cream and cook for 1–2 minutes, until thickened. Stir in the thyme and season. Cool.

7   Divide the dough into two portions, one slightly larger than the other. Roll out the larger portion between two sheets of baking paper to 3 mm (⅛ inch) thick to line the base and side of the pie dish. Spoon in the cooled mushroom filling, levelling the surface. Lightly brush the exposed pastry with egg.

8   Roll out the remaining dough between the sheets of baking paper until about 3 mm (⅛ inch) thick and cover the pie. Pinch the edges together and pierce the top three times with a fork. Trim the edges. Roll the trimmings and cut into mushroom shapes. Arrange over the pie and lightly brush the top with more egg. Place on the hot tray and bake for 35–40 minutes, or until the pastry is golden brown. Set aside for 5 minutes before slicing.

NUTRITION PER SERVE (6)
Protein 14 g; Fat 48 g; Carbohydrate 51 g; Dietary Fibre 8 g; Cholesterol 173 mg; 2900 kJ (695 Cal)

Mix in the cream, using a cutting action, until the mixture comes together in beads.

Add all the mushrooms to the pan and cook them until they are soft.

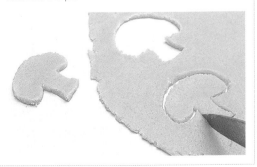
Cut the pastry trimmings into mushroom shapes to decorate the pie.

Shepherd's pie

PREPARATION TIME: 30 MINUTES + COOLING | TOTAL COOKING TIME: 1 HOUR 35 MINUTES | SERVES 6

3 tablespoons olive oil
1 large onion, finely chopped
2 garlic cloves, crushed
2 celery stalks, finely chopped
3 carrots, diced
2 bay leaves
1 tablespoon thyme, chopped
1 kg (2 lb 4 oz) minced (ground) lamb
1½ tablespoons plain (all-purpose) flour
125 ml (4 fl oz/½ cup) dry red wine
2 tablespoons tomato paste (concentrated purée)
400 g (14 oz) tinned chopped tomatoes
800 g (1 lb 12 oz) potatoes, chopped
60 ml (2 fl oz/¼ cup) milk
100 g (3½ oz) butter
½ teaspoon ground nutmeg

1 Heat 2 tablespoons of the oil in a large, heavy-based saucepan and cook the onion for 3–4 minutes, or until softened. Add the garlic, celery, carrot, bay leaves and thyme, and cook for 2–3 minutes. Transfer to a bowl and remove the bay leaves.

2 Add the remaining oil to the same pan and cook the minced lamb over high heat for 5–6 minutes, or until it changes colour. Mix in the flour, cook for 1 minute, then pour in the red wine and cook for 2–3 minutes. Return the vegetables to the pan with the tomato paste and tomato. Reduce the heat, cover and simmer for 45 minutes, stirring occasionally. Season and transfer to a shallow 3 litre (105 fl oz/12 cup) casserole dish and leave to cool. Preheat the oven to 180°C (350°F/Gas 4).

3 Boil the potatoes in salted water for 20–25 minutes, or until tender. Drain, then mash with the milk and butter until smooth. Season with nutmeg and black pepper. Spoon over the mince and fluff with a fork. Bake for 40 minutes, until golden and crusty.

Return the softened vegetables to the pan with the minced lamb.

Spoon the mashed potato over the filling and then fluff with a fork.

NUTRITION PER SERVE
Protein 42 g; Fat 35 g; Carbohydrate 37 g; Dietary Fibre 7 g; Cholesterol 159 mg; 2700 kJ (645 Cal)

Lamb and filo pie

PREPARATION TIME: 20 MINUTES I TOTAL COOKING TIME: 50 MINUTES I SERVES 6

2 tablespoons oil
2 onions, chopped
1 garlic clove, chopped
1 teaspoon ground cumin
1 teaspoon ground coriander
½ teaspoon ground cinnamon
1 kg (2 lb 4 oz) minced (ground) lamb
3 tablespoons chopped parsley
2 tablespoons chopped mint
1 tablespoon tomato paste (concentrated
     purée)
10 sheets filo pastry
250 g (9 oz) unsalted butter, melted

1   Heat the oil in a large frying pan. Add the onion and garlic and cook for 3 minutes, or until just soft. Add the cumin, coriander and cinnamon, and cook, stirring, for 1 minute.

2   Add the minced lamb to the pan and cook over medium–high heat for 10 minutes or until the meat is brown and all the liquid has evaporated. Use a fork to break up any lumps. Add the fresh herbs, tomato paste and a little salt and mix well. Set aside to cool.

3   Preheat the oven to 180°C (350°F/Gas 4) and lightly grease a 33 x 23 cm (13 x 9 inch) ovenproof dish with butter or oil. Remove 3 sheets of filo and cover the rest with a damp tea towel (dish towel) to prevent them drying out. Brush one sheet of pastry with melted butter. Place another 2 sheets of filo on top and brush the top one with butter. Line the dish, letting the excess hang over the side.

4   Spread the filling in the dish and then fold the overhanging pastry over the top. Butter 2 sheets of filo, place one on top of the other and fold in half. Place over the top of the filling and tuck in the edges. Butter the remaining 3 sheets of pastry and cut roughly into squares. Scrunch these over the top of the pie. Bake for 40 minutes or until crisp and golden.

NUTRITION PER SERVE
Protein 47 g; Fat 46 g; Carbohydrate 17 g; Dietary
Fibre 5 g; Cholesterol 105 mg; 2784 kJ (665 Cal)

Spread the lamb over the pastry and then fold the overhanging pastry over the filling.

Scrunch the squares of pastry roughly and arrange them over the top of the pie.

Tourtière

PREPARATION TIME: 40 MINUTES + 20 MINUTES REFRIGERATION + COOLING | TOTAL COOKING TIME: 1 HOUR | SERVES 6

310 g (11 oz/2½ cups) plain (all-purpose) flour
½ teaspoon baking powder
140 g (5 oz) butter, chilled and cubed
½ teaspoon finely chopped thyme
1 teaspoon lemon juice
1 egg, lightly beaten
2–3 tablespoons iced water

FILLING
1 small carrot
1 baby fennel bulb, thick outer leaves removed
4 French shallots (eschalots)
30 g (1 oz) butter
200 g (7 oz) bacon, chopped
3 garlic cloves, crushed
500 g (1 lb 2 ox) minced (ground) pork
1 teaspoon finely chopped thyme
1 teaspoon finely chopped sage
¼ teaspoon ground nutmeg
185 ml (6 fl oz/¾ cup) chicken stock (bouillon)
250 g (9 oz) potatoes, cut into small cubes
1 egg, lightly beaten, to glaze

1   To make the pastry, sift the flour, baking powder and ¼ teaspoon salt into a large bowl and rub in the chilled butter until the mixture resembles fine breadcrumbs. Stir in the thyme, then make a well in the centre and add the lemon juice, egg and a little of the water. Mix with a flat-bladed knife, using a cutting action, until the mixture comes together in beads. Add more water if necessary.

2   Gently gather the dough together and lift onto a lightly floured work surface. Press into a ball and flatten slightly into a disc, wrap in plastic wrap and chill for at least 20 minutes.

3   Finely chop the carrot, fennel and shallots in a food processor. Heat the butter in a large frying pan over medium heat and add the chopped vegetables, bacon, garlic and pork. Cook, stirring often, for 10 minutes, until the pork changes colour, then stir in the thyme, sage and nutmeg. Season well with salt and cracked black pepper. Add 60 ml (2 fl oz/¼ cup) of the stock and simmer for 10 minutes, until it is absorbed. Set aside to cool.

4   Preheat the oven to 200°C (400°F/Gas 6) and heat a baking tray. Grease an 18 cm (7 inch) pie dish. Place the remaining stock in a small saucepan with the potato and simmer for 10 minutes, or until tender. Do not drain. Mash coarsely, then stir into the pork mixture.

5   Divide the dough into two portions, one slightly larger than the other. Roll out the larger portion between two sheets of baking paper until large enough to line the base and side of the dish. Spoon in the filling, levelling the surface. Brush the exposed pastry with the egg.

6   Roll out the remaining dough between the sheets of baking paper until large enough to cover the pie. Trim the edges and crimp to seal. Brush the surface with the egg and make 6–8 small slits over the surface. Bake on the hot baking tray in the centre of the oven for 30 minutes, or until golden.

NUTRITION PER SERVE
Protein 33 g; Fat 30 g; Carbohydrate 42 g; Dietary Fibre 3.5 g; Cholesterol 189 mg; 2350 kJ (560 Cal)

Remove the thick outer leaves from the baby fennel before chopping.

Mash the potato and stock together, then stir into the pork mixture.

Trim the edges of the pastry to fit and then crimp them to seal.

Filo vegetable strudel

PREPARATION TIME: 30 MINUTES + 30 MINUTES STANDING | TOTAL COOKING TIME: 1 HOUR | SERVES 6–8

1 large eggplant (aubergine), thinly sliced
1 red capsicum (pepper)
3 zucchini (courgettes), sliced lengthways
2 tablespoons olive oil
6 sheets filo pastry
50 g (1¾ oz) baby English spinach leaves
60 g (2¼ oz) feta cheese, sliced

1 Preheat the oven to 190°C (375°F/Gas 5). Sprinkle the eggplant slices with a little salt and leave to drain in a colander for 30 minutes. Pat dry with paper towels.

2 Cut the capsicum into quarters and place, skin side up, under a hot grill (broiler) for 10 minutes, or until the skin blackens. Put in plastic bag and let cool. Peel away the skin. Brush the eggplant and zucchini with olive oil and grill for 5–10 minutes, or until golden brown. Set aside to cool.

3 Brush one sheet of filo pastry at a time with olive oil, then lay them on top of each other. Place half the eggplant slices lengthways down the centre of the filo and top with a layer of zucchini, capsicum, spinach and feta cheese. Repeat the layers until the vegetables and cheese are used up. Tuck in the ends of the pastry, then roll up like a parcel. Brush lightly with oil and place on a baking tray. Bake for 35 minutes, or until golden brown.

NOTE: *Unopened packets of filo can be stored in the fridge for up to a month. Once opened, use within 2–3 days.*

Build up layers of eggplant, zucchini, capsicum, spinach and feta cheese.

Tuck in the ends of the pastry, then roll up like a parcel to make a strudel.

NUTRITION PER SERVE (8)
Protein 4 g; Fat 7 g; Carbohydrate 9 g; Dietary Fibre 3 g; Cholesterol 5 mg; 485 kJ (115 Cal)

Brik a l'oeuf

PREPARATION TIME: 30 MINUTES I TOTAL COOKING TIME: 20 MINUTES I MAKES 2

6 sheets filo pastry
30 g (1 oz) butter, melted
1 small onion, finely chopped
200 g (7 oz) tinned tuna in oil, drained
6 pitted black olives, chopped
1 tablespoon chopped parsley
2 eggs

1   Preheat the oven to 200°C (400°F/Gas 6).
Cut the pastry sheets in half widthways. Brush
four sheets with melted butter and lay them on
top of each other. Place half of the combined
onion, tuna, olives and parsley at one end and
make a well in the centre. Break an egg into
the well, being careful to leave the yolk whole.
Season well.

2   Brush two more sheets with melted butter,
place them together and lay them on top of the
tuna and egg. Fold in the sides and roll up into a
neat firm package, still keeping the egg whole.

3   Place on a baking tray and brush with melted
butter. Repeat with the remaining pastry and
filling. Bake for 20 minutes, or until golden.

NOTE: *The yolk will still be soft after 15 minutes
cooking. If you prefer a firmer egg, bake for longer.
Tuna in oil is preferable to brine as it will keep the
filling moist when cooked.*

NUTRITION PER PIE
Protein 35 g; Fat 35 g; Carbohydrate 25 g; Dietary
Fibre 1 g; Cholesterol 260 mg; 2295 kJ (545 Cal)

Carefully break an egg into the centre of the tuna
mixture, without breaking the yolk.

Lay an extra two sheets of filo over the tuna and egg
and fold in the sides.

Roll up the pastry into a neat firm package, keeping
the egg intact.

Rosemary lamb cobbler

PREPARATION TIME: 30 MINUTES | TOTAL COOKING TIME: 2 HOURS | SERVES 4–6

600 g (1 lb 5 oz) boned lamb leg, cut into small chunks
30 g (1 oz/¼ cup) plain (all-purpose) flour, seasoned
30 g (1 oz) butter
2 tablespoons olive oil
8 spring onions (scallions), chopped
3 garlic cloves, crushed
500 ml (17 fl oz/2 cups) beef stock
250 ml (9 fl oz/1 cup) dry white wine
2 teaspoons wholegrain mustard
2 teaspoons finely chopped rosemary
2 celery stalks, sliced
1 teaspoon grated lemon zest
1 teaspoon lemon juice
125 g (4½ oz/½ cup) sour cream

COBBLER TOPPING
185 ml (6 fl oz/¾ cup) milk
1 egg
2 tablespoons melted butter
185 g (6½ oz/1½ cups) plain (all-purpose) flour
2 teaspoons baking powder
1 teaspoon finely chopped rosemary
2 tablespoons finely chopped flat-leaf (Italian) parsley

NUTRITION PER SERVE (6)
Protein 31 g; Fat 28 g; Carbohydrate 31 g; Dietary Fibre 2.5 g; Cholesterol 153 mg; 2180 kJ (520 Cal)

1 Put the lamb pieces and flour in a plastic bag and shake well to evenly coat the lamb. Shake off any excess.

2 Heat the butter and 1 tablespoon of the olive oil in a large saucepan over high heat, and cook the lamb in two batches, for 5 minutes each, until well browned. Add the remaining oil to the second batch if needed.

3 Add half the spring onion to the pan with the garlic and cook for 30 seconds, or until the spring onion is softened. Return all the lamb to the pan with the stock, wine, mustard, rosemary, celery, lemon zest and juice and bring to the boil. Reduce the heat and simmer, stirring occasionally, for 1¼ hours, or until the lamb is tender and the sauce has thickened.

4 Remove from the heat and stir a little of the sauce into the sour cream, then stir it all back into the lamb mixture with the remaining spring onion. Leave to cool. Preheat the oven to 190°C (375°F/Gas 5).

5 Combine the milk, egg and melted butter in a large bowl. Add the combined sifted flour and baking powder with the herbs, cracked black pepper and 1 teaspoon salt. Stir until the batter is thick and sticky, adding a little more flour if it is too wet, or milk if it is too dry.

6 Spoon the lamb into a deep 18 cm (7 inch) pie dish and, using two spoons, cover the top with small dollops of the batter, leaving a little space for spreading. Cook for 30 minutes, or until the topping is risen and golden.

Simmer the mixture until the meat is tender and the sauce has thickened.

Stir a little of the meaty sauce into the sour cream.

Add spoonfuls of the batter to the top of the pie, leaving a little room for spreading.

Cheese and onion pie

PREPARATION TIME: 25 MINUTES + 10 MINUTES COOLING | TOTAL COOKING TIME: 45 MINUTES | SERVES 4

2 tablespoons olive oil
2 onions, chopped
185 g (6½ oz/1½ cups) grated cheddar cheese
1 tablespoon chopped flat-leaf (Italian) parsley
1 teaspoon English mustard
2 teaspoons worcestershire sauce
2 eggs, beaten
2 sheets puff pastry

1 Preheat the oven to 190°C (375°F/Gas 5). Heat the oil in a large frying pan over medium heat, add the onion and cook for 5–7 minutes, or until soft and golden. Transfer to a bowl and allow to cool for 10 minutes.

2 Add the cheese, parsley, mustard and worcestershire sauce to the onion and mix well. Add half the egg to the bowl and season well.

3 Cut each sheet of pastry into a 23 cm (9 inch) circle. Lay one sheet of pastry on a lined baking tray. Spread the filling over the pastry base, piling it higher in the middle and leaving a narrow border. Lightly brush the border with some of the remaining egg and place the second sheet on top, stretching it slightly to neatly fit. Press and seal the edges well and brush the top with the remaining egg. Cut two slits in the top for steam holes.

4 Bake for 10 minutes, then reduce the heat to 180°C (350°F/Gas 4) and cook for another 20–25 minutes, or until the pastry is crisp and golden brown.

Brush the border of the pastry with some of the beaten egg.

Lift the second pastry circle over the cheese and onion filling.

NUTRITION PER SERVE
Protein 21 g; Fat 47 g; Carbohydrate 34 g; Dietary Fibre 2 g; Cholesterol 158 mg; 2625 kJ (630 Cal)

Vegetable and polenta pie

PREPARATION TIME: 20 MINUTES + 15 MINUTES STANDING + REFRIGERATION | TOTAL COOKING TIME: 1 HOUR | SERVES 6

2 eggplants (aubergines), thickly sliced
330 ml (11¼ fl oz/1⅓ cups) vegetable
    (bouillon) stock
150 g (5 oz/1 cup) fine polenta
50 g (1½ oz/½ cup) grated parmesan cheese
1 tablespoon olive oil
1 large onion, chopped
2 garlic cloves, crushed
1 large red capsicum (pepper), diced
2 zucchini (courgettes), thickly sliced
150 g (5 oz) button mushrooms, quartered
400 g (13 oz) tin chopped tomatoes
3 teaspoons balsamic vinegar
olive oil, for brushing

1 Place the eggplant in a colander and sprinkle with salt. Leave for 15 minutes, then rinse, pat dry and cut into cubes.

2 Line a 23 cm (9 inch) round cake tin with foil. Pour the stock and 330 ml (11¼ fl oz/ 1⅓ cups) water into a saucepan. Bring to the boil, add the polenta and stir over low heat for 5 minutes, or until the mixture is thick. Remove from the heat and stir in the cheese until it melts. Spread into the tin and smooth the surface. Refrigerate until set.

3 Preheat the oven to 200°C (400°F/ Gas 6). Heat the oil in a large saucepan and add the onion. Cook over medium heat, stirring occasionally, for 3 minutes, or until soft. Add the garlic and cook for a further minute, then add the vegetables. Bring to the boil, then simmer, covered, for 20 minutes, until the vegetables are tender. Stir in the vinegar and season.

4 Transfer the vegetable mixture to a 23 cm (9 inch) pie dish, piling it up slightly in the centre. Turn out the polenta, peel off the foil and cut into 12 wedges. Arrange the polenta over the vegetables—don't worry about any gaps. Brush lightly with olive oil and bake for 30 minutes, or until lightly brown and crisp.

NUTRITION PER SERVE
Protein 8 g; Fat 8.5 g; Carbohydrate 23 g; Dietary Fibre 4.5 g; Cholesterol 8 mg; 855 kJ (205 Cal)

Cook the polenta, stirring, until all the liquid is absorbed and it is very thick.

Arrange the polenta wedges over the vegetable mixture.

Moroccan beef pies

PREPARATION TIME: 45 MINUTES + 30 MINUTES REFRIGERATION | TOTAL COOKING TIME: 1 HOUR 30 MINUTES | MAKES 4

1 tablespoon oil
2 garlic cloves, crushed
1 onion, cut into thin wedges
2 teaspoons ground cumin
2 teaspoons ground ginger
2 teaspoons paprika
pinch saffron threads
500 g (1 lb 2 oz) round steak, cubed
375 ml (13 fl oz/1½ cups) beef stock
    (bouillon)
1 small cinnamon stick
100 g (3½ oz) pitted prunes, halved
2 carrots, sliced
1 teaspoon grated orange zest

¼ preserved lemon, rinsed, pith and flesh
    removed, finely chopped, optional
200 g (7 oz) Greek-style yoghurt, optional

PASTRY
250 g (9 oz/2 cups) plain (all-purpose) flour
125 g (4½ oz) butter, chilled and cubed
1 egg, lightly beaten
1–2 tablespoons iced water

NUTRITION PER PIE
Protein 40 g; Fat 40 g; Carbohydrate 64 g; Dietary
Fibre 6.5 g; Cholesterol 205 mg; 3183 kJ (760 Cal)

1 Heat the oil in a large saucepan, add the garlic and onion and cook for 3 minutes, or until softened. Add the cumin, ginger, paprika and saffron and stir for 1 minute, or until fragrant. Add the meat and toss until coated. Add the stock, cinnamon stick, prunes and carrot. Bring to the boil, reduce the heat and simmer, covered, for 30 minutes. Increase the heat to medium, add the orange zest and cook, uncovered, for 20 minutes, or until the liquid has reduced and thickened slightly. Remove the cinnamon stick and cool completely.

2 To make the pastry, sift the flour into a large bowl. Rub the butter into the flour until it resembles fine breadcrumbs. Make a well in the centre, add the egg and water and mix with a flat-bladed knife, using a cutting action, until the mixture comes together in beads.

3 Gently gather the dough together and lift onto a lightly floured surface. Press into a ball, wrap in plastic and refrigerate for 30 minutes.

4 Preheat the oven to 200°C (400°F/Gas 6). Grease four 9 cm (3½ inch) pie tins. Divide the dough into four pieces and roll out between two sheets of baking paper to make 20 cm (8 inch) circles. Press into the tins, leaving the excess hanging over the sides.

5 Divide the filling among the tins. Fold over the excess pastry, pleating as you go. Place on a baking tray and bake for 35–40 minutes, or until golden. If using, combine the preserved lemon and yoghurt and serve with the pies.

Cook the beef mixture until the liquid has reduced and thickened slightly.

Gently gather the dough together and press into a ball before chilling.

Fold the overhanging pastry over the filling, pleating as you go.

Chicken coriander pie

PREPARATION TIME: 40 MINUTES | TOTAL COOKING TIME: 45 MINUTES | SERVES 4

50 g (1¾ oz) butter
2 onions, chopped
100 g (3½ oz) button mushrooms, sliced
250 g (9 oz) cooked chicken, chopped
4 hard-boiled eggs
1 tablespoon plain (all-purpose) flour
280 ml (9¾ fl oz) chicken (bouillon) stock
1 egg yolk
3 tablespoons chopped coriander (cilantro)
    leaves
250 g (8 oz) block or packet puff pastry
1 egg, lightly beaten, to glaze

1   Melt half the butter in a large pan. Add the onion and mushrooms and cook for 5 minutes, or until soft, then stir in the chicken. Spoon half the mixture into a 20 cm (8 inch) round, straight-sided pie dish. Slice the eggs and lay over the chicken, then top with the remaining mixture.

2   Preheat the oven to 200°C (400°F/Gas 6). Melt the remaining butter in a saucepan, add the flour and cook for 1 minute. Gradually add the stock and cook for 4 minutes, stirring constantly, then remove from the heat. Stir in the egg yolk and coriander and season. Leave to cool, then pour over the chicken filling in the pie dish.

3   Roll out the pastry into a square larger than the pie dish. Dampen the rim with water and lay the pastry over the top, pressing down firmly to seal. Trim the edges. Roll the leftover pastry into a long strip. Slice it into three equal lengths and make a plait. Brush the top of the pie with egg and place the plait around the edge. Brush again with the remaining egg. Make a few slits in the centre and bake for 35 minutes, until golden.

Slice the hard-boiled eggs and arrange them over the chicken filling.

Lay the decorative plait around the edge of the pie, securing with beaten egg.

NUTRITION PER SERVE
Protein 25 g; Fat 35 g; Carbohydrate 30 g; Dietary
Fibre 3 g; Cholesterol 385 mg; 2220 kJ (530 Cal)

Veal pie with Jerusalem artichoke and potato topping

PREPARATION TIME: 40 MINUTES | TOTAL COOKING TIME: 1 HOUR 20 MINUTES | SERVES 4–6

1 tablespoon olive oil
500 g (1 lb 2 oz) lean minced (ground) veal
2 onions, finely chopped
3 garlic cloves, crushed
150 g (5½ oz) bacon, diced
½ teaspoon dried rosemary
2 tablespoons plain (all-purpose) flour
pinch of cayenne pepper
125 ml (4 fl oz/½ cup) dry white wine
150 ml (5 fl oz) cream
1 egg, lightly beaten
2 hard-boiled eggs, roughly chopped

TOPPING
500 g (1 lb 2 oz) Jerusalem artichokes
400 g (14 oz) potatoes
100 g (3½ oz) butter

1 Heat the oil in a large frying pan and cook the veal, onion, garlic, bacon and rosemary, stirring often, for 10 minutes, or until the veal changes colour. Stir in the flour and cayenne pepper and cook for 1 minute. Pour in the wine and 125 ml (4 fl oz/½ cup) water. Season well. Simmer for 5 minutes, or until the sauce is very thick, then stir in the cream, beaten egg and chopped egg.

2 Preheat the oven to 210°C (415°F/Gas 6–7). Lightly grease a 20 cm (8 inch) spring-form tin. Peel and chop the artichokes and potatoes and boil together for 12–15 minutes, until tender. Drain, add the butter, then mash until smooth.

3 Spoon the filling into the tin then spread with the topping. Bake for 20 minutes, then reduce the heat to 180°C (350°F/Gas 4) and bake for another 30 minutes, or until golden on top.

When the sauce has thickened, stir in the cream, beaten egg and chopped egg.

Mash the cooked potato and artichoke with butter until smooth.

NUTRITION PER SERVE (6)
Protein 31 g; Fat 38 g; Carbohydrate 17 g; Dietary Fibre 4 g; Cholesterol 258 mg; 2265 kJ (540 Cal)

Rich beef pie

PREPARATION TIME: 35 MINUTES + 30 MINUTES REFRIGERATION | TOTAL COOKING TIME: 2 HOURS 45 MINUTES | SERVES 6

FILLING
2 tablespoons oil
1 kg (2 lb 4 oz) chuck steak, cubed
1 large onion, chopped
1 large carrot, finely chopped
2 garlic cloves, crushed
2 tablespoons plain (all-purpose) flour
250 ml (9 fl oz/1 cup) beef stock (bouillon)
2 teaspoons thyme
1 tablespoon worcestershire sauce

PASTRY
250 g (9 oz/2 cups) plain (all-purpose) flour
150 g (5½ oz) butter, chilled and cubed
1 egg yolk
3–4 tablespoons iced water
1 egg yolk and 1 tablespoon milk, to glaze

1 Heat 1 tablespoon of the oil in a large frying pan and brown the meat in batches. Remove from the pan and set aside. Heat the remaining oil, add the onion, carrot and garlic, and cook over medium heat until browned.

2 Return all the meat to the pan and stir in the flour. Cook for 1 minute, then remove the pan from the heat and slowly stir in the stock, mixing the flour in well. Add the thyme and worcestershire sauce, and bring to the boil. Season to taste.

3 Reduce the heat to very low, cover and simmer for 1½–2 hours, or until the meat is tender. During the last 15 minutes of cooking remove the lid and allow the liquid to reduce until very thick. Cool completely.

4 To make the pastry, sift the flour into a large bowl and add the butter. Using your fingertips, rub the butter into the flour until it resembles fine breadcrumbs. Add the egg yolk and 2 tablespoons of iced water, and mix with a flat-bladed knife, using a cutting action, until the mixture comes together in beads, adding a little more water if necessary. Turn out onto a lightly floured surface and gently gather together to form a smooth dough. Cover in plastic wrap and refrigerate for 30 minutes.

5 Preheat the oven to 200°C (400°F/Gas 6). Divide the pastry into two pieces and roll out one piece on a sheet of baking paper until large enough to line a 23 cm (9 inch) pie dish. Fill with the cold filling and roll out the remaining piece of pastry until large enough to fully cover the dish. Dampen the edges of the pastry with a little water. Lay the top piece of pastry over the pie and gently press the pastry together. Trim the edges with a sharp knife and re-roll the trimmings to make decorations for the pie top.

6 Cut a few slits in the top of the pastry to allow the steam to escape. Beat together the egg yolk and milk, and brush over the top of the pie. Bake in the oven for 20–30 minutes, or until the pastry is golden.

NUTRITION PER SERVE
Protein 40 g; Fat 35 g; Carbohydrate 35 g; Dietary Fibre 3 g; Cholesterol 235 mg; 2580 kJ (615 Cal)

The baking paper will help you lift the pastry into the pie dish.

Spoon in the filling then top the pie with the second piece of pastry.

Press the pieces of pastry together and trim off the excess with a sharp knife.

Spinach pie

PREPARATION TIME: 30 MINUTES + 30 MINUTES CHILLING | TOTAL COOKING TIME: 1 HOUR | SERVES 8–10

250 g (9 oz/2 cups) plain (all- purpose) flour
80 ml (2½ fl oz/⅓ cup) olive oil
1 egg, beaten
4–5 tablespoons iced water
1 kg (2 lb 4 oz) spinach, stalks removed, chopped
1 tablespoon olive oil
1 large leek, sliced
4 garlic cloves, crushed
500 g (1 lb 2 oz/2 cups) ricotta cheese
90 g (3¼ oz/1 cup) grated pecorino cheese
300 g (10½ oz) crumbled feta cheese
3 eggs, lightly beaten
3 tablespoons chopped dill
15 g (½ oz/½ cup) chopped flat-leaf (Italian) parsley

1 Sift the flour and ½ teaspoon of salt into a large bowl and make a well in the centre. Mix together the oil, egg and most of the water, and add to the flour. Mix in with a flat-bladed knife until the mixture comes together in beads, adding a little more water if necessary. Gather the dough and press into a ball. Wrap in plastic wrap and chill for at least 30 minutes.

2 Put the spinach in a large saucepan, sprinkle lightly with water, then cover and steam for 5 minutes, or until wilted. Drain well, squeeze out the excess moisture, then chop finely.

3 Preheat the oven to 200°C (400°F/Gas 6) and heat a baking tray. Grease a 25 cm (10 inch) loose-based fluted tart tin. Heat the oil in a frying pan and cook the leek and garlic over low heat for 5 minutes, until soft. Mix with the cheeses, spinach, egg, dill and parsley and season well.

4 Roll out two-thirds of the pastry between two sheets of baking paper until large enough to line the tin. Fill with the spinach mixture. Roll out the remaining pastry and place on the pie. Trim the edges and make three steam holes in the top.

5 Bake the pie on the hot tray for 15 minutes, then reduce the heat to 180°C (350°F/Gas 4) and cook for another 30 minutes. Cover with foil if the pie is over-browning. Leave for 5–10 minutes before slicing.

Drain the wilted spinach well, then finely chop with a large, sharp knife.

NUTRITION PER SERVE (10)
Protein 20 g; Fat 26 g; Carbohydrate 20 g; Dietary Fibre 4 g; Cholesterol 123 mg; 1660 kJ (395 Cal)

Bacon and egg pie

PREPARATION TIME: 20 MINUTES | TOTAL COOKING TIME: 1 HOUR 10 MINUTES | SERVES 4–6

1 sheet shortcrust pastry
2 teaspoons oil
4 bacon slices, chopped
5 eggs, lightly beaten
60 ml (2 fl oz/¼ cup) cream
1 sheet puff pastry
1 egg, lightly beaten, to glaze

1   Preheat the oven to 210°C (415°F/Gas 6–7). Lightly oil a 20 cm (8 inch) loose-based flan (tart) tin. Place the shortcrust pastry in the tin and trim the pastry edges. Cut a sheet of baking paper to cover the pastry-lined tin. Spread a layer of baking beads, dried beans or rice over the paper. Bake for 10 minutes and then discard the paper and rice. Bake the pastry for another 5–10 minutes, or until golden. Allow to cool.

2   Heat the oil in a frying pan. Add the bacon and cook over medium heat for a few minutes, or until lightly browned. Drain on paper towel and allow to cool slightly. Arrange the bacon over the pastry base and pour the mixed eggs and cream over the top.

3   Brush the edges of the pastry with the egg glaze, cover with puff pastry and press on firmly to seal. Trim the pastry edges and decorate the top with trimmings. Brush with remaining egg glaze and bake for 40 minutes, or until puffed and golden brown.

NUTRITION PER SERVE (6)
Protein 14 g; Fat 26 g; Carbohydrate 23 g; Dietary Fibre 1 g; Cholesterol 215 mg; 1569 kJ (375 Cal)

Spread a layer of dried beans or rice over the paper before blind baking.

Carefully pour the combined eggs and cream over the top of the bacon.

Beef and red wine pies

PREPARATION TIME: 50 MINUTES | TOTAL COOKING TIME: 2 HOURS 40 MINUTES | MAKES 6

60 ml (2 fl oz/¼ cup) oil
1.5 kg (3 lb 5 oz) chuck steak, cubed
2 onions, chopped
1 garlic clove, crushed
30 g (1 oz/¼ cup) plain (all-purpose) flour
310 ml (10¾ fl oz/1¼ cups) dry red wine
500 ml (17 fl oz/2 cups) beef stock (bouillon)
2 bay leaves
2 thyme sprigs
2 carrots, chopped
4 sheets shortcrust pastry
1 egg, lightly beaten
4 sheets puff pastry

NUTRITION PER PIE
Protein 60 g; Fat 47 g; Carbohydrate 51 g; Dietary
Fibre 3 g; Cholesterol 200 mg; 3648 kJ (873 Cal)

1 Heat 2 tablespoons of oil in a large frying pan, add the meat and fry in batches until browned. Remove all the meat from the pan. Heat the remaining oil in the same pan, add the onion and garlic and cook, stirring, until golden brown. Add the flour and stir over medium heat for 2 minutes, or until well browned.

2 Remove from the heat and gradually stir in the combined wine and stock. Return to the heat and stir until the mixture boils and thickens. Return the meat to the pan with the bay leaves and thyme, and simmer for 1 hour. Add the carrot and simmer for another 45 minutes, until the meat and carrot are tender and the sauce has thickened. Season to taste, and remove the bay leaves and thyme. Cool.

3 Preheat the oven to 200°C (400°F/Gas 6) and lightly grease six 9 cm (3½ inch) metal pie tins. Cut the shortcrust pastry sheets in half diagonally. Line the base and side of each pie tin with the pastry and trim the edges. Line each pie with baking paper and fill with baking beads. Place on a baking tray and bake for 8 minutes. Remove the paper and beads and bake for a further 8 minutes, or until the pastry is lightly browned. Cool.

4 Spoon the filling into the pastry cases and brush the edges with some of the beaten egg. Cut the puff pastry sheets in half diagonally and cover the tops of the pies. Trim the excess, pressing the edges with a fork to seal. Cut a slit in the top of each pie. Brush the tops with the remaining egg, and bake for 20–25 minutes, or until the pastry is golden brown.

Fry the steak in batches in a large pan until browned all over.

Line the base and side of each pie tin with the shortcrust pastry.

Cover the filling with puff pastry and trim off the excess with a sharp knife.

Cornish pasties

PREPARATION TIME: 1 HOUR + CHILLING | TOTAL COOKING TIME: 45 MINUTES | MAKES 6

310 g (11 oz/2½ cups) plain (all-purpose) flour
125 g (4½ oz) butter, chilled and cubed
4–5 tablespoons iced water
160 g (5½ oz) round steak, diced
1 small potato, finely chopped
1 small onion, finely chopped
1 small carrot, finely chopped
1–2 teaspoons worcestershire sauce
2 tablespoons beef stock (bouillon)
1 egg, lightly beaten, to glaze

1 Grease a baking tray. Process the flour, butter and a pinch of salt in a food processor for 15 seconds, or until crumbly. Add the water and process in short bursts until it comes together. Turn out onto a floured surface and form into a ball. Wrap in plastic and chill for 30 minutes. Preheat the oven to 210°C (415°F/Gas 6–7).

2 Mix together the steak, potato, onion, carrot, worcestershire sauce and stock. Season well.

3 Divide the dough into six portions and roll out to 3 mm (⅛ inch) thick. Cut into six 16 cm (6¼ inch) rounds. Divide the filling evenly and put in the centre of each pastry circle.

4 Brush the pastry edges with the egg and fold over. Pinch to form a frill and place on the tray. Brush with the remaining egg and bake for 15 minutes. Lower the heat to 180°C (350°F/Gas 4) and bake for a further 25–30 minutes, or until golden.

Mix together the steak, potato, onion, carrot, worcestershire sauce and stock.

Fold the pastry over the filling to form a semicircle and pinch to close.

NUTRITION PER PASTY
Protein 15 g; Fat 20 g; Carbohydrate 40 g; Dietary Fibre 3 g; Cholesterol 100 mg; 1665 kJ (395 Cal)

Fisherman's pie

PREPARATION TIME: 40 MINUTES | TOTAL COOKING TIME: 1 HOUR | SERVES 4

800 g (1 lb 12 oz) white fish fillets
375 ml (13 fl oz/1½ cups) milk
1 onion, chopped
2 cloves
50 g (1¾ oz) butter
2 tablespoons plain (all-purpose) flour
pinch of ground nutmeg
2 tablespoons chopped parsley
150 g (5½ oz/1 cup) peas
750 g (1 lb 10 oz) potatoes, quartered
2 tablespoons hot milk
3 tablespoons grated cheddar cheese

1 Place the fish in a wide pan and cover with the milk. Add the onion and cloves and bring to the boil. Reduce the heat and simmer for 5 minutes, or until the fish is cooked and flakes easily with a fork.

2 Preheat the oven to 180°C (350°F/Gas 4). Remove the fish from the pan, reserving the milk and onion. Discard the cloves. Allow the fish to cool then remove any bones and flake into bite-sized pieces with a fork.

3 Heat half of the butter in a pan, stir in the flour and cook, stirring, for 1 minute. Slowly add the reserved milk, stirring constantly until smooth. Cook, stirring, until the sauce begins to bubble, then cook for another minute. Remove from the heat, cool slightly, then add the nutmeg, parsley and peas. Season and gently fold in the fish. Spoon into a 1.25 litre (5 cup) casserole.

4 Cook the potatoes in boiling water until tender. Drain and add the hot milk and remaining butter. Mash until very smooth. Add the cheese. If the mash is very stiff add a little more milk, but it should be fairly firm.

5 Spoon the potato over the top and rough up with a fork, or spoon the potato into a piping bag and neatly pipe over the top. Bake for 45 minutes, until the potato begins to brown.

NUTRITION PER SERVE
Protein 55 g; Fat 25 g; Carbohydrate 40 g; Dietary Fibre 6 g; Cholesterol 200 mg; 2565 kJ (610 Cal)

Cover the fish fillets with the milk and add the onion and cloves.

For a neat topping on the pie, put the mash in a piping bag and pipe over the filling.

Game pie

PREPARATION TIME: 50 MINUTES + OVERNIGHT SETTING I TOTAL COOKING TIME: 4 HOURS I SERVES 6–8

JELLY

any bones reserved from the game meat

2 pig's trotters

1 onion, quartered

1 carrot, roughly chopped

1 celery stalk, chopped

2 bay leaves

6 black peppercorns

FILLING

250 g (9 oz) pork belly, finely diced

4 bacon slices, chopped

400 g (14 oz) game meat (rabbit, pheasant),
    removed from carcass and finely diced
    (bones reserved)

½ small onion, finely chopped

½ teaspoon ground nutmeg

½ teaspoon ground cinnamon

2 dried juniper berries, crushed

1 teaspoon chopped thyme

PASTRY

500 g (1 lb 2 oz/4 cups) plain (all-purpose)
    flour

90 g (3¼ oz) lard

1 egg, lightly beaten, to glaze

1   To make the stock for the jelly, place all the ingredients and 1.75 litres (61 fl oz/7 cups) water in a large saucepan and bring to the boil over high heat. Remove any froth that forms on the surface. Reduce the heat and simmer for 3 hours, skimming off any froth occasionally. Strain, return the liquid to the pan and cook uncovered until it has reduced to about 500 ml (17 fl oz/2 cups). Cool, then refrigerate.

2   To make the filling, combine all the ingredients in a bowl and season well.

3   To make the pastry, sift the flour and ½ teaspoon salt into a large bowl and make a well in the centre. Bring 200 ml (7 fl oz) water and the lard to the boil in a saucepan. Pour the boiling liquid into the flour and mix with a wooden spoon to form a dough. Gather together and lift onto a lightly floured work surface. Press together until smooth. Cover with foil and put in a warm place to keep the dough warm.

4   Preheat the oven to 190°C (375°/Gas 5) and grease an 18 cm (7 inch) spring-form tin. While the pastry is still warm, roll out two-thirds of the warm dough between two sheets of baking paper and line the base and side of the tin, leaving some hanging over the rim. Spoon the filling into the tin, pressing down well. Roll out the remaining dough to about 4 mm (¼ inch) thick and 20 cm (8 inches) across. Place on top of the tin and pinch the edges together to seal. Trim the edges and cut a small hole in the top of the pie.

5   Roll out the pastry trimmings to make decorations, securing to the pie top with a little of the beaten egg. Glaze the top of the pie with egg and bake for 1 hour 20 minutes. Cover the top with foil after about 45 minutes to prevent it colouring too much. Cool.

6   Warm the jelly to a pouring consistency. Place a small piping (icing) nozzle into the hole in the pie and pour in a little of the jelly. Leave to settle, then pour in more jelly until the pie is full. Fill the pie completely so there are no gaps when the jelly sets. Refrigerate overnight and serve at room temperature.

NUTRITION PER SERVE (6)
Protein 40 g; Fat 20 g; Carbohydrate 63 g; Dietary Fibre 3.5 g; Cholesterol 113 mg; 2455 kJ (585 Cal)

Place the dough on top of the filling and pinch the edges together to seal.

Use a small, sharp knife to cut a hole in the top of the pie.

Insert a nozzle into the hole and pour in a little of the liquid jelly.

Family-style meat pie

PREPARATION TIME: 30 MINUTES + COOLING + 20 MINUTES REFRIGERATION | TOTAL COOKING TIME: 1 HOUR 45 MINUTES | SERVES 6

1 tablespoon oil

1 onion, chopped

1 garlic clove, crushed

750 g (1 lb 10 oz) minced (ground) beef

250 ml (9 fl oz/1 cup) beef stock (bouillon)

250 ml (9 fl oz/1 cup) beer

1 tablespoon tomato paste (concentrated purée)

1 tablespoon yeast extract (eg. marmite)

1 tablespoon worcestershire sauce

2 teaspoons cornflour (cornstarch)

375 g (13 oz) shortcrust pastry

375 g (13 oz) puff pastry

1 egg, lightly beaten, to glaze

1   Heat the oil in a large saucepan over medium heat and cook the onion for 5 minutes, until golden. Increase the heat, add the garlic and beef and cook, breaking up any lumps, for about 5 minutes, until the beef changes colour.

2   Add the stock, beer, tomato paste, yeast extract, worcestershire sauce and 125 ml (4 fl oz/ ½ cup) water. Reduce the heat to medium and cook for 1 hour, or until there is little liquid left. Combine the cornflour with 1 tablespoon water, then stir into the meat and cook for 5 minutes, or until thick and glossy. Remove from the heat and cool completely.

3   Lightly grease an 18 cm (7 inch) pie tin. Roll out the shortcrust pastry between two sheets of baking paper until large enough to line the base and side of the tin. Use a small ball of pastry to help press the pastry into the tin, allowing any excess to hang over the side.

4   Roll out the puff pastry between two sheets of baking paper to make a 23 cm (9 inch) circle. Spoon the filling into the pastry shell and smooth it down. Brush the pastry edges with the egg, then place the puff pastry over the top. Cut off any excess with a sharp knife. Press the top and bottom pastries together, then scallop the edges with a fork or your fingers. Refrigerate for 20 minutes. Preheat the oven to 200°C (400°F/Gas 6) and heat a baking tray.

5   Brush the remaining egg over the top of the pie, place on the hot tray on the bottom shelf of the oven and bake for 25–30 minutes, or until golden and well puffed.

NUTRITION PER SERVE
Protein 38 g; Fat 44 g; Carbohydrate 52 g; Dietary Fibre 3 g; Cholesterol 129.5 mg; 3120 kJ (745 Cal)

Spoon the cooled meat filling into the pastry shell.

Trim the edges of the puff pastry pie top with a sharp knife.

Pumpkin and feta pie

PREPARATION TIME: 30 MINUTES + COOLING + 20 MINUTES REFRIGERATION | TOTAL COOKING TIME: 1 HOUR 35 MINUTES | SERVES 6

700 g (1 lb 9 oz) butternut pumpkin
(squash), cubed
4 garlic cloves, unpeeled
100 ml (3½ fl oz/½ cup) olive oil
2 small red onions, halved and sliced
1 tablespoon balsamic vinegar
1 tablespoon soft brown sugar
100 g (3½ oz) feta cheese, broken into
small pieces
1 tablespoon chopped rosemary

PASTRY
250 g (9 oz/2 cups) plain (all-purpose) flour
125 g (4½ oz) butter, chilled and cubed
60 g (2¼ oz/½ cup) grated parmesan cheese
3–4 tablespoons iced water

1 Preheat the oven to 200°C (400°F/Gas 6). Place the pumpkin and garlic cloves on a baking tray, drizzle with 2 tablespoons of the oil and bake for 25–30 minutes, until the pumpkin is tender. Transfer the pumpkin to a large bowl and the garlic to a plate. Leave to cool.

2 Meanwhile, heat 2 tablespoons oil in a pan, add the onion and cook over medium heat, stirring occasionally, for 10 minutes. Add the vinegar and sugar and cook for 15 minutes, or until the onion is caramelised. Remove from the heat and add to the pumpkin. Leave to cool.

3 While the vegetables are cooling, make the pastry. Sift the flour and 1 teaspoon salt into a large bowl and rub in the butter with your fingertips until the mixture resembles fine breadcrumbs. Stir in the cheese. Make a well, add most of the water and mix with a flat-bladed knife, using a cutting action, until the mixture comes together in beads. Add more water if necessary to bring the dough together.

4 Gather the dough together and lift onto a lightly floured work surface. Press into a ball and flatten slightly into a disc. Cover in plastic wrap and refrigerate for 20 minutes.

5 Add the feta cheese and rosemary to the pumpkin. Squeeze out the garlic flesh and mix it through the vegetables. Season to taste.

6 Roll out the dough between two sheets of baking paper to a 35 cm (14 inch) circle. Remove the top sheet of paper and place the bottom paper with the pastry on a tray. Arrange the pumpkin and feta mixture on top, leaving a 6 cm (2½ inch) border. Fold over the edges, pleating as you fold. Bake for 40 minutes, or until crisp and golden.

NUTRITION PER SERVE
Protein 14 g; Fat 39 g; Carbohydrate 42 g; Dietary Fibre 4 g; Cholesterol 73 mg; 2360 kJ (565 Cal)

Place the diced pumpkin and the garlic cloves on a baking tray and drizzle with oil.

Fold the edges of the pastry over the pumpkin and feta filling.

Italian zucchini pie

PREPARATION TIME: 30 MINUTES + 30 MINUTES REFRIGERATION + 30 MINUTES DRAINING | TOTAL COOKING TIME: 1 HOUR | SERVES 6

310 g (11 oz/2½ cups) plain (all-purpose) flour
80 ml (2½ fl oz/⅓ cup) olive oil
1 egg, beaten
3–4 tablespoons iced water
600 g (1 lb 5 oz) zucchini (courgettes)
150 g (5½ oz) provolone cheese, grated
120 g (4¼ oz) ricotta cheese
3 eggs
2 garlic cloves, crushed
2 teaspoons finely chopped basil
pinch of ground nutmeg
1 egg, lightly beaten, to glaze

1 Sift the flour and ½ teaspoon salt into a large bowl and make a well. Combine the oil, egg and almost all the water and add to the flour. Mix with a flat-bladed knife until the mixture forms beads. Add water if needed. Gather into a ball, wrap in plastic and refrigerate for 30 minutes.

2 Preheat the oven to 200°C (400°F/Gas 6) and heat a baking tray. Grease an 18 cm (7 inch) pie dish. Grate the zucchini, toss with ¼ teaspoon of salt and drain in a colander for 30 minutes. Squeeze out any liquid and place in a large bowl with the provolone, ricotta, eggs, garlic, basil and nutmeg. Season well and mix thoroughly.

3 Roll out two-thirds of the pastry between two sheets of baking paper until large enough to line the base and side of the dish.

4 Spoon the filling into the pastry shell and level the surface. Brush the pastry rim with egg. Roll out two-thirds of the remaining dough between the baking paper to make a lid. Cover the filling and press the edges together firmly. Trim and crimp the rim. Prick the top all over with a skewer and brush with egg.

5 Roll the remaining dough into a 30 x 10 cm (12 x 4 inch) long strip. Use a long sharp knife to cut this into nine 1 cm (½ inch) wide lengths. Press three ropes together at one end and then press them onto the work surface to secure them. Plait the ropes and make two more plaits. Trim the ends and space the plaits parallel across the centre of the pie. Brush with egg. Bake on the hot tray for 50 minutes, or until golden.

Spoon the zucchini filling into the pastry shell and level the surface.

NUTRITION PER SERVE
Protein 21 g; Fat 27 g; Carbohydrate 40 g; Dietary Fibre 4 g; Cholesterol 184.5 mg; 2010 kJ (480 Cal)

Potato filo pies

PREPARATION TIME: 1 HOUR | TOTAL COOKING TIME: 1 HOUR 20 MINUTES | MAKES 6

6 roma (plum) tomatoes, halved lengthways
3 tablespoons olive oil
50 g (1¾ oz) butter
3 garlic cloves, crushed
800 g (1 lb 12 oz) potatoes, unpeeled and
   sliced
500 g (1 lb 2 oz) English spinach, trimmed
12 sheets filo pastry
100 g (3½ oz) butter, melted
2 tablespoons sesame seeds

1 Preheat the oven to 200°C (400°F/ Gas 6). Place the tomato halves, cut side up, on a baking tray, drizzle with 1 tablespoon of the oil and sprinkle with a little salt. Bake for 40 minutes.

2 Heat the butter and remaining oil in a large non-stick frying pan and cook the garlic and potato, tossing occasionally, for 10 minutes, or until the potato is tender. Set aside on paper towel. Cook the spinach in the pan for 1–2 minutes, or until wilted. Cool and then squeeze out any excess moisture.

3 Preheat the oven to 180°C (350°F/ Gas 4). Work with one sheet of pastry at a time and cover the rest with a damp tea towel (dish towel). Brush the pastry with melted butter and place another sheet on top. Brush with butter and repeat with another two layers. Cut in half widthways. Place a few potato slices at one end of each half, leaving a wide border on each side. Top with two tomato pieces and some spinach.

4 Fold in the sides of the pastry and roll up. Place on a lightly greased baking tray, brush with melted butter and sprinkle with sesame seeds. Use the remaining filo and filling to make another five parcels. Bake for 25–30 minutes, or until lightly golden.

NUTRITION PER PIE
Protein 9 g; Fat 30 g; Carbohydrate 35 g; Dietary Fibre 6 g; Cholesterol 60 mg; 1940 kJ (465 Cal)

Build up the layers of filo pastry, brushing each with melted butter.

Fold in the sides of the pastry and then roll up around the filling, into a parcel.

Tandoori lamb pie

PREPARATION TIME: 45 MINUTES + 20 MINUTES REFRIGERATION | TOTAL COOKING TIME: 1 HOUR 30 MINUTES | SERVES 4–6

125 g (4½ oz/1 cup) plain (all-purpose) flour

60 g (2¼ oz) butter, chilled and cubed

2 teaspoons coriander seeds

2 teaspoons cumin seeds

2 teaspoons poppy seeds

1 egg yolk

2 tablespoons iced water

FILLING

850 g (1 lb 14 oz) boned lamb shoulder

2 tablespoons oil

2 onions, chopped

1 garlic clove, crushed

2 teaspoons grated ginger

1 teaspoon chilli powder

2 teaspoons garam masala

1 teaspoon ground cumin

½ teaspoon ground turmeric

2 carrots, chopped

310 ml (10¾ fl oz/1¼ cups) beef stock (bouillon)

1 tablespoon plain (all-purpose) flour

1 teaspoon sugar

2 tablespoons lemon juice

200 g (7 oz) plain yoghurt

1 egg yolk, lightly beaten, to glaze

1 To make the pastry, process the flour and butter in a food processor until the mixture is crumbly. Season with a pinch of salt. Add the coriander, cumin and poppy seeds and process until combined. Then add the egg yolk and water. Process in short bursts until the mixture just comes together, adding extra water if necessary. Turn out onto a floured work surface and quickly bring together into a ball. Cover with plastic wrap and refrigerate for at least 20 minutes.

2 To make the filling, trim any excess fat from the lamb and cut into large cubes. Heat the oil in a frying pan and brown the lamb in batches. Return all the lamb to the pan. Add the onion and cook until translucent. Add the garlic, ginger and spices and stir over the heat for about 1 minute, or until aromatic. Stir in the carrot and stock. Bring to the boil, then reduce the heat and simmer, covered, for 50 minutes, or until the lamb is tender. Remove from the heat. Mix together the flour and 2 tablespoons of water, until smooth. Stir into the meat, return to the heat and then stir until the mixture boils and thickens. Add the sugar, lemon juice and yoghurt and stir well. Season with a good pinch of salt.

3 Spoon mixture into a deep 20 cm (8 inch) square or round pie dish and leave to cool. Preheat the oven to 200°C (400°F/Gas 6).

4 Roll out the pastry on a sheet of baking paper until it is large enough to cover the pie dish. Place the pastry over the filling and pinch the edges decoratively with your fingers. Brush with the lightly beaten egg yolk and bake for 25–30 minutes, or until the pastry is browned and crisp.

NUTRITION PER SERVE (6)
Protein 40 g; Fat 25 g; Carbohydrate 25 g; Dietary Fibre 3 g; Cholesterol 185 mg; 1920 kJ (455 Cal)

Add the coriander, cumin and poppy seeds to the food processor.

Stir the chopped carrot and beef stock into the lamb mixture.

Roll out the pastry until it is large enough to cover the pie dish.

Steak and kidney pie

PREPARATION TIME: 20 MINUTES | TOTAL COOKING TIME: 2 HOURS | SERVES 6

750 g (1 lb 10 oz) round steak
4 lamb kidneys
2 tablespoons plain (all-purpose) flour
1 tablespoon oil
1 onion, chopped
30 g (1 oz) butter
1 tablespoon worcestershire sauce
1 tablespoon tomato paste (concentrated
    purée)
125 ml (4 fl oz/½ cup) red wine
250 ml (9 fl oz/1 cup) beef stock (bouillon)
125 g (4½ oz) button mushrooms, sliced
½ teaspoon dried thyme
20 g (¾ oz/⅓ cup) chopped parsley
375 g (13 oz) puff pastry
1 egg, lightly beaten, to glaze

1   Cut the meat into small cubes. Trim the skin from the kidneys. Quarter the kidneys and trim away any fat or sinew. Coat the meat and kidneys with the flour and shake off the excess.

2   Heat the oil in a pan. Add the onion and cook for 5 minutes, or until soft. Remove with a slotted spoon. Add the butter to the pan. Brown the meat and kidneys in batches and then return all the meat and onion to the pan.

3   Add the worcestershire sauce, tomato paste, wine, stock, mushrooms, thyme and parsley to the pan. Bring to the boil then simmer, covered, for 1 hour, or until the meat is tender. Season and leave to cool. Spoon the mixture into a 1.5 litre (52 fl oz/6 cup) pie dish.

4   Preheat the oven to 210°C (415°F/ Gas 6–7). Roll out the puff pastry on a lightly floured surface so that it is 5 cm (2 inches) larger than the dish. Cut thin strips from the pastry and press onto the rim, sealing the joins. Place the pastry on top of the pie. Trim the edges and cut steam holes in the top. Decorate with pastry trimmings and brush the top with the egg. Bake for 35–40 minutes, or until golden brown.

Cook the meat and kidneys in batches and then return it all to the pan.

Roll the puff pastry out on a lightly floured surface until it is a little larger than the dish.

NUTRITION PER SERVE
Protein 38 g; Fat 28 g; Carbohydrate 27 g; Dietary
Fibre 2 g; Cholesterol 244 mg; 2195 kJ (524 Cal)

Potato and salmon parcels

PREPARATION TIME: 30 MINUTES | TOTAL COOKING TIME: 40 MINUTES | MAKES 12

750 g (1 lb 10 oz) floury potatoes, peeled
40 g (1½ oz) butter
60 ml (2 fl oz/¼ cup) cream
125 g (4½ oz/1 cup) grated cheddar cheese
210 g (7½ oz) tinned red salmon, skin and
    bones removed, flaked
1 tablespoon chopped dill
4 spring onions (scallions), finely chopped
3 sheets puff pastry
1 egg, lightly beaten, to glaze

1 Cut the potatoes into small pieces and cook in a saucepan of boiling water until tender. Mash with the butter and the cream until there are no lumps. Lightly grease two oven trays.

2 Add the cheese, salmon, dill and spring onion to the potato and mix well. Preheat the oven to 200°C (400°F/Gas 6). Cut each pastry sheet into four squares. Divide the mixture between the squares (approximately ¼ cup in each). Lightly brush the edges with the egg. Bring all four corners to the centre to form a point and press together to make a parcel.

3 Put the parcels on the greased trays and glaze with the egg. Bake for 15–20 minutes, or until the pastry is golden brown.

NOTE: *Before removing the pastries from the oven, lift them gently off the tray and check that the bottom of the parcels are cooked through. Take care not to overcook the parcels or they may burst open.*

HINT: *If you like your puff pastry to taste extra buttery, brush it with melted butter before baking.*

NUTRITION PER PARCEL
Protein 30 g; Fat 55 g; Carbohydrate 70 g; Dietary Fibre 5 g; Cholesterol 180 mg; 3700 kJ (885 Cal)

Cut each pastry sheet into four squares and then divide the filling among them.

Bring up the corners to the centre and press together to make a parcel.

Rabbit pie

PREPARATION TIME: 45 MINUTES + OVERNIGHT SOAKING + 30 MINUTES REFRIGERATION | TOTAL COOKING TIME: 2 HOURS 30 MINUTES | SERVES 4

1 tablespoon vinegar

1 rabbit, cut into 12 portions

3 tablespoons plain (all-purpose) flour, seasoned with salt and pepper

4 tablespoons olive oil

2 bacon slices, chopped

2 onions, finely chopped

1 green apple, peeled, cored and chopped

12 pitted prunes

1 tablespoon plain (all-purpose) flour

1 tablespoon soft brown sugar

375 ml (13 fl oz/1½ cups) beer or cider

1 teaspoon dried thyme

375 g (13 oz) puff pastry

1 egg yolk mixed with 1 teaspoon water, to glaze

1   Add the vinegar and ½ teaspoon salt to a large bowl of water. Add the rabbit portions and leave to soak overnight in the fridge. Drain and rinse well. Dry with paper towels. Toss the rabbit in the seasoned flour.

2   Preheat the oven to 180°C (350°F/ Gas 4). Heat 3 tablespoons of the oil in a large heavy-based frying pan. Cook the rabbit quickly, in batches, over medium heat until browned. Put the meat in a 2 litre (70 fl oz/ 8 cup) casserole.

3   Heat the remaining oil in the same frying pan and add the bacon, onion, apple and prunes. Cook over medium heat for 5 minutes or until lightly browned. Sprinkle with the flour and brown sugar and stir. Cook, stirring, for 5 minutes. Add the beer or cider and stir constantly for 3 minutes or until thickened. Stir in the thyme. Pour over the rabbit.

4   Cover the dish with a tight-fitting lid and bake for 1½ hours, or until the rabbit is tender.

5   Transfer the rabbit to a deep 1.25 litre (44 fl oz/5 cup) pie dish with a rim. Leave to cool and then refrigerate until cold.

6   Place a pie funnel in the centre of the dish. Roll the pastry out to about 5 cm (2 inches) larger than the top of the dish. Cut small pieces of pastry to fit around the funnel. Mark the pastry to lid size and cut out a hole to fit over the funnel. Cut small strips from the remaining scraps to fit on the rim of the pie plate. Press the joins together. Brush the rim and strips with the egg and water glaze, then position the pastry lid and press to seal. Use the back of a knife to push up the pastry edge at intervals. Refrigerate for at least 30 minutes.

7   Brush the pastry top with the remaining egg glaze. Increase the oven temperature to 210°C (415°F/Gas 6–7). Bake for 30–40 minutes or until the pastry is golden brown and cooked through. Reduce the oven to 180°C (350°F/ Gas 4) during the last 10 minutes of cooking and cover the pie with foil to prevent the top browning too much.

> NUTRITION PER SERVE
> Protein 85 g; Fat 50 g; Carbohydrate 64 g; Dietary Fibre 5 g; Cholesterol 265 mg; 4450 kJ (1063 Cal)

Add the beer or cider and stir constantly with a wooden spoon for 3 minutes.

When the rabbit filling is completely cold, place the pie funnel in the centre of the dish.

Low-fat spinach pie

PREPARATION TIME: 25 MINUTES | TOTAL COOKING TIME: 45 MINUTES | SERVES 6

1.5 kg (3 lb 5 oz) English spinach
2 teaspoons olive oil
1 onion, chopped
4 spring onions (scallions), chopped
750 g (1 lb 10 oz) reduced-fat cottage cheese
2 eggs, lightly beaten
2 garlic cloves, crushed
pinch of ground nutmeg
15 g (½ oz/¼ cup) chopped mint
8 sheets filo pastry
30 g (1 oz) butter, melted
40 g (1½ oz/½ cup) fresh breadcrumbs

1   Preheat the oven to 180°C (350°F/Gas 4) and lightly spray a square 1.5 litre (52 fl oz/6 cup) ovenproof dish with oil. Trim and wash the spinach, then place in a large saucepan with the water clinging to the leaves. Cover and cook for 2–3 minutes, until just wilted. Drain, cool, then squeeze dry and chop.

2   Heat the oil in a small pan. Add the onion and spring onion and cook for 2–3 minutes, until softened. Combine in a bowl with the chopped spinach. Stir in the cottage cheese, egg, garlic, nutmeg and mint. Season and mix thoroughly.

3   Brush a sheet of filo pastry with a little butter. Fold in half widthways and line the base and sides of the dish. Repeat with 3 more sheets. Keep the unused sheets moist by covering with a damp tea towel (dish towel).

4   Sprinkle the breadcrumbs over the pastry. Spread the filling into the dish. Fold over any overlapping pastry. Brush and fold another sheet and place on top. Repeat with 3 more sheets. Tuck the pastry in at the sides. Brush the top with any remaining butter. Score squares or diamonds on top using a sharp knife.

5   Bake for 40 minutes, or until golden. Cut into squares to serve.

Line the base and sides of the dish with the greased and folded pastry.

Cover the top of the pie with pastry and tuck it in at the sides.

NUTRITION PER SERVE
Protein 35 g; Fat 10 g; Carbohydrate 30 g; Dietary Fibre 8 g; Cholesterol 75 mg; 1500 kJ (360 Cal)

Creamy snapper pies

PREPARATION TIME: 25 MINUTES | TOTAL COOKING TIME: 1 HOUR 20 MINUTES | MAKES 6

2 tablespoons olive oil
4 onions, thinly sliced
375 ml (13 fl oz/1½ cups) fish stock
875 ml (30 fl oz/3½ cups) cream
1 kg (2 lb 4 oz) skinless snapper fillets, cut into
    large bite-sized pieces
2 sheets puff pastry
1 egg, lightly beaten, to glaze

1   Preheat the oven to 220°C (425°F/Gas 7).
Heat the oil in a large saucepan, add the onion
and stir over medium heat for 20 minutes, or
until golden brown and slightly caramelised.

2   Add the stock, bring to the boil and cook
for 10 minutes, or until the liquid has nearly
evaporated. Stir in the cream, bring to the boil,
then simmer for 20 minutes, until the liquid
reduces by half or coats the back of a spoon.

3   Divide half the sauce among six 310 ml
(10¾ fl oz/1¼ cup) deep ovenproof dishes. Put
some fish in each dish and top with the sauce.

4   Cut the pastry sheets into rounds slightly
larger than the tops of the dishes. Brush the
edges of the pastry with a little of the egg. Press
onto the dishes. Brush lightly with the remaining
egg. Bake for 30 minutes, or until the pastry is
crisp, golden and puffed.

NUTRITION PER PIE
Protein 43 g; Fat 85 g; Carbohydrate 27 g; Dietary
Fibre 1.6 g; Cholesterol 345 mg; 4347 kJ (1033 Cal)

Reduce the heat and simmer until the liquid coats
the back of a spoon.

Put some fish in each dish, dividing the pieces
equally among the six dishes.

Put a round of pastry on top of each dish and gently
press the edges.

Vegetable pie with cheese topping

PREPARATION TIME: 25 MINUTES + 20 MINUTES REFRIGERATION | TOTAL COOKING TIME: 1 HOUR 30 MINUTES | SERVES 6

125 g (4½ oz/1 cup) plain (all-purpose) flour
60 g (2¼ oz) butter, chilled and cubed
1 egg yolk
2 teaspoons poppy seeds
1–2 tablespoons iced water

FILLING
30 g (1 oz) butter
2 tablespoons oil
1 onion, cut into thin wedges
1 leek, sliced
3 potatoes, peeled and cut into large chunks
300 g (10½ oz) orange sweet potato, cut into
    large chunks
300 g (10½ oz) pumpkin (winter squash),
    cubed
200 g (7 oz) swede (rutabaga), peeled and
    cubed
250 ml (9 fl oz/1 cup) vegetable stock
1 red capsicum (pepper), cubed
200 g (7 oz) broccoli, cut into large florets
2 zucchini (courgettes), cut into large pieces
125 g (4½ oz/1 cup) grated cheddar cheese

NUTRITION PER SERVE
Protein 14 g; Fat 27 g; Carbohydrate 32 g; Dietary
Fibre 6.5 g; Cholesterol 90 mg; 1790 kJ (428 Cal)

1   Preheat the oven to 200°C (400°F/Gas 6). To make the pastry, sift the flour into a large bowl and add the butter. Rub in the butter with your fingertips until it resembles fine breadcrumbs. Make a well in the centre and add the egg yolk, poppy seeds and water and mix with a flat-bladed knife, using a cutting action, until the mixture comes together in beads. Gently gather together and lift onto a lightly floured work surface. Press into a disc, wrap in plastic and refrigerate for 20 minutes.

2   Roll out the dough between two sheets of baking paper, then fit into a 23 cm (9 inch) pie plate. Trim away any excess pastry. Prick the base with a fork and bake for 15–20 minutes, or until dry and golden.

3   To make the filling, heat the butter and oil in a large saucepan and cook the onion and leek over medium heat for 5 minutes, or until soft and golden. Add the potato, sweet potato, pumpkin and swede and cook, stirring occasionally, until the vegetables start to soften. Add the stock and simmer for 30 minutes.

4   Add the remaining vegetables, reduce the heat and simmer for 20 minutes, or until the vegetables are soft—some may break up slightly. The mixture should be just mushy. Season and leave to cool a little.

5   Spoon the filling into the pastry shell and sprinkle with the cheese. Cook under a medium grill (broiler) for 5–10 minutes, or until the cheese is golden brown.

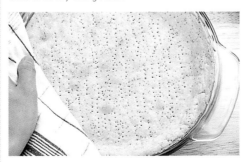

Prick the base of the pastry all over with a fork and bake until dry and golden.

Cook the vegetables until they are very soft when tested with a knife.

Rabbit and mushroom pie with polenta topping

PREPARATION TIME: 30 MINUTES I TOTAL COOKING TIME: 1 HOUR 20 MINUTES I SERVES 6

10 g (¼ oz) dried porcini mushrooms

90 g (3¼ oz) butter

1 kg (2 lb 4 oz) trimmed rabbit meat (fillets or boned saddles), cubed

200 g (7 oz) pancetta or bacon, diced

1 large onion, finely chopped

200 g (7 oz) button mushrooms, quartered

150 g (5½ oz) shimeji mushrooms

1 tablespoon plain (all-purpose) flour

200 g (7 oz) crème fraîche

150 ml (5 fl oz) cream

2 teaspoons chopped thyme

2 tablespoons chopped parsley

TOPPING

500 ml (17 fl oz/2 cups) milk

30 g (1 oz) butter

75 g (2½ oz/½ cup) instant polenta

60 g (2¼ oz/½ cup) grated parmesan cheese

pinch of ground nutmeg

1 egg, lightly beaten

1   Soak the porcini mushrooms in 125 ml (4 fl oz/½ cup) warm water for 15 minutes. Meanwhile, heat half the butter in a large, deep frying pan over medium heat and cook the rabbit in batches for 5 minutes, or until brown all over. Remove from the pan. Add the pancetta to the pan and cook for 4–5 minutes, or until golden. Add the remaining butter and the onion, reduce the heat and cook for 5 minutes, or until softened.

2   Add the button and shimeji mushrooms to the pan and stir well. Squeeze dry the porcini mushrooms and chop. Add to the pan, along with the liquid. Simmer for 10 minutes, or until all the liquid evaporates. Add the flour and stir for 1 minute. Stir in the crème fraîche and cream and season with freshly ground black pepper. Return the rabbit to the pan and simmer for 20 minutes, or until the sauce has reduced and thickened. Add the fresh herbs.

3   Preheat the oven to 200°C (400°F/Gas 6). Grease a 1.25 litre (44 fl oz/5 cup) ovenproof dish. Spoon in the rabbit and mushroom filling.

4   To make the topping, put the milk, butter and ½ teaspoon salt in a saucepan and heat until almost boiling. Add the polenta and stir constantly for 5 minutes, or until thick and smooth and the polenta comes away from the side of the pan. Remove from the heat and stir in the parmesan cheese. Add the nutmeg, beat in the egg and season. Spread over the filling and bake for 20 minutes, or until golden.

VARIATION: *You can use 1 kg (2 lb 4 oz) chicken thigh meat, bones removed, instead of the rabbit.*

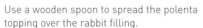

Use a wooden spoon to spread the polenta topping over the rabbit filling.

NUTRITION PER SERVE (6)
Protein 57 g; Fat 53 g; Carbohydrate 10 g; Dietary Fibre 2.5 g; Cholesterol 282 mg; 3260 kJ (780 Cal)

Mediterranean pie

PREPARATION TIME: 25 MINUTES + 20 MINUTES REFRIGERATION | TOTAL COOKING TIME: 35 MINUTES | SERVES 4

375 g (13 oz/3 cups) plain (all-purpose) flour
1 egg, lightly beaten
125 ml (4 fl oz/½ cup) buttermilk
100 ml (3½ fl oz) olive oil

FILLING
2 tablespoons olive oil
100 g (3½ oz) button mushrooms, sliced
400 g (14 oz) tinned tomatoes, drained and
    roughly chopped
100 g (3½ oz) sliced salami
180 g (6¼ oz) jar artichokes, drained
4 tablespoons basil, torn
100 g (3½ oz) grated mozzarella cheese
30 g (1 oz/¼ cup) grated parmesan cheese
milk, to glaze

NUTRITION PER SERVE
Protein 30 g; Fat 52 g; Carbohydrate 75 g; Dietary
Fibre 7 g; Cholesterol 95 mg; 3675 kJ (880 Cal)

1   Preheat the oven to 210°C (415°F/ Gas 6–7). Grease a large baking tray and place in the oven to heat up. Sift the flour into a large bowl and add the egg and buttermilk. Add the oil and mix with a large metal spoon until the mixture comes together and forms a soft dough (add a little water if the mixture is too dry). Turn onto a lightly floured surface and gather together into a smooth ball. Cover with plastic wrap and refrigerate for 20 minutes.

2   Heat the oil in a large frying pan, add the mushrooms and cook over medium heat for 5 minutes, or until they have softened and browned a little.

3   Divide the pastry in half and roll out each portion between two sheets of baking paper, into 30 cm (12 inch) rounds. Layer the tomato, salami, mushrooms, artichokes, basil, mozzarella and parmesan on one of the pastry rounds, leaving a narrow border. Season well.

4   Brush the border with milk. Top with the remaining pastry circle to enclose the filling, then pinch and seal the edges together. Cut three slits in the top. Brush the top with milk. Place on the preheated tray and bake for 30 minutes, or until golden.

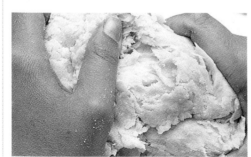
Gently gather the dough together to form a smooth ball.

Brush the pastry border with the milk to help the top layer of pastry stick.

Welsh lamb pie

PREPARATION TIME: 20 MINUTES + COOLING | TOTAL COOKING TIME: 2 HOURS 35 MINUTES | SERVES 6

750 g (1 lb 10 oz) boned lamb shoulder, cubed
90 g (3¼ oz/¾ cup) plain (all-purpose) flour, seasoned
2 tablespoons olive oil
200 g (7 oz) bacon slices, finely chopped
2 garlic cloves, chopped
4 large leeks, sliced
1 large carrot, chopped
2 large potatoes, peeled and diced
310 ml (10¾ fl oz/1¼ cups) beef stock (bouillon)
1 bay leaf
2 teaspoons chopped parsley
375 g (13 oz) quick flaky pastry
1 egg, lightly beaten, to glaze

1 Toss the meat in the flour. Heat the oil in a large frying pan over medium heat and brown the meat in batches for 4–5 minutes, then remove from the pan. Cook the bacon for 3 minutes. Add the garlic and leek and cook for 5 minutes, or until soft.

2 Put the meat in a large saucepan, add the leek and bacon, carrot, potato, stock and bay leaf and bring to the boil, then reduce the heat, cover and simmer for 30 minutes. Uncover and simmer for 1 hour, or until the meat is cooked and the liquid has thickened. Season to taste. Remove the bay leaf, stir in the parsley and set aside to cool.

3 Preheat the oven to 200°C (400°F/Gas 6). Place the filling in an 18 cm (7 inch) pie dish. Roll out the pastry between two sheets of baking paper until large enough to cover the pie. Trim the edges and pinch to seal.

4 Decorate the pie with pastry trimmings. Cut two slits in the top for steam to escape. Brush with egg and bake for 45 minutes, or until the pastry is crisp and golden.

Cook the filling until the liquid has thickened and then remove the bay leaf.

Cut out shapes from the pastry trimmings to decorate the pie.

NUTRITION PER SERVE
Protein 42 g; Fat 28 g; Carbohydrate 43 g; Dietary Fibre 5 g; Cholesterol 147 mg; 2465 kJ (590 Cal)

Ham and chicken pie

PREPARATION TIME: 40 MINUTES | TOTAL COOKING TIME: 1 HOUR | SERVES 8–10

375 g (13 oz/3 cups) plain (all-purpose) flour
180 g (6¼ oz) butter, chilled and cubed
2–3 tablespoons iced water
1 egg, lightly beaten

FILLING
1 kg (2 lb 4 oz) minced (ground) chicken
1 teaspoon dried mixed herbs
2 eggs, lightly beaten
3 spring onions (scallions), finely chopped
2 tablespoons chopped parsley
2 teaspoons French mustard
80 ml (2½ fl oz/⅓ cup) cream
200 g (7 oz) sliced leg ham

1　Preheat the oven to 180°C (350°F/Gas 4). Mix the flour and butter in a food processor for 20 seconds or until fine and crumbly. Add the water and process for 20 seconds or until the mixture comes together. Turn onto a lightly floured surface and press together until smooth. Roll out two-thirds of the pastry to line a 20 cm (8 inch) spring-form tin, leaving some pastry hanging over the side. Cover with plastic wrap and refrigerate until required. Wrap the remaining pastry in plastic wrap and refrigerate.

2　To make the filling, mix together the chicken, herbs, egg, spring onion, parsley, mustard and cream and season well.

3　Spoon a third of the filling into the pastry-lined tin and smooth the surface. Top with half the ham and then another chicken layer, followed by the remaining ham and then a final layer of chicken filling.

4　Brush around the inside edge of pastry with egg. Roll out the remaining pastry to make the pie lid, pressing the pastry edges together. Trim the edge. Decorate the top with pastry trimmings. Brush with beaten egg and bake for 1 hour, or until golden brown.

NUTRITION PER SERVE (8)
Protein 40 g; Fat 29 g; Carbohydrate 39 g; Dietary Fibre 2 g; Cholesterol 215 mg; 2445 kJ (583 Cal)

Combine the chicken, herbs, egg, spring onion, parsley, mustard, cream, salt and pepper.

Layer the chicken filling and the ham in the pastry-lined tin.

Chunky veal and capsicum pie

PREPARATION TIME: 40 MINUTES + 10 MINUTES RESTING + COOLING | TOTAL COOKING TIME: 2 HOURS | SERVES 6

80 ml (2½ fl oz/⅓ cup) olive oil

3 capsicums (peppers), seeded and cut into
    2.5 cm (1 inch) pieces

2 garlic cloves, crushed

1 kg (2 lb 4 oz) neck, shoulder or breast of
    veal, cut into small pieces

30 g (1 oz/¼ cup) plain (all-purpose) flour,
    seasoned

40 g (1½ oz) butter

2 onions, finely chopped

8 French shallots (eschallots), peeled

¼ teaspoon cayenne pepper

2 teaspoons red wine vinegar

185 ml (6 fl oz/¾ cup) chicken stock

2 tablespoons chopped flat-leaf
    (Italian) parsley

375 g (13 oz) shortcrust pastry

1 egg, lightly beaten, to glaze

1 Heat half the oil in a large saucepan and cook the capsicum over medium heat for 2–3 minutes. Add the garlic, cover the pan and reduce the heat to low. Cook gently for 5 minutes, then remove from the pan.

2 Put the veal and flour in a plastic bag and shake until the veal is evenly coated, shaking off any excess flour. Heat the butter and the remaining oil over high heat in the same saucepan and cook the veal in batches until evenly browned. Return all the veal to the pan, add the onion, shallots and cayenne pepper and reduce the heat to low. Cook, covered, for 10 minutes. Stir in the vinegar, cover and turn off the heat. Leave for 10 minutes.

3 Add the capsicum, stock and parsley to the meat, bring to the boil, then reduce the heat to low. Cover and simmer for 20 minutes, or until the meat is tender.

4 Uncover and cook for 30–40 minutes, until the liquid thickens and darkens. Season to taste and cool slightly. Preheat the oven to 200°C (400°F/Gas 6) and heat a baking tray. Lightly grease an 18 cm (7 inch) pie dish.

5 Spoon the filling into the pie dish, levelling the surface. Roll the dough out between two sheets of baking paper to a size slightly larger than the top of the pie dish. Carefully cover the filling and press the pastry over the edge to seal. Trim the edges. Decorate with pastry trimmings and brush the top with egg. Place on the hot tray and bake for 30 minutes, or until golden.

NUTRITION PER SERVE
Protein 44 g; Fat 37 g; Carbohydrate 33 g; Dietary
Fibre 2.5 g; Cholesterol 201 mg; 2660 kJ (635 Cal)

Carefully cover the filling and press the pastry over the edge to seal.

Potato and goat's cheese pies

PREPARATION TIME: 25 MINUTES | TOTAL COOKING TIME: 1 HOUR | MAKES 4

4 potatoes, peeled
4 slices prosciutto
150 g (5½ oz) goat's cheese
250 g (9 oz/1 cup) sour cream
2 eggs, lightly beaten
125 ml (4 fl oz/½ cup) cream

1 Brush four 250 ml (9 fl oz/1 cup) ramekins with melted butter. Preheat the oven to 180°C (350°F/Gas 4).

2 For each pie, thinly slice a potato and pat dry with paper towel. Line the base of a ramekin with a half slice of prosciutto. Layer half the potato slices neatly into the dishes. Put the other half slice of prosciutto on top and crumble a quarter of the goat's cheese over it. Cover with the remaining potato slices and press down firmly. The potato should fill the dish to the top.

3 Mix together the sour cream, egg and cream and season well. Pour into the ramekins, allowing it to seep through the layers. Place on a baking tray and bake for 50–60 minutes, or until the potato is soft when tested with a skewer. Leave for 5 minutes, then run a knife around the edge and turn out onto serving plates.

NUTRITION PER PIE
Protein 25 g; Fat 55 g; Carbohydrate 20 g; Dietary Fibre 2 g; Cholesterol 255 mg; 2645 kJ (630 Cal)

Cut the goat's cheese into four slices, using a sharp knife.

Build up layers of potato, prosciutto and goat's cheese in the ramekin.

Mix together the sour cream, egg and cream and pour over the top.

Pumpkin, leek and corn pie

PREPARATION TIME: 30 MINUTES + COOLING | TOTAL COOKING TIME: 1 HOUR 25 MINUTES | SERVES 6

4 tablespoons olive oil
2 leeks, thinly sliced
2 large garlic cloves, chopped
1 butternut pumpkin (squash), peeled,
    seeded and diced
3 corn cobs
185 g (6½ oz/1½ cups) grated cheddar cheese
1 teaspoon chopped rosemary
15 g (½ oz/½ cup) chopped flat-leaf
    (Italian) parsley
12 sheets filo pastry
5 eggs, lightly beaten

1   Preheat the oven to 180°C (350°F/Gas 4) and grease a 33 x 25 cm (13 x 10 inch) oven dish.

2   Heat 1 tablespoon of the oil in a small saucepan and cook the leek and garlic for 10 minutes, stirring occasionally, until soft and golden. Transfer to a large bowl and cool.

3   Meanwhile, cook the pumpkin in boiling water for 5 minutes, or until just tender. Drain and cool. Cook the corn in boiling water for 7–8 minutes, or until tender. Drain and leave until cool enough to handle. Cut the kernels off the cobs and add them to the bowl with the pumpkin, cheese, rosemary and parsley, then season and mix gently.

4   Cover the filo pastry with a damp tea towel (dish towel) to prevent it drying out. Lightly brush one sheet of filo with oil and place in the dish. Layer five more sheets in the dish, brushing all but the last sheet with oil.

5   Gently stir the egg into the pumpkin mixture, then spoon into the dish. Cover with the remaining filo pastry, again brushing each layer with oil, and tuck in the edges. Bake for 1 hour, or until the pastry is golden brown and the filling has set.

Spoon the pumpkin and corn mixture into the ovenproof dish.

Tuck the edges of the filo pastry into the side of the dish.

NUTRITION PER SERVE
Protein 22 g; Fat 29 g; Carbohydrate 38 g; Dietary Fibre 6 g; Cholesterol 180.5 mg; 2080 kJ (495 Cal)

Chicken and preserved lemon pie

PREPARATION TIME: 40 MINUTES + 20 MINUTES REFRIGERATION + COOLING | TOTAL COOKING TIME: 1 HOUR 15 MINUTES | SERVES 4–6

2 tablespoons olive oil

2 leeks, thinly sliced

¾ preserved lemon, pulp removed, zest
washed and cut into thin strips

1 kg (2 lb 4 oz) boneless chicken thighs, cut
into bite-sized pieces

2 tablespoons plain (all-purpose) flour

250 ml (9 fl oz/1 cup) chicken stock
(bouillon)

250 g (9 oz) potatoes, thinly sliced

2 tablespoons chopped flat-leaf
(Italian) parsley

1 egg, lightly beaten, to glaze

PASTRY
100 g (3½ oz) self-raising flour
150 g (5½ oz) plain (all-purpose) flour
60 g (2¼ oz) butter, chilled and cubed
60 g (2¼ oz) lard, chilled and cubed
3–4 tablespoons iced water
1 egg, lightly beaten, to glaze

1 Heat the oil in a large frying pan, and cook the leek for 2–3 minutes, or until golden. Add the preserved lemon and cook for 3 minutes, or until fragrant. Remove from the pan.

2 Add a little extra oil to the pan if necessary and brown the chicken in batches, stirring, for 5 minutes. Return all the chicken to the pan with the leek and lemon. Sprinkle with flour and cook, stirring, for 2 minutes.

3 Gradually stir in the chicken stock, then add the potato. Bring to the boil, then reduce the heat and simmer for 7 minutes, or until thickened slightly. Stir in the parsley. Transfer to a bowl and allow to cool completely.

4 To make the pastry, sift the flours and a pinch of salt into a large bowl and rub in the chopped butter and lard with your fingertips until the mixture resembles fine breadcrumbs. Make a well, add almost all the water and mix with a flat-bladed knife, using a cutting action, until the mixture forms beads, adding more water if necessary. Turn onto a lightly floured surface, gather into a ball, cover in plastic wrap and refrigerate for 20 minutes. Preheat the oven to 200°C (400°F/Gas 6) and heat a baking tray.

5 Spoon the filling into a 16 cm (6¼ inch) pie plate. Roll out the dough between baking paper until large enough to cover the pie. Trim away excess pastry, then press the rim to seal. Cut a few steam holes in the top and decorate with pastry trimmings. Brush with the egg, place on the hot tray and bake for 35–40 minutes, or until the crust is crisp and golden.

NUTRITION PER SERVE (6)
Protein 40 g; Fat 39 g; Carbohydrate 40 g; Dietary
Fibre 4 g; Cholesterol 240 mg; 2795 kJ (665 Cal)

When the chicken mixture has thickened slightly, stir in the parsley.

Spoon the chicken filling into a pie dish and level the surface.

Salmon pie

PREPARATION TIME: 25 MINUTES + REFRIGERATION | TOTAL COOKING TIME: 50 MINUTES | SERVES 4–6

60 g (2¼ oz) butter
1 onion, finely chopped
200 g (7 oz) button mushrooms, sliced
2 tablespoons lemon juice
220 g (7¾ oz) salmon fillet, boned, skinned
   and cubed
2 hard-boiled eggs, chopped
2 tablespoons chopped dill
2 tablespoons chopped parsley
185 g (6½ oz/1 cup) cooked rice
60 ml (2 fl oz/¼ cup) cream
375 g (13 fl oz) puff pastry
1 egg, lightly beaten, to glaze

1 Lightly oil an oven tray. Melt half the butter in a frying pan and cook the onion for 5 minutes, or until soft but not browned. Add the mushrooms and cook for 5 minutes. Stir in the lemon juice and transfer to a bowl.

2 Melt the remaining butter in the pan, add the salmon and cook for 2 minutes. Remove from the heat, cool slightly and add the egg, dill, parsley, salt and pepper. Stir gently and set aside. Stir together the rice and cream.

3 Roll out half the pastry to a rectangle measuring 18 x 30 cm (7 x 12 inches) and place on the tray. Spread with half the rice mixture, leaving a small border all the way around. Top with the salmon mixture, then the mushroom mixture, and finish with the remaining rice.

4 Roll out the remaining pastry to 20 x 33 cm (8 x 13 inches) to cover the filling. Crimp the edges to seal. Refrigerate for 30 minutes. Preheat the oven to 210°C (415°F/Gas 6–7). Brush with the egg and bake for 15 minutes. Reduce the heat to 180°C (350°F/Gas 4) and bake for a further 15–20 minutes until golden.

Spread the salmon mixture evenly over the layer of creamy rice.

Hang the pastry top over a rolling pin to make it easy to place over the filling.

NUTRITION PER SERVE (6)
Protein 30 g; Fat 60 g; Carbohydrate 70 g; Dietary Fibre 4 g; Cholesterol 180 mg; 3700 kJ (885 Cal)

Italian Easter pie

PREPARATION TIME: 40 MINUTES + 20 MINUTES COOLING | TOTAL COOKING TIME: 1 HOUR 5 MINUTES | SERVES 6–8

450 g (1 lb) spinach or silverbeet (Swiss chard), stalks removed
90 g (3¼ oz) fresh white breadcrumbs
250 ml (9 fl oz/1 cup) milk
500 g (1 lb 2 oz) ricotta cheese (see NOTE)
200 g (7 oz) grated parmesan cheese
8 eggs
pinch of ground nutmeg
pinch of cayenne pepper
10 small marjoram leaves
150 g (5½ oz) butter
20 sheets filo pastry

1 Bring 500 ml (17 fl oz/2 cups) salted water to the boil in a large saucepan. Add the spinach or silverbeet, cover and cook, stirring occasionally, for 5 minutes, or until wilted. Drain well. When cool enough to handle, wring out all the liquid in a clean tea towel (dish towel). Chop well.

2 Preheat the oven to 180°C (350°F/Gas 4). Put the breadcrumbs and milk in a large bowl and leave for 5 minutes. Add the ricotta, half the parmesan, 4 eggs, the nutmeg, cayenne, marjoram and chopped spinach. Season and mix.

3 Melt the butter and lightly brush a 23 cm (9 inch) spring-form tin. Line the base and the side with a sheet of filo pastry. Brush with the melted butter and place another filo sheet on top, positioned so that any exposed wall of the tin is covered. Continue in this way, using a total of 10 sheets of filo. Don't worry about the filo forming folds on the tin walls, just push them flat as you brush with the butter.

4 Spoon the filling into the tin. Make four deep indentations in the surface around the edge of the pie, then break an egg into each. Season and sprinkle with the remaining parmesan. Fold over any overhanging pastry. Cover with the remaining filo, buttering each layer.

5 Bake for 40 minutes, cover the top with foil, then bake for another 20 minutes. Cool in the tin for 20 minutes before serving.

NOTE: *Use ricotta from a wheel as pre-packaged ricotta tends to be too moist.*

Gently break an egg into each of the four indentations.

NUTRITION PER SERVE (8)
Protein 29 g; Fat 38 g; Carbohydrate 29 g; Dietary Fibre 3 g; Cholesterol 286 mg; 2360 kJ (565 Cal)

Raised pork pie

PREPARATION TIME: 20 MINUTES + CHILLING + OVERNIGHT SETTING | TOTAL COOKING TIME: 1 HOUR | SERVES 6–8

1.2 kg (2 lb 10 oz) minced (ground) pork
90 g (3¼ oz/⅔ cup) chopped pistachio nuts
2 green apples, peeled and finely chopped
6 sage leaves, finely chopped
500 g (1 lb 2 oz/4 cups) plain (all-purpose)
    flour
150 g (5½ oz) butter
2 eggs, lightly beaten
1 egg yolk, to glaze
200 ml (7 fl oz) vegetable stock
200 ml (7 fl oz) unsweetened apple juice
2 teaspoons gelatine

1 Mix together the pork, pistachio nuts, apple and sage and season. Fry a piece of the mixture to taste and adjust the seasoning. Cover and refrigerate. Wrap a piece of plastic wrap around a 6 cm (2½ inch) high, 20 cm (8 inch) straight-sided tin, then turn the tin over and grease the outside base and side.

2 Put the flour and 1 teaspoon salt in a bowl and make a well in the centre. Put the butter in a pan with 210 ml (7½ fl oz) water, bring to the boil and add to the flour with the egg. Mix with a wooden spoon until combined, then turn out onto a work surface and bring together to form a smooth dough. Wrap in plastic wrap and refrigerate for 10 minutes.

3 Cut off a third of the pastry and wrap in plastic wrap—do not refrigerate. Roll the remainder into a circle large enough to just cover the outside of the tin. Lift onto a rolling pin and place over the tin, working fast before the pastry sets. Refrigerate until the pastry hardens (about 3 hours).

4 Preheat the oven to 200°C (400°F/Gas 6). Carefully pull the tin out from the pastry case and remove the plastic wrap. Attach a paper collar made of two layers of greased baking paper around the outside of the pastry so it fits snugly and secure with a paper clip at the top and bottom. Fill the pie with the pork mixture, then roll out the remaining pastry to form a lid. Attach it to the base with some water, pressing or crimping it to make it look neat. Cut a small hole in the top of the pie.

5 Put the pie on a baking tray, bake for 40 minutes and check the pastry top. If it is still pale, bake for a further 10 minutes, then remove the paper. Brush with the egg yolk mixed with 1 tablespoon water and bake for another 15 minutes, or until the sides are brown. Cool completely.

6 Bring the stock and half the apple juice to the boil. Sprinkle the gelatine over the surface of the remaining apple juice in a bowl and leave to go spongy, then pour into the stock and mix until the gelatine dissolves. Place a small funnel (a piping (icing) nozzle works well) in the hole of the pie and pour in a little of the gelatine, leave to settle and then pour in some more until the pie is full. Fill the pie completely so there are no gaps when the gelatine sets. Leave in the fridge overnight.

STORAGE: *If wrapped tightly with plastic wrap, pork pies will last for 4–5 days in the fridge.*

NUTRITION PER SERVE (6)
Protein 60 g; Fat 35 g; Carbohydrate 72 g; Dietary Fibre 5.5 g; Cholesterol 257 mg; 3545 kJ (845 Cal)

Cover the outside of the tin with the pastry, working fast so that it does not set.

The greased paper collar should fit snugly around the outside of the pastry.

Gradually pour the gelatine mixture into the cooked and cooled pie until it is full.

Moroccan lamb pie

PREPARATION TIME: 30 MINUTES + COOLING | TOTAL COOKING TIME: 2 HOURS 40 MINUTES | SERVES 6–8

3 tablespoons olive oil
2 onions, finely chopped
4 garlic cloves, crushed
1¼ teaspoons each ground cinnamon, cumin and coriander
½ teaspoon ground ginger
large pinch of cayenne pepper
1.2 kg (2 lb 10 oz) boned lamb leg, cut into small cubes
375 ml (13 fl oz/1½ cups) chicken stock (bouillon)
2 teaspoons grated lemon zest
1 tablespoon lemon juice
2 carrots, cut into small cubes
60 g (2¼ oz) ground almonds
30 g (1 oz/⅔ cup) chopped coriander leaves
500 g (1 lb 2 oz) puff pastry
1 egg, lightly beaten, to glaze

1   Heat the oil in a large saucepan. Add the onion, garlic and spices and cook, stirring, over medium heat for 40 seconds. Add the lamb and stir until coated. Add the stock, lemon zest and juice and cook, covered, over low heat for 45 minutes. Add the carrot. Simmer, covered, for 45 minutes. Stir in the almonds. Boil for 30 minutes, until the sauce becomes very thick. Stir in the chopped coriander, season and cool.

2   Preheat the oven to 200°C (400°F/Gas 6) and heat a baking tray. Grease a 20 cm (8 inch) pie dish. Roll out the pastry to a 40 cm (16 inch) round and neaten the edge. Line the dish, leaving the pastry overhanging the rim. Spoon in the filling and level the surface. Fold the overhanging pastry into loose pleats over the filling. Using scissors, cut out Vs of pastry where it falls into deep folds so the pastry can bake evenly.

3   Brush with egg and bake on the hot tray in the centre of the oven for 20 minutes. Reduce the oven to 180°C (350°F/Gas 4), cover the pie with foil and bake for another 20 minutes.

Boil the lamb mixture for a further 30 minutes, or until the sauce becomes very thick.

Fold the overhanging pastry up and over the filling, in loose pleats.

NUTRITION PER SERVE (8)
Protein 39 g; Fat 31 g; Carbohydrate 26 g; Dietary Fibre 3 g; Cholesterol 115 mg; 2230 kJ (535 Cal)

Chicken and leek pie

PREPARATION TIME: 20 MINUTES | TOTAL COOKING TIME: 50 MINUTES | SERVES 4–6

60 g (2¼ oz) butter

2 large leeks, finely sliced

4 spring onions (scallions), sliced

1 garlic clove, crushed

30 g (1 oz/¼ cup) plain (all-purpose) flour

375 ml (13 fl oz/1½ cups) chicken stock

125 ml (4 fl oz/½ cup) cream

1 barbecued chicken, skin and bones
    removed, chopped

2 sheets puff pastry

60 ml (2 fl oz/¼ cup) milk

1 Preheat the oven to 200°C (400°F/
Gas 6). In a large saucepan, melt the butter and
add the leek, spring onion and garlic. Cook
over low heat for 6 minutes, or until the leek is
soft but not browned. Sprinkle in the flour and
mix well. Pour in the stock gradually and cook,
stirring well, until thick and smooth. Stir in the
cream and add the chicken.

2 Put the mixture in a shallow 20 cm (8 inch)
pie dish and set aside to cool.

3 Cut a circle out of one of the sheets of pastry
to cover the top of the pie. Paint around the rim
of the pie dish with a little of the milk. Put the
pastry on top and seal around the edge firmly.
Trim off any overhanging pastry and decorate the
edge with a fork.

4 Cut the other sheet of pastry into 1 cm
(½ inch) strips and loosely roll up each strip
like a snail. Arrange the spirals on top of the
pie, starting from the middle and leaving gaps
between them. The spirals may not cover the
whole surface of the pie. Make a few small
holes between the spirals to let out any steam
and brush the top of the pie lightly with the
remaining milk. Bake for 35–40 minutes, or
until the top is brown and crispy. Make sure the
spirals are well cooked and are not raw in the
middle.

Seal the edge firmly and trim off any overhanging
pastry with a sharp knife.

Roll up the strips of pastry into spirals and arrange
them on top of the pie.

NUTRITION PER SERVE (4)
Protein 25 g; Fat 55 g; Carbohydrate 40 g; Dietary
Fibre 3 g; Cholesterol 185 mg; 3105 kJ (740 Cal)

Spinach and feta triangles

PREPARATION TIME: 30 MINUTES | TOTAL COOKING TIME: 45 MINUTES | MAKES 8

1 kg (2 lb 4 oz) English spinach
60 ml (2 fl oz/¼ cup) olive oil
1 onion, chopped
10 spring onions (scallions), sliced
20 g (¾ oz/⅓ cup) chopped flat-leaf
    (Italian) parsley
1 tablespoon chopped dill
large pinch of ground nutmeg
35 g (1¼ oz/⅓ cup) grated parmesan cheese
150 g (5½ oz/1 cup) crumbled feta cheese
90 g (3¼ oz/ ⅓ cup) ricotta cheese
4 eggs, lightly beaten
40 g (1½ oz) butter, melted
1 tablespoon olive oil, extra
12 sheets filo pastry

1   Trim any coarse stems from the spinach. Wash the leaves thoroughly, roughly chop and place in a large saucepan with just a little water clinging to the leaves. Cover and cook gently over low heat for 5 minutes, or until the leaves have wilted. Drain well and allow to cool slightly before squeezing tightly to remove the excess water. Chop.

2   Heat the oil in a frying pan. Add the onion and cook over low heat for 10 minutes, or until soft and golden. Add the spring onion and cook for a further 3 minutes. Remove from the heat. Stir in the drained spinach, parsley, dill, nutmeg, cheeses and egg. Season well.

3   Preheat the oven to 180°C (350°F/Gas 4). Grease two baking trays. Combine the melted butter with the extra oil. Work with three sheets of pastry at a time, keeping the rest covered with a damp tea towel (dish towel). Brush each sheet with butter mixture and lay on top of each other. Cut in half lengthways.

4   Place 4 tablespoons of the filling on an angle at the end of each strip. Fold the pastry over to enclose the filling and form a triangle. Continue folding over until you reach the end of the pastry. Put on the baking trays and brush with the remaining butter mixture. Bake for 20–25 minutes, or until the pastry is golden brown.

VARIATION: *If you are unable to buy English spinach, silverbeet (Swiss chard) can be used instead. Use the same quantity and trim the coarse white stems from the leaves.*

NOTE: *Feta is a traditional Greek-style salty cheese. Any leftover should be stored immersed in lightly salted water and kept refrigerated. Rinse and pat dry before using.*

NUTRITION PER TRIANGLE
Protein 15 g; Fat 25 g; Carbohydrate 10 g; Dietary Fibre 4.5 g; Cholesterol 125 mg; 1325 kJ (315 Cal)

Brush each sheet of filo pastry with the mixture of melted butter and oil.

Fold the pastry over the spinach filling to enclose it and form a triangle.

Continue folding the triangle over until you reach the end of the pastry sheet.

Chargrilled vegetable and parmesan pie

PREPARATION TIME: 45 MINUTES + 1 HOUR STANDING I TOTAL COOKING TIME: 1 HOUR 30 MINUTES I SERVES 6

1 garlic clove, crushed
300 ml (10½ fl oz) olive oil
1 large eggplant (aubergine)
1 medium orange sweet potato
3 large zucchini (courgettes)
2 red capsicums (peppers)
2 yellow capsicums (peppers)
2 tablespoons polenta
90 g (3¼ oz) parmesan cheese, grated
1 egg, lightly beaten

PASTRY
450 g (1 lb) plain (all-purpose) flour
2 teaspoons cumin seeds
2 teaspoons paprika
100 g (3½ oz) butter, chopped

1 Mix the garlic and oil together. Cut the eggplant and sweet potato into 5 mm (¼ inch) slices and the zucchini into 5 mm (¼ inch) lengths, then brush with the garlic oil. Quarter the capsicums and place, skin side up, under a hot grill (broiler) for 10 minutes, or until the skins blacken and blister. Cool in a plastic bag, then peel.

2 Cook the eggplant, sweet potato and zucchini in batches in a chargrill pan over high heat, turning often, for 5–6 minutes, or until brown and tender. Set aside to cool. Preheat the oven to 180°C (350°F/Gas 4) and grease a deep 20 cm (8 inch) spring-form tin.

3 To make the pastry, sift the flour into a bowl and add the cumin, paprika and ½ teaspoon salt. Gently heat the butter in a saucepan with 225 ml (7¾ fl oz) water. Bring to the boil, pour into the flour and mix with a wooden spoon. When cool enough to handle, tip onto a floured surface and press gently together. Rest for 5 minutes.

4 Set aside one-quarter of the dough and roll out the rest between two sheets of baking paper until large enough to line the base and side of the tin, leaving some pastry overhanging. Sprinkle the polenta over the base, then layer the red capsicum, zucchini, eggplant, sweet potato and yellow capsicum in the pie, brushing each layer with a little garlic oil, sprinkling with parmesan and seasoning with salt and pepper, and pressing the layers down firmly as you go.

5 Roll out the remaining pastry between two sheets of baking paper to fit the top of the tin. Brush the edges of the bottom layer of pastry with egg. Cover with the pastry lid. Brush the edges with egg and trim with a sharp knife, crimping the edges to seal. Cut a small steam hole in the centre of the pie. Roll out the trimmings and use to decorate. Cook for 1 hour, or until crisp and golden (cover with foil if it browns too quickly). Cool for 1 hour before serving at room temperature.

NUTRITION PER SERVE
Protein 18 g; Fat 54 g; Carbohydrate 68 g; Dietary Fibre 7 g; Cholesterol 86 mg; 3445 kJ (820 Cal)

Pour the melted butter into the flour mixture and stir with a wooden spoon.

Layer the chargrilled vegetables and grated parmesan cheese in the pastry case.

Chilli con carne pie

PREPARATION TIME: 25 MINUTES + 20 MINUTES REFRIGERATION | TOTAL COOKING TIME: 2 HOURS 15 MINUTES | SERVES 6–8

185 g (6½ oz/1½ cups) plain (all-purpose) flour
100 g (3½ oz) butter, chilled and cubed
90 g (3¼ oz/¾ cup) grated cheddar cheese
1–2 tablespoons iced water

FILLING
2 tablespoons olive oil
1 onion, chopped
2 garlic cloves, chopped
¼ teaspoon chilli powder
2 teaspoons ground cumin
1 teaspoon ground coriander
¼ teaspoon cayenne pepper
1 teaspoon paprika
1 teaspoon dried oregano
750 g (1 lb 10 oz) minced (ground) beef
2 tablespoons tomato paste (tomato purée)
125 ml (4 fl oz/½ cup) dry red wine
425 g (14 oz) tinned chopped tomatoes
1 tablespoon wholegrain mustard
300 g (10½ oz) tinned red kidney beans, drained and rinsed
2 tablespoons chopped flat-leaf (Italian) parsley
1 tablespoon chopped oregano
170 g (6 oz/⅔ cup) sour cream

NUTRITION PER SERVE (8)
Protein 27 g; Fat 32 g; Carbohydrate 24 g; Dietary Fibre 4 g; Cholesterol 111 mg; 2085 kJ (500 Cal)

1 Sift the flour into a bowl and rub in the butter with your fingertips until the mixture resembles fine breadcrumbs. Stir in the cheese. Make a well in the centre and add almost all the water. Mix with a flat-bladed knife, using a cutting action, until the dough comes together, adding more water if necessary.

2 Gather the dough together and lift onto a lightly floured surface. Press into a ball and flatten slightly into a disc. Cover in plastic wrap and refrigerate for at least 20 minutes.

3 To make the filling, heat the oil in a large saucepan over medium heat and cook the onion for 5 minutes, until softened. Add the garlic, spices and oregano and cook for 2 minutes. Add the beef and cook over high heat for 5 minutes, until brown. Stir in the tomato paste and cook for 1 minute. Pour in the wine and simmer for 3 minutes. Add the tomato and mustard, bring to the boil, then reduce the heat and simmer for 30 minutes. Add the kidney beans and cook for 30 minutes, or until any excess moisture has evaporated. Stir in the fresh herbs. Season well.

4 Preheat the oven to 200°C (400°F/Gas 6). Lightly grease a 23 cm (9 inch) pie dish and spoon in the filling. Roll out the pastry to fit the top of the dish, then trim away the excess pastry and crimp the edges. Make two or three cuts in the top to let the steam escape. Bake for 10 minutes, then reduce the oven to 180°C (350°F/ Gas 4) and cook for 40–45 minutes, or until the top is golden. Cover the top with foil if it is browning too much. Serve with sour cream.

Simmer the chilli con carne filling until the excess liquid has evaporated.

Use a rolling pin to help you lift the pastry top over the filling.

Chicken and corn pies

PREPARATION TIME: 25 MINUTES + 2 HOURS REFRIGERATION | TOTAL COOKING TIME: 50 MINUTES | MAKES 6

1 tablespoon olive oil
650 g (1 lb 7 oz) chicken thigh fillets, cut into
    small pieces
1 tablespoon grated ginger
400 g (14 oz) oyster mushrooms, halved
3 corn cobs, kernels removed
125 ml (4 fl oz/½ cup) chicken stock
2 tablespoons kecap manis (see NOTE)
2 tablespoons cornflour (cornstarch)
90 g (3¼ oz) coriander (cilantro) leaves,
    chopped
6 sheets shortcrust pastry
milk, to glaze

1 Grease six 10 cm (4 inch) metal pie tins. Heat the oil in a large frying pan over high heat and add the chicken. Cook for 5 minutes, or until golden. Add the ginger, mushrooms and corn and cook for 5–6 minutes, until the chicken is just cooked through. Add the stock and kecap manis. Mix the cornflour with 2 tablespoons water, then stir into the pan. Boil for 2 minutes before adding the coriander. Cool and then chill for 2 hours.

2 Preheat the oven to 180°C (350°F/Gas 4). Using a saucer as a guide, cut a 15 cm (6 inch) round from each sheet of shortcrust pastry and line the pie tins. Fill the shells with the cooled filling, then cut out another six rounds large enough to make the lids. Trim away any extra pastry and seal the edges with a fork. Decorate with pastry scraps. Prick a few holes in the top of each pie, brush with a little milk and bake for 35 minutes, until golden.

NOTE: *Kecap manis is a thick, sweet soy sauce. If you can't find it, use regular soy sauce mixed with a little soft brown sugar.*

Add the cornflour and then boil for 2 minutes to let it thicken the filling.

Cut out six rounds of pastry to fit the tops of the pie tins, then cover the filling.

NUTRITION PER PIE
Protein 36 g; Fat 58 g; Carbohydrate 85 g; Dietary Fibre 8 g; Cholesterol 145 mg; 4145 kJ (990 Cal)

Beef, stout and potato pie

PREPARATION TIME: 30 MINUTES | TOTAL COOKING TIME: 3 HOURS 20 MINUTES | SERVES 6

2 tablespoons olive oil
1.25 kg (2 lb 12 oz) chuck steak, cut into
    small cubes
2 onions, sliced
2 bacon slices, roughly chopped
4 garlic cloves, crushed
2 tablespoons plain (all-purpose) flour
435 ml (15¼ fl oz) tin stout
375 ml (13 fl oz/1½ cups) beef stock
1½ tablespoons chopped thyme
2 large potatoes, thinly sliced

1   Heat 1 tablespoon of the oil over high heat in
a large flameproof casserole dish. Add the beef in
batches and cook, stirring, for 5 minutes, or until
the meat is browned. Remove from the dish.
Reduce the heat to low, add the remaining oil,
then cook the onion and bacon for 10 minutes,
stirring occasionally. Add the garlic and cook for
another minute. Return the beef to the dish.

2   Sprinkle the flour over the beef, cook for
a minute, stirring, and then gradually add the
stout, stirring constantly. Add the stock, increase
the heat to medium–high and bring to the boil.
Stir in the thyme, season well, then reduce the
heat and simmer for 2 hours, or until the beef is
tender and the mixture has thickened.

3   Preheat the oven to 200°C (400°F/Gas 6).
Lightly grease a 1.25 litre (44 fl oz/5 cup)
ovenproof dish and pour in the beef filling.
Arrange the potato slices in a single overlapping
layer over the top to cover the meat. Brush lightly
with olive oil and sprinkle with salt. Bake for
45–50 minutes, or until the topping is golden.

NUTRITION PER SERVE
Protein 49 g; Fat 13 g; Carbohydrate 14 g; Dietary
Fibre 2 g; Cholesterol 146 mg; 1665 kJ (400 Cal)

Gradually add the stout to the beef mixture, stirring
constantly.

Arrange the potato slices in a single overlapping
layer to cover the meat.

Asparagus pie

PREPARATION TIME: 40 MINUTES + 45 MINUTES REFRIGERATION I TOTAL COOKING TIME: 30 MINUTES I SERVES 6

350 g (12 oz) plain (all-purpose) flour
250 g (9 oz) butter, chilled and cubed
170 ml (5½ fl oz/⅔ cup) iced water

FILLING
800 g (1 lb 10 oz) asparagus
30 g (1 oz) butter
½ teaspoon chopped thyme
1 French shallot (eschallot), chopped
60 g (2¼ oz) sliced ham
80 ml (2½ fl oz/⅓ cup) cream
2 tablespoons grated parmesan cheese
1 egg
pinch of ground nutmeg
1 egg, extra, lightly beaten, to glaze

1 To make the pastry, mix the flour and a pinch of salt in a food processor for 3 seconds. Add the butter and mix until it is cut finely but not entirely blended into the flour—a few lumps are desirable. With the motor running on the processor, gradually pour in the iced water until the dough comes together. It should still have some small pebbles of butter.

2 Transfer the dough to a lightly floured work surface and press into a rectangle about 30 x 12 cm (12 x 4½ inches). Fold one end into the centre, then the opposite end over to cover the first. Roll into a rectangle again and repeat the folding three or four times. Wrap in plastic wrap and chill for 45 minutes.

3 Remove the woody ends from the asparagus and slice the thick spears in half lengthways. Heat the butter in a large frying pan and cook the asparagus, thyme and shallot with a tablespoon of water for 3 minutes, stirring often, until the asparagus is tender. Season well.

4 Preheat the oven to 200°C (400°F/Gas 6) and grease a 20 cm (8 inch) fluted, loose-based flan tin. Roll the pastry out to a circle about 30 cm (12 inches) diameter and line the tin, leaving the rest of the pastry hanging over the edge. Place half the asparagus in the dish, top with the ham, then the remaining asparagus.

5 Combine the cream, parmesan, egg and nutmeg. Season well and pour over the asparagus. Fold the excess pastry over the filling, forming loose pleats. Brush with the egg and bake for 25 minutes, or until golden.

NUTRITION PER SERVE
Protein 15 g; Fat 46 g; Carbohydrate 46 g; Dietary Fibre 4 g; Cholesterol 200 mg; 2730 kJ (650 Cal)

Fold the ends of the dough over and press into a rectangle. Repeat several times.

Pour the combined cream, egg, parmesan and nutmeg over the asparagus.

Salmon filo pie with dill butter

PREPARATION TIME: 25 MINUTES + COOLING | TOTAL COOKING TIME: 1 HOUR | SERVES 6–8

150 g (5½ oz/¾ cup) medium-grain white rice
90 g (3¼ oz) butter, melted
8 sheets filo pastry
500 g (1 lb 2 oz) fresh salmon fillet, cut into small cubes
2 French shallots (eschallots), finely chopped
1½ tablespoons baby capers
150 g (5½ oz) Greek-style yoghurt
1 egg
1 tablespoon grated lemon zest
3 tablespoons chopped dill
30 g (1 oz/¼ cup) dry breadcrumbs
1 tablespoon sesame seeds
2 teaspoons lemon juice

NUTRITION PER SERVE (6)
Protein 23 g; Fat 20 g; Carbohydrate 35 g; Dietary Fibre 1 g; Cholesterol 110 mg; 1705 kJ (410 Cal)

1 Put the rice in a large saucepan and add enough water to cover it by 2 cm (1 inch). Bring to the boil over medium heat, then reduce the heat to low, cover and cook for 20 minutes, or until all the water has been absorbed and tunnels appear on the surface of the rice. Set aside to cool.

2 Preheat the oven to 180°C (350°F/Gas 4). Grease a 20 x 30 cm (8 x 12 inch) baking tin with melted butter. Cover the filo pastry with a damp tea towel (dish towel). Mix the salmon with the shallots, capers, rice, yoghurt and egg. Add the lemon zest, 1 tablespoon of the dill and season well.

3 Layer four sheets of pastry in the base of the tin, brushing each one with melted butter and leaving the sides of the pastry hanging over the edge of the tin. Spoon in the salmon filling and pat down well. Fold the pastry over the filling.

4 Top with four sheets of filo, brushing each one with melted butter and sprinkling all but the top layer with a tablespoon of breadcrumbs. Sprinkle the top with sesame seeds.

5 Score the top of the pie into diamonds without cutting right through the pastry. Bake for 35–40 minutes on the lowest shelf until golden brown. Reheat the remaining butter, add the lemon juice and remaining dill and pour a small amount over each portion of pie.

Combine the salmon, shallots, capers, rice, yoghurt, egg, lemon zest and dill.

Sprinkle the pie with sesame seeds, then score the top into diamonds.

Beef and caramelised onion pie

PREPARATION TIME: 40 MINUTES + 20 MINUTES COOLING I TOTAL COOKING TIME: 2 HOURS 30 MINUTES I SERVES 6–8

80 ml (2½ fl oz/⅓ cup) oil

2 large red onions, thinly sliced

1 teaspoon dark brown sugar

1 kg (2 lb 4 oz) lean rump steak, diced

30 g (1 oz/¼ cup) plain (all-purpose) flour, seasoned

2 garlic cloves, crushed

225 g (8 oz) button mushrooms, sliced

250 ml (9 fl oz/1 cup) beef stock

150 ml (5 fl oz) stout

1 tablespoon tomato paste (concentrated purée)

1 tablespoon worcestershire sauce

1 tablespoon chopped thyme

350 g (12 oz) potatoes, diced

2 carrots, diced

600 g (1 lb 5 oz) quick flaky pastry

1 egg, lightly beaten, to glaze

NUTRITION PER SERVE (8)
Protein 36 g; Fat 32 g; Carbohydrate 47 g; Dietary Fibre 4 g; Cholesterol 113 mg; 2615 kJ (625 Cal)

1 Heat 2 tablespoons of the oil in a frying pan over medium heat and cook the onion for 5 minutes, or until light brown. Add the sugar and cook for another 7–8 minutes, or until the onion caramelises. Remove from the pan, set aside and wipe the pan clean.

2 Toss the beef in the flour and shake off the excess. Heat the remaining oil in the same pan and cook the meat in batches over high heat until browned. Return all the meat to the pan, add the garlic and mushrooms and cook for 2 minutes. Add the stock, stout, tomato paste, worcestershire sauce and thyme. Bring to the boil, then reduce the heat and simmer, covered, for 1 hour. Add the potato and carrot and simmer for 30 minutes. Remove from the heat and allow to cool.

3 Preheat the oven to 190°C (375°F/Gas 5). Grease a 1.25 litre (44 fl oz/5 cup) pie dish. Pour in the filling and top with the onion. Roll the pastry out between two sheets of baking paper until it is 2.5 cm (1 inch) wider than the pie dish. Cut a 2 cm (¾ inch) strip around the edge of the pastry, brush with water and then place damp side down on the rim of the dish.

4 Cover with the remaining pastry and press the edges together. Knock up the rim by making small slashes in the edges of the pastry with the back of a knife. Re-roll the trimmings and use them to decorate the pie. Brush with egg and bake for 35 minutes, or until golden.

Spoon the caramelised onion over the filling in the pie dish.

Place the strip of pastry damp side down on the rim of the dish.

Chicken and mushroom pithivier

PREPARATION TIME: 45 MINUTES + 30 MINUTES REFRIGERATION I TOTAL COOKING TIME: 40 MINUTES I SERVES 4

50 g (1¾ oz) butter
2 bacon slices, sliced
4 spring onions (scallions), chopped
100 g (3½ oz) button mushrooms, sliced
1 tablespoon plain (all-purpose) flour
185 ml (6 fl oz/¾ cup) milk
1 tablespoon cream
180 g (6¼ oz/1 cup) chopped cooked chicken
    breast
20 g (¾ oz/⅓ cup) chopped parsley
2 sheets puff pastry
1 egg yolk, lightly beaten, to glaze

1   Melt the butter in a pan and cook the bacon and spring onion, stirring, for 2–3 minutes. Add the mushrooms and cook, stirring, for 3 minutes. Stir in the flour and cook for 1 minute. Add the milk all at once and stir for 2–3 minutes, or until thickened. Simmer for 1 minute then remove from the heat. Stir in the cream, chicken and parsley. Set aside to cool.

2   Cut two 23 cm (9 inch) circles from the pastry sheets. Place one circle on a greased baking tray. Pile the chicken filling in the centre, mounding slightly in the middle and leaving a small border. Combine the egg yolk with 1 teaspoon water, and brush the pastry edge.

3   Using a small pointed knife and starting from the centre of the second pastry circle, mark curved lines at regular intervals. Take care not to cut through the pastry. Place this sheet over the other and stretch it a little to fit evenly. Press the edges together to seal. Using the back of a knife, push up the outside edge at 1 cm (½ inch) intervals. Cover and refrigerate for at least 30 minutes. Preheat the oven to 210°C (415°F/ Gas 6–7). Brush the pie with egg and make a hole in the centre for steam to escape. Bake for 25 minutes, or until golden.

Draw curved lines from the centre to the edge of the pastry.

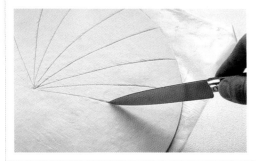

Use the back of a knife to push up the edge of the pastry.

NUTRITION PER SERVE
Protein 25 g; Fat 40 g; Carbohydrate 35 g; Dietary Fibre 2 g; Cholesterol 160 mg; 2395 kJ (570 Cal)

Cottage pie

PREPARATION TIME: 30 MINUTES | TOTAL COOKING TIME: 1 HOUR 45 MINUTES | SERVES 6–8

2 tablespoons olive oil

2 onions, chopped

2 carrots, diced

1 celery stalk, diced

1 kg (2 lb 4 oz) minced (ground) beef

2 tablespoons plain (all-purpose) flour

375 ml (13 fl oz/1½ cups) beef stock

1 tablespoon soy sauce

1 tablespoon worcestershire sauce

2 tablespoons tomato sauce (ketchup)

1 tablespoon tomato paste (concentrated purée)

2 bay leaves

2 teaspoons chopped flat-leaf (Italian) parsley

TOPPING

400 g (14 oz) potatoes, peeled and diced

400 g (14 oz) parsnips, peeled and diced

30 g (1 oz) butter

125 ml (4 fl oz/½ cup) milk

1   Heat the oil in a large frying pan over medium heat and cook the onion, carrot and celery, stirring occasionally, for 5 minutes, until softened and lightly coloured. Add the beef and cook for 7 minutes, then stir in the flour and cook for 2 minutes. Add the stock, soy sauce, worcestershire sauce, tomato sauce and paste and bay leaves and simmer over low heat for 30 minutes, stirring occasionally. Leave to cool. Remove the bay leaves and stir in the parsley.

2   To make the topping, boil the potato and parsnip in salted water for 15–20 minutes, or until cooked through. Drain, return to the pan and mash with the butter and enough of the milk to make a firm mash.

3   Preheat the oven to 180°C (350°F/Gas 4) and lightly grease a 2.5 litre (87 fl oz/10 cup) ovenproof dish. Spoon the filling into the dish and spread the topping over it. Fluff with a fork. Bake for 40 minutes, or until golden.

Mash the potato and parsnip together with a potato masher.

Spoon the cooled meat filling into the lightly greased dish.

NUTRITION PER SERVE (8)
Protein 31 g; Fat 18 g; Carbohydrate 27 g; Dietary Fibre 4 g; Cholesterol 78 mg; 1640 kJ (390 Cal)

Vegetable lattice pie

PREPARATION TIME: 40 MINUTES + REFRIGERATION | TOTAL COOKING TIME: 1 HOUR | SERVES 6

185 g (6½ oz) butter
250 g (9 oz/ 2 cups) plain (all-purpose) flour
3 tablespoons iced water

FILLING

1 tablespoon oil
1 small onion, finely chopped
1 small red capsicum (pepper), chopped
1 small green capsicum (pepper), chopped
150 g (5½ oz) pumpkin (winter squash), chopped
1 small potato, chopped
100 g (3½ oz) broccoli, cut into small florets
1 carrot, chopped
3 tablespoons plain (all-purpose) flour
250 ml (9 fl oz/1 cup) milk
2 egg yolks
60 g (2¼ oz/½ cup) grated cheddar cheese
1 egg, lightly beaten, to glaze

1 Chop 125 g (4½ oz) of the butter. Sift the flour into a large bowl and add the chopped butter. Rub the butter into the flour with your fingertips until the mixture is fine and crumbly. Add almost all the water and use a knife to mix to a firm dough, adding more water if necessary. Turn onto a lightly floured surface and press together until smooth. Divide the dough in half, roll out one portion and line a deep 20 cm (8 inch) fluted flan (tart) tin. Refrigerate for 20 minutes. Roll the remaining pastry out to a 25 cm (10 inch) diameter circle. Cut into strips and lay half of them on a sheet of baking paper, leaving a 2 cm (¾ inch) gap between each strip. Interweave the remaining strips to form a lattice pattern. Cover with plastic wrap and refrigerate, keeping flat, until firm.

2 Preheat the oven to 180°C (350°F/ Gas 4). Line the pastry in the flan tin with baking paper and spread with a layer of baking beads or rice. Bake for 10 minutes, remove from the oven and discard the paper and beans. Bake for another 10 minutes or until golden. Allow to cool.

3 To make the filling, heat the oil in a frying pan. Add the onion and cook for 2 minutes or until soft. Add the capsicum and cook, stirring, for another 3 minutes. Steam or boil the remaining vegetables until just tender; drain and cool. Combine the onion, capsicum and the other vegetables in a large bowl.

4 Heat the remaining butter in a small saucepan. Add the flour and cook, stirring, for 2 minutes. Add the milk gradually, stirring until smooth after each addition. Stir until the sauce boils and thickens. Boil for 1 minute and then remove from the heat. Add the egg yolks and cheese and stir until smooth. Pour over the vegetables and stir together. Pour into the pastry case and brush the edges with a little of the beaten egg. Using the baking paper to help, invert the lattice over the vegetables, trim the edges and brush with a little egg. Press the edges lightly to seal to the cooked pastry. Brush the top with egg and bake for 30 minutes or until the pastry is golden.

NUTRITION PER SERVE
Protein 17 g; Fat 39 g; Carbohydrate 48 g; Dietary Fibre 4 g; Cholesterol 190 mg; 2535 kJ (605 Cal)

Add almost all the water to the bowl, mixing with a knife until a firm dough is formed.

Invert the lattice over the pie and slowly pull away the baking paper.

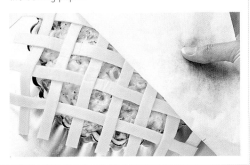

Savoury tarts

Pissaladière

PREPARATION TIME: 50 MINUTES + 50 MINUTES STANDING | TOTAL COOKING TIME: 2 HOURS | SERVES 8

7 g (¼ oz) dried yeast
1 teaspoon caster (superfine) sugar
375 g (13 oz/3 cups) plain (all-purpose) flour
2 tablespoons powdered milk
1 tablespoon oil

TOPPING
80 ml (2½ fl oz/⅓ cup) olive oil
3–4 garlic cloves, finely chopped
6 onions, cut into thin rings
425 g (15 oz) tinned chopped tomatoes
1 tablespoon tomato paste (concentrated
   purée)
15 g (½ oz/¼ cup) chopped flat-leaf
   (Italian) parsley
1 tablespoon chopped thyme
olive oil, for brushing
3 x 45 g (1½ oz) tins anchovy fillets, drained
   and halved lengthways
36 small black olives

1 Lightly grease two 30 cm (12 inch) pizza trays. Place the yeast, sugar and 250 ml (4½ fl oz/½ cup) warm water in a small bowl. Set aside in a warm place for 5–10 minutes, or until frothy (if the yeast doesn't froth, then start again with a fresh batch). Sift the plain flour, ½ teaspoon salt and the milk powder into a large bowl and make a well in the centre. Add the oil and yeast and mix thoroughly.

2 Turn onto a lightly floured surface and knead for 10 minutes, gradually adding small amounts of flour if necessary, until the dough is smooth and elastic. Place in an oiled bowl and brush the surface with a little oil, cover with plastic wrap and set aside in a warm place for 30 minutes, or until doubled in size.

3 To make the topping, heat the oil in a saucepan. Add the garlic and onion and cook, covered, over low heat for about 40 minutes, stirring frequently. The onion should be softened but not browned. Remove the lid and cook, stirring often, for a further 30 minutes, or until lightly golden. Take care not to burn. Set aside to cool.

4 Cook the chopped tomato in a pan, stirring frequently, for 20 minutes, or until thick and reduced to about 250 ml (9 fl oz/1 cup). Remove from the heat and stir in the tomato paste and herbs. Season with freshly ground black pepper. Cool, then stir into the cooled onion mixture.

5 Preheat the oven to 220°C (425°F/Gas 7). Punch down the dough, then turn onto a lightly floured surface and knead for 2 minutes. Divide the dough in half. Return one portion to the bowl and cover. Roll out the other portion to a 30 cm (12 inch) circle and press evenly onto the pizza tray. Brush with some olive oil. Spread half the onion and tomato mixture evenly onto the dough, leaving a small border. Arrange half the anchovy fillets over the top in a lattice pattern and place an olive in each square. Repeat with the rest of the dough and topping. Bake for 15–20 minutes, or until the dough is cooked through and lightly browned (if you bake both tarts in the oven at the same time, they will take a little longer to cook).

NUTRITION PER SERVE
Protein 9 g; Fat 17 g; Carbohydrate 35 g; Dietary Fibre 5 g; Cholesterol 8 mg; 1390 kJ (330 Cal)

Stir the tomato paste and herbs into the cooked tomatoes, then season with pepper.

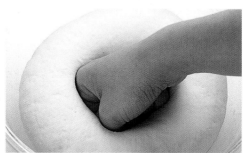
Punch down the dough to expel any excess air before kneading.

Arrange half of the anchovy fillets in a lattice pattern over the top.

Mediterranean ricotta tarts

PREPARATION TIME: 20 MINUTES + 20 MINUTES COOLING | TOTAL COOKING TIME: 30 MINUTES | MAKES 6

30 g (1 oz/⅓ cup) dry breadcrumbs
2 tablespoons olive oil
1 garlic clove, crushed
½ red capsicum (pepper), quartered and cut into thin strips
1 zucchini (courgette), cut into thin strips
3 slices prosciutto, cut into thin strips
375 g (13 oz) firm ricotta cheese (see NOTE)
40 g (1½ oz/⅓ cup) grated cheddar cheese
30 g (1 oz/⅓ cup) grated parmesan cheese
2 tablespoons shredded basil
4 black olives, pitted and sliced

1   Preheat the oven to 180°C (350°F Gas 4). Lightly grease six 10 cm (4 inch) fluted (tart) flan tins. Lightly sprinkle 1 teaspoon breadcrumbs over the base and side of each tin.

2   Heat half the oil in a frying pan, add the garlic, capsicum and zucchini and cook, stirring, over medium heat for 5 minutes, or until the vegetables are soft. Remove from the heat and add the prosciutto. Season to taste.

3   Place the ricotta in a large bowl and add the other cheeses and remaining breadcrumbs. Season. Press the mixture into the tins and smooth the surface.

4   Bake for 20 minutes, or until the tarts are slightly puffed and golden. Cool completely (the tarts will deflate on cooling) and remove from the tins. Do not refrigerate.

5   Sprinkle the bases with basil and divide the vegetable mixture between them. Top with the olives then drizzle with the remaining oil.

NOTE: *Use firm ricotta or very well-drained ricotta, or the tarts will be difficult to remove from the tins.*

Sprinkle breadcrumbs over the base and sides of each tin.

Bake the tarts until they are puffed and golden around the edges.

NUTRITION PER TART
Protein 20 g; Fat 27 g; Carbohydrate 8 g; Dietary Fibre 1 g; Cholesterol 66 mg; 1457 kJ (348 Cal)

Cheese and chive soufflé tart

PREPARATION TIME: 40 MINUTES | TOTAL COOKING TIME: 55 MINUTES | SERVES 6–8

80 g (2¾ oz) butter
40 g (1½ oz/⅓ cup) plain (all-purpose) flour
250 ml (9 fl oz/1 cup) cream
160 g (5½ oz/⅔ cup) sour cream
4 eggs, separated
130 g (4½ oz/1 cup) grated gruyère cheese
3 tablespoons chopped chives
¼ teaspoon ground nutmeg
pinch of cayenne pepper
12 sheets filo pastry

1 Preheat the oven to 190°C (375°F/ Gas 5). Grease a deep 20 cm (8 inch) loose-based fluted flan (tart) tin or pie dish. Melt half the butter in a saucepan. Sift in the flour and cook, stirring, for 1 minute. Remove from the heat and gradually whisk in the cream and sour cream.

2 Return to the heat and whisk constantly until the mixture boils and thickens. Remove from the heat and whisk in the egg yolks. Then cover the surface with plastic wrap and set aside to allow to cool slightly. Whisk in the cheese, chives, nutmeg and cayenne pepper.

3 Melt the remaining butter and brush some over each sheet of pastry. Fold each one in half and use to line the flan tin, allowing the edges to overhang.

4 Beat the egg whites until stiff peaks form, then stir a spoonful into the cheese mixture to loosen it up. Gently fold in the rest of the beaten egg white. Spoon the mixture into the pastry shell and then fold the pastry over the top. Brush the top with the remaining melted butter and bake for 40–45 minutes, or until puffed and golden. Serve immediately.

Fold each buttered sheet of filo in half, and use to line the tart tin.

Carefully fold the filo pastry over the top of the filling, then brush with melted butter.

NUTRITION PER SERVE (8)
Protein 10 g; Fat 40 g; Carbohydrate 15 g; Dietary Fibre 1 g; Cholesterol 200 mg; 1895 kJ (450 Cal)

Spicy pumpkin and cashew tarts

PREPARATION TIME: 1 HOUR + 20 MINUTES REFRIGERATION | TOTAL COOKING TIME: 1 HOUR | SERVES 4

250 g (9 oz/2 cups) plain (all-purpose) flour
100 g (3½ oz) butter, chilled and cubed
1½ tablespoons coriander seeds, lightly crushed
1 egg
2 teaspoons iced water

CASHEW NUT TOPPING
40 g (1 oz/¼ cup) roasted cashews, chopped
¼ teaspoon paprika
1 teaspoon cumin seeds
1 teaspoon sesame seeds

SPICY PUMPKIN FILLING
600 g (1 lb 5 oz) butternut pumpkin (squash)
1 tablespoon oil
1 onion, thinly sliced
1 garlic clove, crushed
¼ teaspoon ground cumin
¼ teaspoon ground coriander
½ teaspoon garam masala
¼ teaspoon chilli flakes
1 tablespoon honey
1 tablespoon soy sauce
200 g (7 oz) ricotta cheese

1 Process the flour, butter, coriander seeds and a pinch of salt in a food processor for 15 seconds, or until the mixture resembles fine breadcrumbs. Add the egg and water. Process in short bursts until the mixture just comes together, adding a little more water if necessary. Turn onto a floured surface and gather into a ball. Wrap in plastic and refrigerate for at least 20 minutes.

2 Preheat the oven to 200°C (400°F/Gas 6) and grease four shallow 11 cm (4¼ inch) loose-based flan (tart) tins. Divide the pastry into quarters and roll out on baking paper to line the tins, pressing well into the base and side. Trim off the excess pastry with a sharp knife or by rolling a rolling pin over the top of the tin. Prick all over the bases with a fork and bake for 18–20 minutes, or until browned. Set aside to cool. Reduce the oven to 180°C (350°F/Gas 4).

3 To make the cashew nut topping, mix the cashews and paprika. Place the cumin and sesame seeds in a dry frying pan and stir over low heat until lightly toasted, add to the cashew mixture and set aside to cool.

4 To make the spicy pumpkin filling, cut the pumpkin into 2.5 cm (1 inch) cubes. Heat the oil in a pan, add the pumpkin, onion, garlic and spices and cook, stirring, over medium heat, until the onion is soft and translucent. Add the honey and 2 tablespoons water. Bring to the boil, then reduce the heat and simmer, covered, for 10–15 minutes, or until the pumpkin is tender. Stir in the soy sauce.

5 Place a quarter of the ricotta cheese into the base of each pastry shell. Spoon the spicy pumpkin filling and its liquid over the cheese and then sprinkle with the cashew nut topping. Place the tarts in the oven to reheat for 10 minutes. Serve warm.

NUTRITION PER SERVE
Protein 20 g; Fat 40 g; Carbohydrate 70 g; Dietary Fibre 6 g; Cholesterol 135 mg; 2955 kJ (705 Cal)

Lightly crush the coriander seeds using a mortar and pestle.

Chop the roasted cashew nuts and then mix with the paprika in a bowl.

Lightly toast the cumin and sesame seeds in a dry frying pan.

Roasted tomato and zucchini tartlets

PREPARATION TIME: 45 MINUTES | TOTAL COOKING TIME: 1 HOUR 20 MINUTES | MAKES 6

3 roma (plum) tomatoes, halved lengthways
1 teaspoon balsamic vinegar
1 teaspoon olive oil
3 small zucchini (courgettes), sliced
3 sheets ready-rolled puff pastry
1 egg yolk, beaten, to glaze
12 small black olives
24 capers, rinsed and drained

PISTACHIO MINT PESTO
75 g (2½ oz/½ cup) unsalted shelled pistachio
  nuts
40 g (1½ oz/2 cups) firmly packed mint leaves
2 garlic cloves, crushed
80 ml (2½ fl oz/⅓ cup) olive oil
50 g (1¾ oz/½ cup) grated parmesan cheese

1 Preheat the oven to 150°C (300°F/Gas 2). Place the tomatoes, cut side up, on a baking tray. Roast for 30 minutes, brush with the combined vinegar and oil and roast for a further 30 minutes. Increase the oven temperature to 210°C (415°F/Gas 6–7).

2 To make the pesto, place the pistachios, mint and garlic in a food processor and process for 15 seconds. With the motor running, slowly pour in the olive oil. Add the parmesan and process briefly.

3 Preheat the grill (broiler) and line with foil. Place the zucchini in a single layer on the foil and brush with the remaining balsamic vinegar and oil. Grill for about 5 minutes, turning once.

4 Roll out the pastry to 25 x 40 cm (10 x 16 inches) and cut out six 12 cm (4 inches) circles. Put the circles on a greased baking tray and brush with egg yolk. Spread a tablespoon of pesto on each, leaving a 2 cm (¾ inch) border. Divide the zucchini among the pastries and top with tomato halves. Bake for 15 minutes, or until golden. Top with olives, capers and black pepper.

Roast the tomatoes for 30 minutes, then brush with the vinegar and oil.

Arrange a few grilled zucchini slices over the pesto, leaving a clear border.

NUTRITION PER TARTLET
Protein 15 g; Fat 60 g; Carbohydrate 35 g; Dietary Fibre 6 g; Cholesterol 80 mg; 3040 kJ (725 Cal)

Salami, eggplant and artichoke tart

PREPARATION TIME: 20 MINUTES + 30 MINUTES REFRIGERATION | TOTAL COOKING TIME: 55 MINUTES | SERVES 4–6

125 g (4½ oz/1 cup) plain (all-purpose) flour
60 g (2¼ oz) butter, chilled and cubed
1 egg yolk
1–2 tablespoons iced water

FILLING
2 tablespoons oil
250 g (9 oz) eggplant (aubergine), cubed
110 g (3¾ oz/½ cup) quartered marinated
   artichokes
125 g (4½ oz) piece salami, cubed
1 tablespoon chopped chives
1 tablespoon chopped parsley
1 egg, lightly beaten
60 ml (2 fl oz/¼ cup) cream

1 Put the flour and butter in a food processor and process for 15 seconds, or until crumbly. Add the egg yolk and water and process in short bursts until the mixture just comes together, adding a little more water if necessary. Turn the mixture onto a floured surface and gather together into a ball. Wrap in plastic and refrigerate for at least 20 minutes. Preheat the oven to 200°C (400°F/Gas 6). Grease a shallow 20 cm (8 inch) loose-based flan (tart) tin.

2 Roll out the pastry on a sheet of baking paper to line the tin and trim off any excess. Refrigerate for 10 minutes. Prick the pastry with a fork and bake for 10 minutes, until lightly browned. Cool.

3 Heat the oil and toss the eggplant over high heat until it begins to brown and soften; drain on paper towels. Mix the eggplant, artichokes, salami and herbs and press firmly into the pastry case. Pour over the combined egg and cream and bake for 45 minutes, or until browned and set.

Cut the salami and eggplant into cubes. You can use plain or flat-leaf (Italian) parsley.

Press the filling firmly into the base and pour over the egg and cream.

NUTRITION PER SERVE (6)
Protein 8 g; Fat 25 g; Carbohydrate 15 g; Dietary Fibre 2 g; Cholesterol 75 mg; 1300 kJ (310 Cal)

Italian summer tart

PREPARATION TIME: 40 MINUTES + 50 MINUTES REFRIGERATION | TOTAL COOKING TIME: 1 HOUR | SERVES 4–6

185 g (6½ oz/1½ cups) plain (all-purpose) flour
90 g (3¼ oz) butter, chilled and cubed
1 egg yolk
2–3 tablespoons iced water

FILLING
1 tablespoon olive oil
2 small red onions, sliced
1 tablespoon balsamic vinegar
1 teaspoon soft brown sugar
1 tablespoon thyme leaves
170 g (6 oz) jar marinated quartered artichokes, drained
4 slices prosciutto, cut into strips
12 black olives

1 Place the flour and butter in a food processor and process for 15 seconds, or until the mixture resembles fine breadcrumbs. Add the egg yolk and water. Process in short bursts until the mixture just comes together, adding a little extra water if necessary. Turn onto a lightly floured work surface and gather together into a ball. Cover with plastic wrap and refrigerate for at least 30 minutes.

2 Roll the pastry between two sheets of baking paper until large enough to fit a 35 x 10 cm (14 x 4 inch) loose-based flan tin. Press it well into the sides and trim off the excess. Cover and refrigerate for 20 minutes.

3 Preheat the oven to 190°C (375°F/Gas 5). Cover the pastry shell with baking paper and fill evenly with baking beads or rice. Bake for 15 minutes. Remove the paper and beads and bake for a further 15 minutes, or until the pastry is golden and dry. Cool on a wire rack.

4 To make the filling, heat the oil in a saucepan, add the onion slices and cook, stirring occasionally, for 15 minutes. Add the vinegar and sugar and cook for a further 15 minutes. Remove from the heat, stir through the thyme leaves and set aside to cool.

5 Spread the onion mixture evenly over the pastry shell. Arrange the quartered artichoke pieces on top, then fill the spaces between the artichokes with rolled-up pieces of prosciutto and the black olives. Serve the tart at room temperature.

NUTRITION PER SERVE (6)
Protein 6 g; Fat 15 g; Carbohydrate 25 g; Dietary Fibre 2 g; Cholesterol 70 mg; 1155 kJ (275 Cal)

Once the mixture resembles fine breadcrumbs, add the egg yolk and a little water.

Fill the spaces with rolled-up pieces of prosciutto and black olives.

Vol-au-vents

PREPARATION TIME: 20 MINUTES + 15 MINUTES REFRIGERATION | TOTAL COOKING TIME: 30 MINUTES | MAKES 4

250 g (9 oz) puff pastry
1 egg, lightly beaten
40 g (1½ oz) butter
2 spring onions (scallions), finely chopped
2 tablespoons plain (all-purpose) flour
375 ml (13 fl oz/1½ cups) milk
your choice of filling (see NOTE)

1 Preheat the oven to 220°C (425°F/Gas 7) and line a baking tray with baking paper. Roll out the pastry to a 20 cm (8 inch) square. Cut four circles of pastry with a 10 cm (4 inch) cutter. Place the rounds onto the tray and score 6 cm (2½ inch) circles into the centre of the rounds with a cutter, taking care not to cut right through the pastry. Refrigerate for 15 minutes.

2 Use a floured knife blade to knock up the sides of each pastry round by indenting every 1 cm (½ inch) around the rim. Brush with the egg, carefully avoiding the edge as any glaze spilt on the side will stop the pastry from rising.

3 Bake for 20 minutes, until golden brown and crisp. Cool on a wire rack. Remove the centre from each pastry circle and pull out and discard any partially cooked pastry from the centre. Return to the oven for 2 minutes to dry out if the centre is undercooked.

4 Melt the butter in a saucepan, add the spring onion and stir over low heat for 2 minutes, or until soft. Add the flour and stir for 2 minutes, or until lightly golden. Gradually add the milk, stirring until smooth. Stir constantly over medium heat for 4 minutes, or until the mixture boils and thickens. Season well. Remove from the heat and stir in your choice of filling before spooning into the cases to serve.

NOTE: *Add 350 g (12 oz) of any of the following to the sauce: sliced, cooked mushrooms; peeled, cooked prawns; chopped, cooked chicken breast; poached, flaked salmon; dressed crabmeat; oysters; steamed asparagus spears.*

Cut out four circles from the puff pastry with a 10 cm (4 inch) cutter.

Make indentations around the outside of the pastry with a knife.

NUTRITION PER VOL-AU-VENT (UNFILLED)
Protein 9 g; Fat 27 g; Carbohydrate 31 g; Dietary Fibre 1 g; Cholesterol 100 mg; 1680 kJ (400 Cal)

Sweet potato, potato and onion tart

PREPARATION TIME: 45 MINUTES + 15 MINUTES REFRIGERATION | TOTAL COOKING TIME: 1 HOUR 20 MINUTES | SERVES 4–6

125 g (4½ oz/1 cup) plain (all-purpose) flour
90 g (3¼ oz) butter, chilled and cubed
1–2 tablespoons iced water

FILLING
400 g (14 oz) orange sweet potato, peeled
400 g (14 oz) potatoes, peeled
1 onion, thinly sliced
250 ml (9 fl oz/1 cup) cream
2 eggs
1 tablespoon wholegrain mustard

1 Mix the flour and butter in a food processor until the mixture resembles fine breadcrumbs. Add the water and process for 5 seconds to combine. Turn onto a lightly floured surface and gather into a smooth ball.

2 Roll out the pastry on a sheet of baking paper large enough to fit the base and sides of a 23 cm (9 inch) flan (tart) tin. Trim away the excess and chill for 15 minutes. Preheat the oven to 190°C (375°F/Gas 5).

3 Cover the pastry with a piece of baking paper, fill with baking beads or uncooked rice and bake for 10 minutes. Discard the paper and beads and bake for another 10 minutes. Cool.

4 Thinly slice the sweet potato and potato. Cook in a steamer for 15 minutes, or until just tender. Drain off any liquid, cover and set aside.

5 Layer the sweet potato and potato in the pastry shell, in an overlapping pattern, with the onion, gently pushing the layers in to compact them, finishing with onion. Combine the cream, eggs and mustard, season and pour over the tart. Bake for 45 minutes, or until golden.

Roll out the pastry and use to line the base and side of the tin.

Mix together the cream, egg and mustard and pour over the tart.

NUTRITION PER SERVE (6)
Protein 9 g; Fat 30 g; Carbohydrate 40 g; Dietary Fibre 4 g; Cholesterol 155 mg; 2035 kJ (485 Cal)

Ratatouille tarts

PREPARATION TIME: 40 MINUTES + 15 MINUTES REFRIGERATION + 20 MINUTES STANDING | TOTAL COOKING TIME: 1 HOUR 10 MINUTES | MAKES 12

375 g (13 oz/3 cups) plain (all-purpose) flour
170 g (6 oz) butter, chilled and chopped
125 ml (4 fl oz/½ cup) iced water

RATATOUILLE FILLING
1 eggplant (aubergine) (about 500 g/1 lb 6 oz)
60 ml (2 fl oz/¼ cup) oil
1 onion, chopped
2 garlic cloves, crushed
2 zucchini (courgettes), sliced
1 red capsicum (pepper), chopped
1 green capsicum (pepper), chopped
250 g (9 oz) cherry tomatoes, halved
1 tablespoon balsamic vinegar
125 g (4½ oz/1 cup) grated cheddar cheese

1   Sift the flour into a bowl and add the butter. Using your fingertips, rub the butter into the flour until the mixture resembles fine breadcrumbs. Make a well in the centre and add most of the water. Mix together with a flat-bladed knife, using a cutting action, until the dough just comes together, adding a little more water if necessary.

2   Turn the dough onto a work surface, gather into a ball and divide into 12 portions. Grease twelve 8 cm (3¼ inch) loose-based fluted flan (tart) tins. Roll out each portion of dough on a sheet of baking paper to a circle a little larger than the tins. Lift the pastry into the tins and press well into the sides, then trim away any excess pastry. Refrigerate for 15 minutes. Preheat the oven to 200°C (400°F/Gas 6).

3   Put the tins on baking trays, prick the pastry bases all over with a fork and bake for 20–25 minutes, or until the pastry is fully cooked and lightly golden. Cool completely.

4   Meanwhile, to make the ratatouille filling, cut the eggplant into 2 cm (¾ inch) cubes, put into a colander and sprinkle generously with salt. Leave for 20 minutes, then rinse, drain and pat dry with paper towels.

5   Heat 2 tablespoons of the oil in a large frying pan and cook the eggplant for 8–10 minutes, or until browned. Drain on paper towels. Heat the remaining oil and add the onion. Cook over medium heat for 5 minutes, or until very soft. Add the garlic and cook for 1 minute, then add the zucchini and capsicum and cook, stirring frequently, for 10 minutes, or until softened. Add the eggplant and tomatoes. Cook, stirring, for 2 minutes. Transfer to a bowl, stir in the vinegar, then cover and cool completely.

6   Preheat the oven to 180°C (350°F/ Gas 4). Divide the filling among the shells using a slotted spoon, draining off any excess liquid. Sprinkle with the cheese and bake for 10–15 minutes, or until the cheese has melted and the tarts are warmed through.

NOTE: *The ratatouille filling can be made a day ahead and stored in an airtight container in the refrigerator.*

NUTRITION PER TART
Protein 7.5 g; Fat 20 g; Carbohydrate 25 g; Dietary Fibre 3.5 g; Cholesterol 45 mg; 1328 kJ (317 Cal)

Rub the butter into the sifted flour until the mixture resembles fine breadcrumbs.

Sprinkle a generous amount of salt on the eggplant cubes.

Pour the balsamic vinegar over the vegetables and mix well.

Tomato, parmesan and anchovy tart

PREPARATION TIME: 10 MINUTES + COOLING | TOTAL COOKING TIME: 1 HOUR 45 MINUTES | SERVES 6–8

3 tablespoons olive oil
1 onion, finely chopped
2 tablespoons chopped parsley
1 teaspoon dried basil
1 teaspoon sugar
2 x 800 g (1 lb 12 oz) tins tomatoes, drained
2 sheets shortcrust pastry
2 teaspoons chopped anchovy fillets
2 tablespoons grated parmesan cheese
3 eggs, lightly beaten

1 Heat the oil in a frying pan and gently fry the onion for 15 minutes, or until golden. Add the parsley, basil and sugar and cook for 20–30 seconds, stirring constantly.

2 Drain the tomatoes and chop into a pulp. Add to the pan, then reduce the heat and simmer for 30 minutes, or until dark and quite dry. Cool.

3 Preheat the oven to 180°C (350°F/Gas 4) and grease a 23 cm (9 inch) shallow fluted loose-based flan (tart) tin. Roll the pastry sheets together, one on top of the other, to 3 mm (⅛ inch) thick. Line the tin with the pastry and prick with a fork. Line with baking paper, fill with baking beads or rice and bake for 10 minutes. Remove the baking paper and beads and bake for a further 10 minutes, or until dry.

4 Stir the anchovies, parmesan cheese and eggs through the filling, then spoon into the pastry case and level the surface. Bake for 40 minutes, or until set.

Line the tart tin with pastry and prick the base with a fork to reduce puffing.

Stir the chopped anchovies, parmesan and eggs through the filling.

NUTRITION PER SERVE (6)
Protein 6 g; Fat 17 g; Carbohydrate 18 g; Dietary Fibre 2 g; Cholesterol 65 mg; 1045 kJ (250 Cal)

Feta tart with beetroot

PREPARATION TIME: 40 MINUTES + 15 MINUTES REFRIGERATION | TOTAL COOKING TIME: 1 HOUR | SERVES 6

110 g (3¾ oz/¾ cup) plain wholemeal
 (whole-wheat) flour
90 g (3½ oz/¾ cup) plain (all-purpose) flour
125 g (4½ oz) butter, chilled and cubed
1 egg yolk
1–2 tablespoons iced water
300 g (10½ oz) ricotta cheese
300 g (10½ oz) crumbled feta cheese
3 eggs, lightly beaten
300 g (10½ oz) baby beetroot (beets), with
 short stalks attached
1 tablespoon walnut or olive oil
1 tablespoon red wine vinegar
30 g (1 oz/¼ cup) chopped pecans
2 tablespoons coriander (cilantro) leaves

1   Place the flours, butter and a pinch of salt in
a food processor and mix for 15 seconds, until
crumbly. Add the egg yolk and most of the water.
Process in short bursts until the mixture just
comes together, adding more water if needed.
Turn onto a floured surface and gather into a
ball. Wrap in plastic and chill for 15 minutes.
Preheat the oven to 180°C (350°F/Gas 4).

2   Mix the cheeses together with a fork. Add
the eggs and mix well. Grease a 23 cm (9 inch)
loose-based flan (tart) tin. Roll out the pastry
on a floured surface to line the tin, press it into
the sides and trim off any excess pastry. Cover
with baking paper, fill with baking beads or rice
and bake for 10 minutes. Remove the paper and
beads and bake for a further 10 minutes.

3   Spoon the filling into the base and bake for
30 minutes, or until the filling is firm and puffed
(the filling will flatten slightly when removed
from the oven).

4   Boil or steam the beetroots until tender, then
peel and cut in half. Drizzle with the combined
oil and vinegar, and season well. Serve the
beetroot, chopped pecans and coriander with
the tart.

NUTRITION PER SERVE
Protein 25 g; Fat 45 g; Carbohydrate 25 g; Dietary
Fibre 4 g; Cholesterol 230 mg; 2455 kJ (585 Cal)

The baby beetroots should be well scrubbed and trimmed, leaving just a short stem.

Blind-bake the pastry shell, then add the ricotta and feta filling.

Caramelised onion, rocket and blue cheese tarts

PREPARATION TIME: 30 MINUTES + 30 MINUTES REFRIGERATION | TOTAL COOKING TIME: 1 HOUR 10 MINUTES | MAKES 6

250 g (9 oz/2 cups) plain (all-purpose) flour
125 g (4½ oz) butter, chilled and cubed
30 g (1 oz/¼ cup) grated parmesan cheese
1 egg, lightly beaten
60 ml (2 fl oz/¼ cup) iced water

FILLING
2 tablespoons olive oil
3 onions, thinly sliced
100 g (3½ oz) baby rocket leaves
100 g (3½ oz) blue cheese, crumbled
3 eggs, lightly beaten
60 ml (2 fl oz/¼ cup) cream
60 g (2¼ oz/½ cup) grated parmesan cheese
pinch of grated nutmeg

NUTRITION PER TART
Protein 18 g; Fat 40 g; Carbohydrate 33 g; Dietary
Fibre 2.5 g; Cholesterol 215 mg; 2388 kJ (570 Cal)

1   In a large bowl, rub the butter into the sifted flour until it resembles fine breadcrumbs. Stir in the parmesan. Make a well in the centre, add the egg and water and mix with a flat-bladed knife, using a cutting action, until the mixture forms beads. Turn onto a lightly floured work surface, press into a disc, wrap in plastic and chill for 30 minutes.

2   Preheat the oven to 200°C (400°F/Gas 6). Divide the pastry into six portions. Roll the dough out between two sheets of baking paper to fit six 8 cm (3¼ inch) fluted loose-based flan (tart) tins, trimming off the excess.

3   Line the pastry shells with baking paper large enough to cover the base and side of each tin and cover with baking beads or rice. Bake for 10 minutes, then remove the paper and beads and bake for a further 10 minutes, or until the base is dry and golden. Cool slightly. Reduce the oven to 180°C (350°F/Gas 4).

4   Heat the oil in a large frying pan, add the onion and cook over medium heat for 20 minutes, or until the onion is caramelised. Add the rocket and stir until wilted. Remove from the pan and cool.

5   Divide the mixture between the tart bases and sprinkle with the blue cheese. Whisk together the eggs, cream, parmesan and nutmeg and pour evenly over each of the tarts. Place on a baking tray and bake for 20–30 minutes. Serve hot or cold.

Rub the butter into the flour until the dough resembles fine breadcrumbs.

Use a small ball of pastry to help you press the pastry neatly into the tins.

Tomato and thyme tart

PREPARATION TIME: 35 MINUTES + 15 MINUTES REFRIGERATION I TOTAL COOKING TIME: 30 MINUTES I SERVES 6–8

250 g (9 oz/2 cups) plain (all-purpose) flour
125 g (4½ oz) butter, chilled and cubed
125 g (4½ oz) cream cheese, chopped
1 tablespoon thyme leaves

FILLING
40 g (1½ oz/½ cup) fresh breadcrumbs
30 g (1 oz/¼ cup) grated parmesan cheese
2 tablespoons lemon thyme leaves
6 roma (plum) tomatoes, sliced
3 spring onions (scallions), sliced
1 egg yolk, beaten with 1 teaspoon of water,
    to glaze

1 Mix the flour, butter, cream cheese and thyme in a food processor. Add 2 tablespoons of water and process in short bursts until the mixture just comes together, adding more water if needed. Turn onto a floured surface and gather together into a ball. Press into a large triangle, cover with plastic wrap and chill for 15 minutes. Place on a greased baking tray and prick all over with a fork.

2 Preheat the oven to 210°C (415°F/Gas 6–7). Place the breadcrumbs, most of the parmesan and 1 tablespoon of the lemon thyme on the pastry, leaving an 8 cm (3¼ inch) border. Overlap the tomatoes and scatter some of the spring onions on top, maintaining the border. Add freshly ground black pepper, the remaining spring onions, parmesan cheese and lemon thyme. Fold the pastry border over the filling, pleating as you go, and press to seal. Brush with the egg and water glaze and bake for 10 minutes. Reduce the oven temperature to 180°C (350°F/Gas 4) and cook for a further 15–20 minutes, or until golden.

Press the pastry dough into a rough triangle shape before chilling.

Turn the pastry border up and over the filling to make a traditional free-form tart.

NUTRITION PER SERVE (6)
Protein 10 g; Fat 30 g; Carbohydrate 40 g; Dietary Fibre 3 g; Cholesterol 110 mg; 1840 kJ (440 Cal)

French shallot tatin

PREPARATION TIME: 45 MINUTES + 20 MINUTES REFRIGERATION | TOTAL COOKING TIME: 1 HOUR | SERVES 4–6

750 g (1 lb 10 oz) French shallots (eschallots)
50 g (1¾ oz) butter
2 tablespoons olive oil
60 g (2¼ oz/⅓ cup) soft brown sugar
3 tablespoons balsamic vinegar
125 g (4½ oz/1 cup) plain (all-purpose) flour
60g (2¼ oz) butter, chilled and cubed
2 teaspoons wholegrain mustard
1 egg yolk
1–2 tablespoons iced water

1   Peel the shallots, leaving the bases intact and tips exposed. Heat the butter and olive oil in a large saucepan and cook the shallots over low heat for 15 minutes, then remove. Add the sugar, vinegar and 3 tablespoons water and stir to dissolve the sugar. Return the shallots to the pan and simmer over low heat for 15–20 minutes, turning occasionally.

2   Preheat the oven to 200°C (400°F/Gas 6). Process the flour and butter in a food processor until crumbly. Add the mustard, egg yolk and most of the water. Process in short bursts until the mixture comes together, adding more water if necessary. Turn onto a floured surface and gather into a ball. Wrap in plastic and refrigerate for 20 minutes.

3   Grease a shallow 20 cm (8 inch) round sandwich tin. Tightly pack the shallots into the tin and pour over syrup from the pan. Roll out the pastry on a sheet of baking paper to a circle, 1 cm (½ inch) larger than the tin. Lift the pastry into the tin and lightly push it down so it is slightly moulded over the shallots. Bake for 20–25 minutes, or until golden brown. Cool for 5 minutes on a wire rack. Place a plate over the tin and turn the tart out.

HINT: *Put the unpeeled shallots in boiling water for 30 seconds to make them easier to peel.*

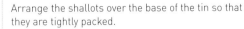

Arrange the shallots over the base of the tin so that they are tightly packed.

Lightly push the edges of the pastry down so that it moulds over the shallots.

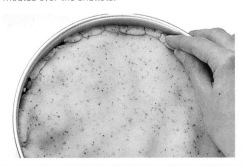

NUTRITION PER SERVE (6)
Protein 5 g; Fat 25 g; Carbohydrate 25 g; Dietary Fibre 2 g; Cholesterol 75 mg; 1360 kJ (325 Cal)

Red capsicum, tomato and onion tart

PREPARATION TIME: 35 MINUTES + 20 MINUTES REFRIGERATION | TOTAL COOKING TIME: 1 HOUR 10 MINUTES | SERVES 6–8

150 g (5½ oz/1¼ cups) plain (all-purpose) flour

100 g (3½ oz/⅔ cup) wholemeal (whole-wheat) plain flour

125 g (4½ oz) butter, chilled and cubed

1 tablespoon sesame seeds

1 egg, lightly beaten

1–2 tablespoons iced water

FILLING

500 g (1 lb 2 oz) tomatoes, finely chopped

2 tablespoons tomato paste (concentrated purée)

1 teaspoon dried oregano

½ teaspoon sugar

1 tablespoon olive oil

3 red onions, sliced

1 teaspoon chopped thyme

3 red capsicums (peppers)

35 g (1¼ oz/⅓ cup) grated parmesan cheese

1　Process the flours, butter and sesame seeds in a food processor for about 15 seconds, or until the mixture resembles fine breadcrumbs. Add the egg and process in short bursts until the mixture just comes together. Add iced water if necessary. Turn onto a lightly floured surface and gather into a ball. Wrap in plastic and refrigerate for at least 20 minutes. Preheat the oven to 200°C (400°F/Gas 6) and grease a shallow 19 x 28 cm (7½ x 11¼ inch) loose-based fluted flan (tart) tin.

2　Roll out the pastry on baking paper until large enough to line the tin. Press into the sides and trim off the excess. Prick the pastry all over with a fork and bake for 12 minutes, or until just brown and dry. Allow to cool.

3　To make the filling, heat the tomatoes, tomato paste, oregano and sugar in a saucepan. Bring to the boil, then reduce the heat and simmer for 15–20 minutes, or until thick. Allow to cool. Season well.

4　Heat the oil in a saucepan and add the onion and thyme. Cook for 30 minutes, or until the onion is soft and transparent.

5　Quarter the capsicums and remove the seeds and membrane. Grill (broil), skin side up, until the skins have blistered. Cool in a plastic bag. Remove the skins and cut into rectangular strips.

6　Spread the onion evenly over the base of the pastry shell and top with the tomato sauce. Sprinkle with the parmesan cheese then decorate with the capsicum. Bake for 30 minutes, or until heated through and the pastry is crisp. Serve hot.

STORAGE: *The pastry can be made in advance and kept in the freezer for up to 3 months; or in the fridge for a day. Make sure it is well covered. Allow enough time to bring the pastry to room temperature before rolling out.*

NUTRITION PER SERVE (6)
Protein 10 g; Fat 20 g; Carbohydrate 30 g; Dietary Fibre 5 g; Cholesterol 80 mg; 1485 kJ (355 Cal)

Slice the red onions into large pieces to add texture to the tart filling.

Lift the pastry into the prepared tin and press it well into the sides.

Spread the onions over the pastry shell and top with the tomato sauce.

Spicy chicken tarts

PREPARATION TIME: 50 MINUTES | TOTAL COOKING TIME: 55 MINUTES | MAKES 8

2 large onions, finely chopped
400 g (14 oz) eggplant (aubergine), cubed
2 garlic cloves, crushed
2 x 410 g (14½ oz) tins chopped tomatoes
1 tablespoon tomato paste (concentrated
    purée)
3 teaspoons soft brown sugar
1 tablespoon red wine vinegar
3 tablespoons chopped parsley
4 sheets shortcrust pastry
2 teaspoons ground cumin seeds
2 teaspoons ground coriander
1 teaspoon paprika
400 g (14 oz) chicken breast fillets
olive oil
sour cream and coriander (cilantro) leaves,
    to serve

1 Fry the onion in a little oil until golden. Add the eggplant and garlic and cook for a few minutes. Stir in the tomato, tomato paste, sugar and vinegar. Bring to the boil, reduce the heat, cover and simmer for 20 minutes. Uncover and simmer for 10 minutes, or until thickened. Add the parsley and season. Preheat the oven to 190°C (375°F/Gas 5).

2 Grease eight 7.5 cm (3 inch) pie tins, line with the pastry and decorate the edges with a spoon. Prick the bases with a fork. Bake for 15 minutes, or until golden.

3 Mix the cumin seeds, coriander and paprika on baking paper. Coat the chicken breasts in the spices. Heat some oil in a frying pan and cook the chicken for 10 minutes, turning regularly, or until brown and cooked through. Slice the fillets diagonally.

4 Fill the pie shells with the eggplant mixture and decorate with the sliced chicken, sour cream and coriander leaves.

It is quick and simple to decorate the edge of the pastry cases with a spoon.

Detach the tenderloin from the breast as it will cook much more quickly.

NUTRITION PER TART
Protein 20 g; Fat 35 g; Carbohydrate 45 g; Dietary
Fibre 5 g; Cholesterol 65 mg; 2315 kJ (550 Cal)

Mushroom and ricotta filo tart

PREPARATION TIME: 35 MINUTES I TOTAL COOKING TIME: 40 MINUTES I SERVES 6

60 g (2¼ oz) butter
270 g (9½ oz) field mushrooms, sliced
2 garlic cloves, crushed
1 tablespoon Marsala
1 teaspoon thyme leaves
½ teaspoon chopped rosemary leaves
pinch of grated nutmeg
5 sheets filo pastry
75 g (2½ oz) butter, melted
200 g (7 oz) ricotta cheese
2 eggs, lightly beaten
125 g (4½ oz/½ cup) sour cream
1 tablespoon chopped flat-leaf (Italian) parsley

1 Preheat the oven to 180°C (350°F/Gas 4). Melt the butter in a frying pan and cook the mushrooms over high heat for a few minutes, until they begin to soften. Add the garlic, cook for another minute, then stir in the Marsala, thyme, rosemary and nutmeg. Remove the mushrooms from the pan and drain off any liquid.

2 Work with 1 sheet of filo pastry at a time, keeping the rest covered with a damp tea towel (dish towel) to stop them drying out. Brush the sheets with melted butter and fold in half. Place on top of each other to line a shallow 23 cm (9 inch) loose-based flan (tart) tin, allowing the pastry to hang over the rim.

3 Beat the ricotta, eggs and sour cream together and season to taste. Spoon half the mixture into the tin, then layer the mushrooms. Top with the rest of the ricotta mixture. Loosely fold the overhanging pastry over the filling. Bake for 35 minutes, or until firm. Sprinkle with the parsley.

Remove the mushrooms from the pan, draining off as much liquid as possible.

Layer half the ricotta filling into the pastry, then the mushroom mixture.

NUTRITION PER SERVE
Protein 9 g; Fat 35 g; Carbohydrate 9 g; Dietary Fibre 2 g; Cholesterol 160 mg; 1515 kJ (360 Cal)

Potato and zucchini tart

PREPARATION TIME: 25 MINUTES + 15 MINUTES REFRIGERATION | TOTAL COOKING TIME: 1 HOUR 5 MINUTES | SERVES 6–8

185 g (6½ oz/1½ cups) plain (all-purpose) flour
125 g (4½ oz) butter, chilled and cubed
1 egg yolk
1–2 tablespoons iced water

FILLING
450 g (1 lb) floury potatoes, peeled and roughly chopped
40 g (1½ oz/⅓ cup) plain (all-purpose) flour
125 g (4½ oz) jarlsberg cheese, grated
80 ml (2½ fl oz/⅓ cup) cream
2 eggs, separated
2 small zucchini (courgettes), thinly sliced lengthways
4 thyme sprigs, to garnish

NUTRITION PER SERVE (6)
Protein 15 g; Fat 30 g; Carbohydrate 40 g; Dietary Fibre 3 g; Cholesterol 185 mg; 2105 kJ (500 Cal)

1 Put the flour in a bowl with ½ teaspoon salt. Rub in the butter with your fingertips, until the mixture resembles fine breadcrumbs. Add the egg yolk and most of the water and mix with a knife to form a rough dough, adding more water if necessary. Turn onto a lightly floured surface and work into a smooth ball, then wrap in plastic wrap and refrigerate for 15 minutes. Preheat the oven to 190°C (375°F/Gas 5).

2 Grease a 25 cm (10 inch) loose-based flan (tart) tin. On a lightly floured surface, roll out the dough large enough to fit the tin, and trim off the excess pastry. Cover with baking paper and fill with baking beads or rice. Bake for 10 minutes and discard the paper and beads. Bake for another 5–10 minutes.

3 To make the filling, boil the potato until tender. Drain, cool for 5 minutes and mash. Mix in the flour and cheese, stir in 170 ml (5½ fl oz/⅔ cup) water and, when loosely incorporated, add the cream. Whisk until smooth, then add the egg yolks and combine well. Season with salt and white pepper. Beat the egg whites in a small bowl until stiff peaks form, fold into the potato mixture and gently pour into the pie crust.

4 Arrange the zucchini over the pie in a decorative pattern. Decorate with thyme and bake for 35–45 minutes, until set and golden brown. Serve hot or at room temperature.

The easiest way to line the tin is to lift the pastry using a rolling pin.

Blind-bake the pastry base before filling it with the potato mixture.

Arrange the thin slices of zucchini over the pie in a decorative pattern.

Fried green tomato tart

PREPARATION TIME: 35 MINUTES + 15 MINUTES REFRIGERATION | TOTAL COOKING TIME: 40 MINUTES | SERVES 6

4 green tomatoes
1 tablespoon olive oil
20 g (¾ oz) butter
1 teaspoon ground cumin
2 garlic cloves, crushed
1 sheet puff pastry
60 g (2¼ oz/¼ cup) sour cream
1 tablespoon chopped basil
2 tablespoons chopped parsley
60 g (2¼ oz/½ cup) grated cheddar cheese

1 Cut the tomatoes into thin slices. Heat the oil and butter in a frying pan and fry the cumin and garlic for 1 minute. Fry the tomatoes in batches for 2–3 minutes, until slightly softened. Drain on paper towels.

2 Preheat the oven to 200°C (400°F/Gas 6). Cut a 24 cm (9½ inch) round from the puff pastry and place on a greased baking tray. Make a 2 cm (¾ inch) border by scoring gently around the edge. Make small cuts inside the border. Refrigerate for 15 minutes, then bake for 10–15 minutes.

3 Combine the sour cream, basil and half the parsley. Sprinkle the cheddar cheese over the centre of the pastry. Arrange a layer of tomatoes around the inside edge of the border and then add the rest. Bake for 20 minutes, or until the pastry is golden. Spoon the cream mixture into the middle and sprinkle over the remaining parsley.

Using the tip of a knife, make small cuts in the area inside the border.

Arrange the tomatoes around the inside edge of the border.

NUTRITION PER SERVE
Protein 5 g; Fat 20 g; Carbohydrate 10 g; Dietary Fibre 2 g; Cholesterol 40 mg; 1025 kJ (245 Cal)

Pesto and anchovy tart

PREPARATION TIME: 35 MINUTES | TOTAL COOKING TIME: 30 MINUTES | SERVES 6

PESTO
75 g (2½ oz/1½ cups) basil leaves,
  firmly packed
2 garlic cloves
50 g (1¾ oz/½ cup) grated parmesan cheese
80 g (2¾ oz/⅓ cup) pine nuts, toasted
60 ml (2 fl oz/¼ cup) olive oil

375 g (13 oz) ready-made puff pastry
1 egg yolk, lightly beaten
45 g (1½ oz) tin anchovies, drained
50 g (1¾ oz/⅓ cup) grated mozzarella cheese
35 g (1¼ oz/⅓ cup) grated parmesan cheese

1 To make the pesto, put the basil, garlic, parmesan and pine nuts in a food processor and chop finely. With the motor running, slowly add the oil and process until well combined.

2 Preheat the oven to 200°C (400°F/Gas 6). Roll the pastry into a rectangle 18 x 35 cm (7 x 14 inches), and 5 mm (¼ inch) thick. Cut a 2 cm (¾ inch) strip from all the way round the edge of the pastry. Combine the egg yolk with 1 teaspoon water and brush the edge of the pastry. Trim the pastry strips to fit around the rectangle and attach them to form a crust. Place on a lightly floured baking tray and, using the tip of a sharp knife, make small cuts all over the base. Bake for 15 minutes. Press the centre of the pastry down with the back of a spoon and bake for a further 5 minutes, or until lightly golden. Allow to cool.

3 Spread the pesto evenly over the base of the pastry. Cut the anchovies into strips and arrange over the pesto. Sprinkle the grated mozzarella and parmesan over the top and bake for 10 minutes, or until golden.

Attach the strips of pastry around the edge of the rectangle to make a crust.

Spread the pesto evenly into the shaped pastry base.

NUTRITION PER SERVE
Protein 15 g; Fat 40 g; Carbohydrate 25 g; Dietary Fibre 2 g; Cholesterol 70 mg; 2155 kJ (515 Cal)

Vegetable tart with salsa verde

PREPARATION TIME: 30 MINUTES + 30 MINUTES REFRIGERATION | TOTAL COOKING TIME: 50 MINUTES | SERVES 6

215 g (7¾ oz/1¾ cups) plain (all-purpose) flour
120 g (4¼ oz) chilled butter, cubed
60 ml (2 fl oz/¼ cup) cream
1–2 tablespoons iced water

SALSA VERDE

1 garlic clove
40 g (1½ oz/2 cups) flat-leaf (Italian) parsley
80 ml (2½ fl oz/⅓ cup) extra virgin olive oil
3 tablespoons chopped dill
1½ tablespoons dijon mustard
1 tablespoon red wine vinegar
1 tablespoon drained baby capers

FILLING

1 large (250 g/9 oz) waxy potato, cut into
    2 cm (¾ inch) cubes
1 tablespoon olive oil
2 garlic cloves, crushed
1 red capsicum (pepper), cut into cubes
1 red onion, sliced
2 zucchini (courgettes), sliced
2 tablespoons chopped dill
1 tablespoon chopped thyme
1 tablespoon drained baby capers
150 g (5½ oz) marinated quartered artichoke
    hearts, drained
30 g (1 oz/⅔ cup) baby English spinach leaves

1 Sift the flour and ½ teaspoon salt into a large bowl. Add the butter and rub in with your fingertips until it resembles fine breadcrumbs. Add the cream and most of the water and mix with a knife until it comes together in beads, adding more water if necessary. Gather together on a lightly floured work surface, press into a disc, wrap in plastic wrap and chill for 30 minutes.

2 Preheat the oven to 200°C (400°F/Gas 6) and grease a 27 cm (10¾ inch) loose-based flan (tart) tin. Roll the dough out between two sheets of baking paper until large enough to line the tin, trimming off the excess. Cover with baking paper, then add baking beads and bake for 15–20 minutes. Remove the paper and beads, reduce the heat to 180°C (350°F/Gas 4) and bake for 20 minutes, or until golden.

3 Mix all the salsa verde ingredients in a food processor until almost smooth.

4 Boil the potato until just tender. Drain. Heat the oil in a large frying pan and cook the garlic, capsicum and onion for 3 minutes, stirring often. Add the zucchini, dill, thyme and capers and cook for 3 minutes. Reduce the heat, add the potato and artichokes, and heat through. Season to taste.

5 Spread 3 tablespoons of the salsa verde over the pastry. Spoon the filling into the case and drizzle with half the remaining salsa. Pile the spinach leaves in the centre and drizzle over the last of the salsa verde.

NUTRITION PER SERVE
Protein 5.5 g; Fat 30 g; Carbohydrate 27 g; Dietary Fibre 3.5 g; Cholesterol 50 mg; 1590 kJ (380 Cal)

Use a flat-bladed knife to mix the water into the dough until it comes together in beads.

Mix together the slasa verde ingredients in a food processor until almost smooth.

Goat's cheese and sweet potato tart

PREPARATION TIME: 30 MINUTES + 30 MINUTES REFRIGERATION I TOTAL COOKING TIME: 40 MINUTES I SERVES 2–3

2 teaspoons fine semolina
125 g (4½ oz/1 cup) self-raising flour
60 g (2¼ oz) butter, chilled and cubed
1 egg yolk
2 tablespoons iced water

FILLING
2 tablespoons olive oil
1 small leek, chopped
50 g (1¾ oz) goat's cheese, crumbled
1 egg, lightly beaten
2 tablespoons cream
150 g (5½ oz) sweet potato, thinly sliced
½ teaspoon cumin seeds

1   Put the flour and butter in a food processor and process for 15 seconds, or until the mixture resembles fine breadcrumbs. Add the egg yolk and water. Process in short bursts until the mixture just comes together, adding a little more water if necessary. Turn out onto a floured surface and gather together into a ball. Wrap in plastic wrap and chill for 20 minutes.

2   Lightly grease a 25 cm (10 inch) pizza tray or baking tray and sprinkle with the semolina. Roll out the dough to a 20 cm (8 inch) circle. Lift onto the tray and roll over the outside edge to make a small rim; pinch this decoratively with your fingers. Prick the base with a fork and refrigerate for 10 minutes. Preheat the oven to 200°C (400°F/Gas 6). Bake for 12 minutes, or until just brown.

3   To make the filling, heat half the oil in a saucepan, add the leek and cook until soft, then allow to cool. Spread the leek over the base of the pastry case, top with the cheese and season. Pour over the combined egg and cream and lay the sweet potato on top. Brush with the remaining oil and scatter over the cumin seeds. Bake for 20–25 minutes, or until the filling is set. Leave for 5 minutes before cutting.

Turn over the edge of the pastry circle to make a small rim.

Pinch the rim between your fingers to make a decorative edging.

NUTRITION PER SERVE (3)
Protein 15 g; Fat 45 g; Carbohydrate 40 g; Dietary Fibre 3 g; Cholesterol 200 mg; 2475 kJ (590 Cal)

Roasted tomato and garlic tart

PREPARATION TIME: 40 MINUTES | TOTAL COOKING TIME: 1 HOUR 10 MINUTES | SERVES 4

4 roma (plum) tomatoes, halved
1 tablespoon olive oil
1 teaspoon balsamic vinegar
1 teaspoon salt
5–10 garlic cloves, unpeeled
2 sheets puff pastry
1 egg, lightly beaten
10 bocconcini (fresh baby mozzarella cheese),
   halved

1   Preheat the oven to 200°C (400°F/Gas 6).
Put the tomatoes, cut side up, on a baking tray
and drizzle with the olive oil, balsamic vinegar
and salt. Bake for 20 minutes. Add the garlic and
bake for a further 15 minutes. Cool and squeeze
or peel the garlic from its skin.

2   Grease a 35 x 10 cm (14 x 4 inch) loose-
based fluted flan (tart) tin. Lay a sheet of pastry
over each end of the tin, so that they overlap in
the middle and around the edges. Seal the sheets
together with egg and trim the edges. Cover with
baking paper and fill with baking beads or rice
and bake for 15 minutes. Remove the paper and
beads and bake for 10 minutes.

3   Place the roasted tomatoes along the centre
of the tart and fill the gaps with the garlic and
bocconcini. Bake for a further 10 minutes and
serve.

NUTRITION PER SERVE (4)
Protein 25 g; Fat 40 g; Carbohydrate 30 g; Dietary
Fibre 3 g; Cholesterol 115 mg; 2580 kJ (615 Cal)

Place the tomatoes on a baking tray and drizzle with oil, vinegar and salt.

Let the roasted garlic cloves cool, then squeeze or peel them from their skins.

Place a sheet of pastry over each end of the tin, so they overlap in the middle.

Spinach and ricotta lattice tart

PREPARATION TIME: 50 MINUTES + 15 MINUTES REFRIGERATION | TOTAL COOKING TIME: 40 MINUTES | SERVES 6

250 g (9 oz/2 cups) plain (all-purpose) flour

125 g (4½ oz) butter, chilled and cubed

1 egg

2 tablespoons sesame seeds

2–3 tablespoons iced water

FILLING

50 g (1¾ oz) butter

120 g (4¼ oz/1 cup) finely chopped spring onions (scallions)

2 garlic cloves, crushed

500 g (1 lb 2 oz) English spinach, trimmed, washed and roughly shredded

2 tablespoons chopped mint

185 g (6½ oz) ricotta cheese

50 g (1¾ oz) grated parmesan cheese

3 eggs, beaten

1–2 tablespoons milk, to glaze

1   Place the flour and butter in a food processor and process for 15 seconds, or until the mixture resembles fine breadcrumbs. Add the egg, sesame seeds and most of the water and process in short bursts until the mixture just comes together, adding a little extra water if needed. Turn onto a lightly floured surface and quickly gather into a ball. Cover the pastry with plastic wrap and refrigerate for at least 15 minutes. Place a baking tray in the oven and preheat the oven to 180°C (350°F/Gas 4).

2   To make the filling, melt the butter in a large saucepan, add the spring onion and garlic and cook until soft. Add the spinach a little at a time, then stir in the mint. Remove from the heat and allow to cool slightly before stirring in the cheeses and the egg. Season and mix well.

3   Grease a shallow 23 cm (9 inch) round or 22 cm (8½ inch) square loose-based flan (tart) tin. Roll out two-thirds of the pastry on a sheet of baking paper to thinly line the tin, pressing it well into the sides. Spoon the filling into the pastry shell.

4   Roll out the remaining pastry and cut into 1.5 cm (⅝ inch) strips. Interweave the strips in a lattice pattern over the top of the tart. Dampen the edge of the pastry base and gently press the strips down. Trim the edges of the pastry by pressing down with your thumb or by rolling a rolling pin across the top of the tin. Brush with milk. Place on the baking tray and bake for about 40 minutes, or until the pastry is golden.

NOTE: *Depending on how thick you like to roll your pastry, there may be about 100 g (3½ oz) of pastry trimmings left over. It is easier to have this little bit extra when making the lattice strips as they will be long enough to cover the top of the pie. The extra pastry can be covered and frozen for future use as decorations, or made into small tart shells.*

NUTRITION PER SERVE (6)
Protein 20 g; Fat 35 g; Carbohydrate 35 g; Dietary Fibre 5 g; Cholesterol 215 mg; 2220 kJ (530 Cal)

Roll out the remaining pastry and cut into thin strips for the lattice.

Interweave the lattice strips over the top of the spinach and ricotta filling.

Dampen the edge pf the pastry shell and press down the lattice and trim.

Fresh herb tart

PREPARATION TIME: 40 MINUTES + 30 MINUTES REFRIGERATION I TOTAL COOKING TIME: 1 HOUR 10 MINUTES I SERVES 4–6

150 g (5½ oz/1¼ cups) plain (all-purpose) flour
100 g (3½ oz) butter, chilled and cubed
1–2 tablespoons iced water
250 g (9 oz/1 cup) light sour cream
125 ml (4 fl oz/½ cup) thick (double/heavy) cream
2 eggs, lightly beaten
1 tablespoon chopped thyme
2 tablespoons chopped parsley
1 tablespoon chopped oregano

1 Put the flour and butter in a food processor and process for 15 seconds, or until the mixture resembles fine breadcrumbs. Add most of the water and process in short bursts until the mixture just comes together, adding a little more water if needed. Turn onto a floured surface and gather into a ball. Cover with plastic wrap and chill for at least 20 minutes.

2 Roll out the pastry on a sheet of baking paper to line a 35 x 10 cm (14 x 4 inch) loose-based flan (tart) tin and trim away the excess pastry. Refrigerate for 10 minutes. Preheat the oven to 200°C (400°F/Gas 6).

3 Cover the pastry shell with baking paper and fill evenly with baking beads or rice. Place on a baking tray and bake for 20 minutes. Remove the paper and beads and reduce the oven temperature to 180°C (350°F/Gas 4). Cook for 15–20 minutes, or until golden and dry. Cool.

4 Whisk together the sour cream, thickened cream and eggs until smooth. Then stir in the herbs and season.

5 Place the pastry shell on a baking tray and pour in the filling. Bake for 25–30 minutes, or until set. Allow to stand for 15 minutes before serving and cutting.

If you don't have baking beads for blind baking, use dry rice or beans.

Put the pastry shell on a baking tray before cooking to catch any drips.

NUTRITION PER SERVE (6)
Protein 6 g; Fat 25 g; Carbohydrate 20 g; Dietary Fibre 1 g; Cholesterol 130 mg; 1340 kJ (320 Cal)

Roast capsicum risotto tarts

PREPARATION TIME: 45 MINUTES I TOTAL COOKING TIME: 1 HOUR 15 MINUTES I SERVES 6

20 g (¾ oz) butter
95 g (3¼ oz/½ cup) wild rice
220 g (7¾ oz/1 cup) short-grain brown rice
1 litre (35 fl oz/4 cups) vegetable stock
2 eggs, beaten
50 g (1¾ oz) grated parmesan cheese
2 green capsicums (peppers)
2 red capsicums (peppers)
2 yellow capsicums (peppers)
150 g (5½ oz) camembert cheese, thinly sliced
2 tablespoons oregano leaves

1   Melt the butter in a large saucepan, add the rice and stir over low heat until the rice is well coated. In a separate pan, heat the stock. Add 125 ml (4 fl oz/½ cup) of stock to the rice, stirring well. Increase the heat to medium and add the remaining stock, 250 ml (9 fl oz/1 cup) at a time, stirring until it has been absorbed. This will take about 30–40 minutes. Remove the pan from the heat and cool before adding the eggs and the parmesan cheese. Season.

2   Grease six 10 cm (4 inch) loose-based fluted flan (tart) tins. Divide the risotto among the tins and press into the base and side. Allow to cool completely.

3   Cut the capsicums into large flat pieces and grill (broil), skin side up, until the skins have blackened and blistered. Cool in a plastic bag, remove the skins and slice.

4   Preheat the oven to 200°C (400°F/Gas 6). Place the camembert cheese slices in the bottom of the lined tins and bake until bubbly, about 20 minutes. Divide the capsicum evenly between the tarts. Bake for 30 minutes. Sprinkle with the oregano leaves and serve hot or at room temperature.

Using a spoon, press the risotto into the base and side of the flan tins.

Divide the slices of camembert between the lined flan tins.

NUTRITION PER SERVE
Protein 15 g; Fat 15 g; Carbohydrate 40 g; Dietary Fibre 3 g; Cholesterol 100 mg; 1515 kJ (360 Cal)

Quiches

Quiche lorraine

PREPARATION TIME: 35 MINUTES + 35 MINUTES REFRIGERATION | TOTAL COOKING TIME: 1 HOUR 5 MINUTES | SERVES 4–6

185 g (6½ oz/1½ cups) plain (all-purpose)
    flour
90 g (3¼ oz) butter, chilled and cubed
1 egg yolk
2–3 tablespoons iced water

FILLING
20 g (¾ oz) butter
1 onion, chopped
4 bacon slices, cut into thin strips
2 tablespoons chopped chives
2 eggs
185 ml (6 fl oz/¾ cup) cream
60 ml (2 fl oz/¼ cup) milk
100 g (3½ oz) Swiss cheese, grated

1 Mix the flour and butter in a food processor
for 15 seconds, or until crumbly. Add the egg
yolk and water. Process in short bursts until the
mixture just comes together. Add a little more
water if needed. Turn out onto a floured surface
and gather together into a ball. Wrap the dough
in plastic and refrigerate for at least 15 minutes.

2 Roll the pastry between two sheets of
baking paper until large enough to line a
shallow 25 cm (10 inch) loose-based flan (tart)
tin. Press well into the side of the tin and trim
off any excess pastry. Refrigerate the pastry-
lined tin for 20 minutes. Preheat the oven to
190°C (375°F/Gas 5).

3 Cover the pastry shell with baking paper,
spread with a layer of baking beads or rice and
bake for 15 minutes. Remove the paper and
beads and bake the pastry shell for 10 minutes,
or until the pastry is golden and dry. Reduce the
oven temperature to 180°C (350°F/Gas 4).

4 To make the filling, heat the butter in a
frying pan. Add the onion and bacon and
cook for 10 minutes, stirring frequently, until
the onion is soft and the bacon is cooked. Stir
through the chives and leave to cool.

5 Beat together the eggs, cream and milk.
Season with freshly ground black pepper.
Spread the filling evenly into the pastry shell.
Pour the egg mixture over the top and sprinkle
with the cheese. Bake for 30 minutes, or until
the filling is set and golden.

NUTRITION PER SERVE (6)
Protein 15 g; Fat 40 g; Carbohydrate 25 g; Dietary
Fibre 2 g; Cholesterol 210 mg; 2185 kJ (520 Cal)

Roll out the pastry between two sheets of baking
paper so it doesn't stick.

Pour the egg mixture over the onion and bacon in
the base of the pastry shell.

Blue cheese and onion quiche

PREPARATION TIME: 40 MINUTES + 20 MINUTES REFRIGERATION | TOTAL COOKING TIME: 1 HOUR 40 MINUTES | SERVES 8

2 tablespoons olive oil
1 kg (2 lb 4 oz) red onions, very thinly sliced
1 teaspoon soft brown sugar
250 g (9 oz/2 cups) plain (all-purpose) flour
100 g (3½ oz) butter, chilled and cubed
1–2 tablespoons iced water
185 ml (6 fl oz/¾ cup) cream
3 eggs
100 g (3½ oz) blue cheese, crumbled
1 teaspoon chopped thyme

1 Heat the oil in a pan over low heat and cook the onion and sugar, stirring regularly, for 45 minutes, or until the onion is lightly golden.

2 Process the flour and butter in a food processor for 15 seconds, or until crumbly. Add most of the water and process in short bursts until the mixture just comes together, adding more water if necessary. Turn out onto a floured surface and gather into a ball. Wrap in plastic wrap and refrigerate for 10 minutes.

3 Preheat the oven to 180°C (350°F/Gas 4). Roll out the pastry thinly on a lightly floured surface to fit a greased 22 cm (8½ inch) loose-based flan (tart) tin. Trim away the excess pastry. Refrigerate for 10 minutes.

4 Line the pastry with baking paper and spread with a layer of baking beads or rice. Put on a baking tray and bake for 10 minutes. Remove the paper and beads, then bake for another 10 minutes, or until lightly golden and dry.

5 Cool, then gently spread the onion in the pastry shell. Whisk together the cream, eggs, blue cheese, thyme and some freshly ground black pepper to taste. Pour into the base and bake for 35 minutes, or until firm.

Roll the pastry out thinly and line the greased tart tin, trimming away any excess.

Spread the onion over the cooled pastry base, then pour in the cream mixture.

NUTRITION PER SERVE
Protein 9 g; Fat 30 g; Carbohydrate 25 g; Dietary Fibre 1.5 g; Cholesterol 145 mg; 1718 kJ (410 Cal)

Feta, basil and olive quiche

PREPARATION TIME: 40 MINUTES + 25 MINUTES REFRIGERATION | TOTAL COOKING TIME: 40 MINUTES | SERVES 6

150 g (5½ oz/1¼ cups) flour, sifted
90 g (3¼ oz) butter, melted and cooled
60 ml (2 fl oz/¼ cup) milk

FILLING
200 g (7 oz) feta cheese, cubed
15 g (½ oz/¼ cup) basil leaves, shredded
30 g (1 oz/¼ cup) sliced black olives
3 eggs, lightly beaten
80 ml (2½ fl oz/⅓ cup) milk
90 g (3¼ oz/⅓ cup) sour cream

1 Grease a deep 23 cm (9 inch) loose-based flan (tart) tin. Place the flour in a large bowl and make a well in the centre. Add the butter and milk and stir until the mixture comes together to form a dough. Turn out onto a floured surface and gather into a ball. Refrigerate for 5 minutes. Roll out the pastry and place in the tin, press it well into the sides and trim the edge. Refrigerate for 20 minutes. Preheat the oven to 200°C (400°F/ Gas 6).

2 To make the filling, spread the feta evenly over the base of the pastry and top with the basil and olives.

3 Whisk the eggs, milk and sour cream until smooth, then pour into the pastry shell. Bake for 15 minutes, then reduce the oven temperature to 180°C (350°F/Gas 4) and cook for a further 25 minutes, or until the filling is firmly set. Serve at room temperature.

Cut the feta into cubes and shred the basil leaves.

Sprinkle the shredded basil and sliced olives over the quiche.

NUTRITION PER SERVE
Protein 15 g; Fat 35 g; Carbohydrate 20 g; Dietary Fibre 2 g; Cholesterol 180 mg; 1750 kJ (415 Cal)

Spicy sweet potato quiche

PREPARATION TIME: 30 MINUTES + 20 MINUTES REFRIGERATION | TOTAL COOKING TIME: 1 HOUR 35 MINUTES | SERVES 6

250 g (9 oz/2 cups) plain (all-purpose) flour
125 g (4½ oz) butter, chilled and cubed
1 egg yolk
2–3 tablespoons iced water

FILLING
30 g (1 oz) butter
1 onion, sliced
1 garlic clove, crushed
2 teaspoons black mustard seeds
2 teaspoons ground cumin
1 teaspoon soft brown sugar
450 g (1 lb) orange sweet potato, chopped
2 eggs, lightly beaten
60 ml (2 fl oz/¼ cup) milk
60 ml (2 fl oz/¼ cup) cream
2 tablespoons chopped parsley
2 tablespoons chopped chives

NUTRITION PER SERVE
Protein 10 g; Fat 30 g; Carbohydrate 45 g; Dietary
Fibre 4 g; Cholesterol 140 mg; 2015 kJ (480 Cal)

1   Process the flour and butter in a food processor for 15 seconds, or until crumbly. Add the egg yolk and most of the water. Process in short bursts until the mixture comes together, adding more water if necessary. Turn out onto a floured surface and gather into a ball. Roll the pastry between two sheets of baking paper until large enough to line a shallow 23 cm (9 inch) loose-based fluted flan (tart) tin. Trim away the excess pastry. Refrigerate for 20 minutes.

2   For the filling, heat the butter in a large saucepan and cook the onion and garlic for 5 minutes, or until golden. Add the mustard seeds, cumin and sugar and stir for 1 minute. Add the sweet potato and cook for 10 minutes over low heat until it has softened slightly. Stir gently, or the sweet potato will break up.

3   Preheat the oven to 180°C (350°F/Gas 4). Cover the pastry shell with baking paper and spread with a layer of baking beads or rice. Bake for 15 minutes, then remove the paper and beads and bake for a further 15 minutes.

4   Put the sweet potato mixture into the pastry shell. Mix together the egg, milk, cream and herbs and pour over the sweet potato. Bake for 50 minutes, or until set.

Peel the sweet potato and cut into bite-sized chunks for the filling.

Add the mustard seeds, cumin and brown sugar to the onion and garlic.

Pour the combined egg, milk, cream and herbs over the sweet potato mixture.

Artichoke and provolone quiches

PREPARATION TIME: 40 MINUTES + 30 MINUTES REFRIGERATION | TOTAL COOKING TIME: 35 MINUTES | MAKES 6

250 g (9 oz/2 cups) plain (all-purpose) flour
125 g (4½ oz) butter, chilled and cubed
1 egg yolk
3 tablespoons iced water

FILLING
1 small eggplant (aubergine), sliced
olive oil
6 eggs, lightly beaten
3 teaspoons wholegrain mustard
150 g (5½ oz) provolone cheese, grated
200 g (7 oz) marinated artichokes, sliced
125 g (4½ oz) semi-dried (sun-blushed)
    tomatoes

1 Process the flour and butter in a food processor for 15 seconds, or until crumbly. Add the egg yolk and most of the water. Process in short bursts until the mixture comes together. Add a little more water if needed. Turn onto a floured surface and gather into a ball. Wrap in plastic and refrigerate for at least 30 minutes.

2 Preheat the oven to 190°C (375°F/ Gas 5) and grease six 11 cm (4¼ inch) oval or round pie tins.

3 To make the filling, brush the eggplant with olive oil and grill until golden. Mix together the egg, mustard and cheese.

4 Roll out the pastry to line the tins. Trim away the excess pastry and decorate the edges. Place one eggplant slice in each tin and top with the artichokes and tomatoes. Pour the egg mixture over the top and bake for 25 minutes, or until golden.

Brush each slice of eggplant with a little olive oil and then grill until golden.

Place one slice of eggplant in the bottom of each tin, then top with artichokes and tomatoes.

NUTRITION PER QUICHE
Protein 20 g; Fat 30 g; Carbohydrate 35 g; Dietary Fibre 4 g; Cholesterol 290 mg; 2025 kJ (480 Cal)

Tomato and thyme quiche

PREPARATION TIME: 35 MINUTES + 30 MINUTES REFRIGERATION | TOTAL COOKING TIME: 45 MINUTES | SERVES 8

185 g (6½ oz/1½ cups) plain (all-purpose)
   flour
125 g (4½ oz) butter, chilled and cubed
1 egg yolk
2–3 tablespoons iced water

FILLING
425 g (15 oz) tin tomatoes
4 eggs
300 g (10½ oz) sour cream
25 g (1 oz/¼ cup) grated parmesan cheese
2 spring onions (scallions), finely chopped
1–2 tablespoons chopped thyme

1   Preheat the oven to 210°C (415°F/Gas 6–7).
Sift the flour into a bowl and rub in the butter
until the mixture resembles fine breadcrumbs.
Add the combined egg yolk and most of the
water and mix to a soft dough, adding more
water if necessary. Turn onto a lightly floured
surface and gather into a ball. Wrap in plastic
and refrigerate for 30 minutes.

2   Roll out the pastry to line a shallow 23 cm
(9 inch) flan (tart) tin, trimming off the excess.
Cover with baking paper and spread with a layer
of baking beads or rice. Bake for 10 minutes,
then discard the paper and beads and cook for a
further 5 minutes, or until golden.

3   Drain the tomatoes and halve lengthways.
Place, cut side down, on paper towels to drain.
Beat together the eggs and sour cream and stir in
the cheese and spring onion.

4   Pour the filling into the pastry shell. Arrange
the tomatoes, cut side down, over the filling.
Sprinkle with thyme and black pepper. Reduce
the oven to 180°C (350°F/Gas 4) and bake for 30
minutes, or until the filling is set and golden.

STORAGE: *The pastry shell can be blind-baked a*
day in advance and stored in an airtight container.

NUTRITION PER SERVE
Protein 9 g; Fat 25 g; Carbohydrate 20 g; Dietary
Fibre 2 g; Cholesterol 105 mg; 1345 kJ (320 Cal)

Drain the tinned tomatoes and cut them in half
lengthways. Put on paper towel to drain further.

Blind-bake the pastry shell until it is dry and
golden before pouring in the filling.

Mustard chicken and asparagus quiche

PREPARATION TIME: 25 MINUTES + 40 MINUTES REFRIGERATION | TOTAL COOKING TIME: 1 HOUR 20 MINUTES | SERVES 6

250 g (9 oz/2 cups) plain (all-purpose) flour
100 g (3½ oz) butter, chilled and cubed
1 egg yolk
3 tablespoons iced water

FILLING
150 g (5½ oz) asparagus, chopped
25 g (1 oz) butter
1 onion, chopped
60 g (2¼ oz/¼ cup) wholegrain mustard
200 g (7 oz) soft cream cheese
125 ml (4 fl oz/½ cup) cream
3 eggs, lightly beaten
200 g (7 oz) cooked chicken, chopped
½ teaspoon black pepper

NUTRITION PER SERVE
Protein 15 g; Fat 30 g; Carbohydrate 25 g; Dietary
Fibre 2 g; Cholesterol 190 mg; 1860 kJ (440 Cal)

1 Process the flour and butter in a food processor until crumbly. Add the egg yolk and most of the water. Process in short bursts until the mixture comes together. Add a little more water if needed. Turn onto a floured surface and gather into a ball. Wrap in plastic and refrigerate for 30 minutes. Grease a deep 20 cm (8 inch) loose-based flan (tart) tin.

2 Preheat the oven to 200°C (400°F/Gas 6). Roll out the pastry and line the tin. Trim off any excess. Place the tin on a baking tray and chill for 10 minutes. Cover the pastry with baking paper and spread with a layer of baking beads or rice. Bake for 10 minutes. Remove the paper and beads and bake for another 10 minutes, or until the pastry is lightly browned and dry. Cool. Reduce the oven to 180°C (350°F/Gas 4).

3 To make the filling, boil or steam the asparagus until tender. Drain and pat dry with paper towel. Heat the butter in a pan and cook the onion until translucent. Remove from the heat and add the wholegrain mustard and cream cheese. Stir until the cheese has melted, then leave to cool. Add the cream, eggs, chicken and asparagus and mix well.

4 Spoon the filling into the pastry shell and sprinkle with the black pepper. Bake for 50 minutes–1 hour, or until puffed and set. Cover the surface with foil if it browns before the quiche is set. Cool for at least 15 minutes before cutting.

When the mixture is crumbly add the egg yolk and enough iced water to bring together.

Dry the asparagus well to avoid excess moisture in the filling.

Add the mustard and cream cheese and stir until the cheese has melted.

Leek and ham quiche with polenta pastry

PREPARATION TIME: 45 MINUTES + 50 MINUTES REFRIGERATION | TOTAL COOKING TIME: 1 HOUR 15 MINUTES | SERVES 6

125 g (4½ oz/1 cup) plain (all-purpose) flour
75 g (2½ oz/½ cup) polenta
90 g (3¼ oz) butter, chilled and cubed
90 g (3¼ oz) cream cheese, chilled and cubed

FILLING
50 g (1¾ oz) butter
2 leeks, thinly sliced
3 eggs, lightly beaten
375 ml (13 fl oz/1½ cups) cream
½ teaspoon ground nutmeg
80 g (2¾ oz) ham, chopped
75 g (2½ oz) Swiss cheese, grated

1 Process the flour and polenta briefly to mix together. Add the butter and cream cheese and process for about 15 seconds, until the mixture comes together. Add 1–2 tablespoons of iced water if needed. Turn out onto a floured surface and gather into a ball. Wrap in plastic wrap and refrigerate for 30 minutes.

2 Heat the butter in a pan and add the leeks. Cover and cook for 10–15 minutes, stirring often, until soft but not brown. Cool. Mix together the egg, cream and nutmeg and season with pepper.

3 Grease a shallow 21 x 28 cm (8¼ x 11¼ inch) loose-based flan (tart) tin with melted butter. Roll the pastry between baking paper until large enough to fit the tin and trim off any excess pastry. Refrigerate for 20 minutes. Preheat the oven to 190°C (375°F/Gas 5).

4 Cover the pastry shell with baking paper and baking beads or rice. Bake for 15 minutes. Remove the paper and beads and bake for 15 minutes, until the pastry is golden and dry. Reduce the oven to 180°C (350°F/Gas 4).

5 Spread the leek over the pastry shell and sprinkle with the ham and cheese. Pour in the cream mixture. Bake for 30 minutes, or until golden and set.

Cook the leek, stirring frequently, until it is soft but not brown..

Spread the leek over the pastry shell and sprinkle with ham and cheese.

NUTRITION PER SERVE
Protein 15 g; Fat 50 g; Carbohydrate 25 g; Dietary Fibre 2 g; Cholesterol 210 mg; 2495 kJ (595 Cal)

Eggplant and sun-dried capsicum quiches

PREPARATION TIME: 30 MINUTES + 45 MINUTES REFRIGERATION | TOTAL COOKING TIME: 1 HOUR | MAKES 6

185 g (6 oz/1½ cups) plain (all-purpose) flour
125 g (4½ oz) butter, chilled and cubed
1 egg yolk
1 tablespoon iced water

FILLING
100 g (3½ oz) slender eggplant (aubergine),
    thinly sliced
30 g (1 oz) butter
4 spring onions (scallions), finely chopped
1–2 garlic cloves, crushed
½ small red capsicum (pepper), finely chopped
40 g (1½ oz/¼ cup) sun-dried capsicums
    (peppers), drained and chopped
2 eggs, lightly beaten
185 ml (6 fl oz/¾ cup) cream

1 Process the flour and butter for about
15 seconds until crumbly. Add the egg yolk
and water. Process in short bursts until the
mixture comes together. Add a little extra water
if needed. Turn out onto a floured surface and
gather into a ball. Wrap in plastic and refrigerate
for at least 30 minutes.

2 Brush the eggplant slices with olive oil and
grill until browned. Heat the butter in a pan and
cook the spring onion, garlic and capsicum for
5 minutes, stirring frequently, until soft. Add the
sun-dried capsicum and leave to cool. Combine
egg and cream in a bowl and season well.

3 Grease six 8 cm (3 inch) fluted tart tins. Roll
out the pastry thinly to line the tins, and trim.
Cover and refrigerate for 15 minutes. Preheat the
oven to 190°C (375°F/Gas 5). Cover the pastry
shells with baking paper and a layer of baking
beads or rice. Bake for 10 minutes. Remove the
paper and beads and bake for 10 minutes.

4 Divide the filling among the pastry shells, top
with the eggplant and pour over the cream and
egg mixture. Bake for 25–30 minutes, or until set.

NUTRITION PER QUICHE
Protein 7 g; Fat 35 g; Carbohydrate 25 g; Dietary
Fibre 2 g; Cholesterol 200 mg; 1940 kJ (460 Cal)

Cut the slender eggplant into thin slices on the diagonal.

Mix together the egg and cream and then pour into the pastry shells.

Low-fat roast vegetable quiche

PREPARATION TIME: 45 MINUTES + 25 MINUTES REFRIGERATION | TOTAL COOKING TIME: 2 HOURS 30 MINUTES | SERVES 6–8

1 small potato, peeled

200 g (7 oz) pumpkin (winter squash), peeled

100 g (3½ oz) orange sweet potato, peeled

1 large parsnip, peeled

½ red capsicum (pepper)

1 onion, cut into wedges

3 garlic cloves, halved

1 teaspoon olive oil

200 g (7 oz/1⅔ cups) plain (all-purpose) flour

55 g (2 oz) butter, chilled and cubed

60 g (2¼ oz) ricotta cheese

250 ml (9 fl oz/1 cup) skim milk

3 eggs, lightly beaten

30 g (1 oz/¼ cup) grated reduced-fat cheddar cheese

NUTRITION PER SERVE (6)
Protein 15 g; Fat 10 g; Carbohydrate 45 g; Dietary Fibre 5.5 g; Cholesterol 115 mg; 1440 kJ (345 Cal)

1 Preheat the oven to 180°C (350°F/Gas 4). Lightly grease a 23 cm (9 inch) loose-based flan (tart) tin. Cut the potato, pumpkin, sweet potato, parsnip and capsicum into bite-sized chunks, place in a baking dish with the onion and garlic and drizzle with the oil. Season and bake for 1 hour, or until tender. Leave to cool.

2 Process the flour, butter and ricotta in a food processor until crumbly, then gradually add 4 tablespoons of the milk, or enough to form a soft dough. Turn out onto a lightly floured surface and gather into a smooth ball. Cover and refrigerate for 15 minutes.

3 Roll out the pastry on a lightly floured surface and then ease into the tin, bringing it gently up the side. Trim the edge and refrigerate for another 10 minutes. Increase the oven to 200°C (400°F/Gas 6). Cover the pastry with baking paper and spread with a layer of baking beads or rice. Bake for 10 minutes, then remove the paper and beads and bake for 10 minutes, or until golden brown and dry.

4 Combine the remaining milk, the egg and cheese. Place the vegetables in the pastry base and pour the mixture over the top. Reduce the oven to 180°C (350°F/Gas 4) and bake for 1 hour 10 minutes, or until set in the centre. Leave for 5 minutes before removing from the tin to serve.

Put the vegetables in a baking dish and drizzle with the olive oil.

Ease the pastry into the tin, bringing it up the side and then trimming the edge.

Fresh salmon and dill quiche

PREPARATION TIME: 35 MINUTES + 30 MINUTES REFRIGERATION | TOTAL COOKING TIME: 1 HOUR | SERVES 4–6

200 g (7 oz/1⅔ cups) plain (all-purpose) flour
125 g (4½ oz) butter, chilled and cubed
1 teaspoon icing sugar
1–2 tablespoons iced water

FILLING
2 eggs
1 egg yolk
250 ml (9 fl oz/1 cup) cream
1 teaspoon finely grated lemon zest
2 tablespoons finely chopped spring onions
     (scallions)
450 g (1 lb) fresh salmon fillet, bones and skin
     removed and cut into bite-sized chunks
1 tablespoon chopped dill

1   Process the flour, butter and icing sugar
in a food processor for about 15 seconds until
crumbly. Add most of the water. Process in short
bursts until the mixture just comes together. Add
a little more water if needed. Turn out onto a
floured surface and gather into a ball. Wrap in
plastic and refrigerate for 15 minutes.

2   Roll the pastry between two sheets of baking
paper until large enough to fit a 23 cm (9 inch)
loose-based flan (tart) tin. Trim away the excess
pastry and refrigerate for 15 minutes. Preheat the
oven to 180°C (350°F/Gas 4).

3   To make the filling, lightly beat the eggs and
egg yolk. Add the cream, lemon zest and spring
onion and season well. Cover and set aside.

4   Prick the base of the pastry shell with a fork.
Cover with baking paper and a layer of baking
beads or rice. Bake for 15 minutes, or until
lightly golden. Remove the paper and beads and
arrange the salmon over the base. Scatter with
the dill and then pour in the egg mixture. Bake
for 40 minutes, or until the salmon is cooked
and the filling has set. Serve warm or cool.

Cut the boned and skinned salmon into bite-sized chunks.

Scatter the chopped dill over the salmon in the pastry case.

NUTRITION PER SERVE (6)
Protein 25 g; Fat 45 g; Carbohydrate 25 g; Dietary
Fibre 1 g; Cholesterol 255 mg; 2535 kJ (605 Cal)

Mediterranean quiche

PREPARATION TIME: 50 MINUTES + 15 MINUTES REFRIGERATION | TOTAL COOKING TIME: 1 HOUR 25 MINUTES | SERVES 6–8

2 sheets shortcrust pastry
3 tablespoons olive oil
2 garlic cloves, crushed
1 onion, diced
1 small chilli, seeded and finely chopped
1 red capsicum (pepper), chopped into
    bite-sized pieces
1 yellow capsicum (pepper), chopped into
    bite-sized pieces
400 g (14 oz) tinned tomatoes, drained and
    chopped
2 tablespoons chopped oregano
4 eggs, lightly beaten
35 g (1¼ oz/⅓ cup) grated parmesan cheese

1   Grease a 23 cm (9 inch) loose-based fluted flan (tart) tin. Place the sheets of pastry so that they are slightly overlapping and roll out until large enough to fit the tin. Press well into the sides and trim off the excess pastry. Cover and refrigerate for 15 minutes. Preheat the oven to 190°C (375°F/Gas 5).

2   Cover the pastry shell with baking paper and spread with a layer of baking beads or rice. Bake for 10 minutes. Remove the paper and beads and bake for another 10 minutes, or until golden. Cool on a wire rack.

3   Heat the oil in a frying pan and cook the garlic and onion until soft. Add the chilli, red and yellow capsicum and cook for 6 minutes. Stir in the tomatoes and oregano and simmer, covered, for 10 minutes. Remove the lid and cook until the liquid has evaporated. Remove from the heat and leave to cool.

4   Stir the egg and cheese into the tomato mixture and spoon into the pastry shell. Bake for 35–45 minutes, or until the filling has set.

NUTRITION PER SERVE (8)
Protein 9 g; Fat 25 g; Carbohydrate 20 g; Dietary
Fibre 2 g; Cholesterol 105 mg; 1345 kJ (320 Cal)

Cook the vegetable filling until all the liquid has evaporated. Leave to cool.

Spoon the tomato and capsicum filling into the baked pastry shell.

Spinach and red capsicum quiches with chive pastry

PREPARATION TIME: 40 MINUTES + 45 MINUTES REFRIGERATION | TOTAL COOKING TIME: 1 HOUR | MAKES 4

215 g (7¾ oz/1¼ cups) plain (all-purpose) flour
2 tablespoons chopped chives
125 g (4½ oz) butter, chilled and cubed
1 egg yolk
3 tablespoons iced water

FILLING
500 g (1 lb 2 oz) English spinach
30 g (1 oz) butter
6 spring onions (scallions), finely sliced
1–2 garlic cloves, finely chopped
1 small red capsicum (pepper), finely chopped
2 eggs, lightly beaten
250 ml (9 fl oz/1 cup) cream
100 g (3½ oz) firm camembert or brie cheese, cut into 8 slices

1   Place the flour and chives in a food processor, add the butter and process for about 15 seconds, or until the mixture is crumbly. Add the egg yolk and most of the water. Process in short bursts until the mixture just comes together, adding a little more water if necessary. Turn out onto a floured surface and gather into a ball. Wrap in plastic wrap and refrigerate for at least 30 minutes.

2   To make the filling, wash the spinach thoroughly and put in a saucepan with just the water clinging to the leaves. Cover and cook for 5 minutes, or until wilted. Drain and allow to cool. Squeeze as much moisture from the spinach as possible and chop roughly.

3   Heat the butter in a saucepan and cook the spring onion, garlic and capsicum for 5–7 minutes, stirring frequently. Stir in the spinach and allow to cool. In a bowl, combine the egg and cream and season well.

4   Grease four 11 cm (4¼ inch) loose-based fluted flan (tart) tins. Divide the pastry into quarters and roll out to fit the tins. Trim away the excess pastry, then cover the tins and refrigerate for 15 minutes. Preheat the oven to 190°C (375°F/Gas 5).

5   Cover the pastry shells with baking paper and spread with a layer of baking beads or rice. Bake for 10 minutes. Remove the paper and beads and bake for a further 10 minutes.

6   Divide the spinach filling evenly among the pastry shells. Pour the egg mixture over the filling. Place 2 slices of the cheese on top of each quiche. Bake for 25–30 minutes, or until the filling is golden brown and set.

VARIATION: *You can replace the camembert or brie with mature cheddar, mozzarella or fontina (a semi-firm, creamy cheese).*

NUTRITION PER QUICHE
Protein 15 g; Fat 45 g; Carbohydrate 30 g; Dietary Fibre 4 g; Cholesterol 230 mg; 2440 kJ (580 Cal)

Turn the dough onto a floured surface and gather into a ball.

Use your hands to squeeze as much moisture as possible from the spinach.

Cook the spring onion, garlic and capsicum, stirring frequently.

Asparagus and artichoke quiches

PREPARATION TIME: 40 MINUTES + 30 MINUTES REFRIGERATION | TOTAL COOKING TIME: 40 MINUTES | MAKES 6

150 g (5½ oz/1¼ cups) plain (all-purpose) flour
90 g (3¼ oz) butter, chilled and cubed
60 g (2¼ oz/½ cup) grated cheddar cheese
2–3 tablespoons iced water

FILLING
155 g (5½ oz) asparagus, trimmed and cut into bite-sized pieces
2 eggs
80 ml (2½ fl oz/⅓ cup) cream
40 g (1½ oz/⅓ cup) grated gruyère cheese
150 g (5½ oz) marinated artichoke hearts, quartered
1 tablespoon rosemary leaves

1 Process the flour and butter in a food processor for about 15 seconds, until crumbly. Add the cheese and water. Process in short bursts until the mixture just comes together, adding a little more water if needed. Turn onto a floured surface and gather into a ball. Wrap in plastic wrap and refrigerate for 30 minutes.

2 Preheat the oven to 190°C (375°F/Gas 5) and grease six 8 cm (3¼ inch) loose-based fluted flan (tart) tins. Roll out the pastry to fit the tins, trimming away excess. Prick pastry bases with a fork, place on a baking tray and bake for 10–12 minutes, or until the pastry is light and golden.

3 To make the filling, blanch the asparagus pieces in boiling salted water. Drain and refresh in iced water. In a bowl, lightly beat the eggs, cream and half the cheese together and season with salt and freshly ground black pepper.

4 Divide the artichoke and asparagus among the pastry shells, pour the egg and cream mixture over the top and sprinkle with the remaining cheese. Bake for 25 minutes, or until the filling is set and golden. If the pastry is over-browning, cover with foil.

Cut the marinated artichoke hearts into quarters.

Divide the artichoke and asparagus evenly between the pastry shells.

NUTRITION PER QUICHE
Protein 10 g; Fat 30 g; Carbohydrate 20 g; Dietary Fibre 2 g; Cholesterol 150 mg; 1665 kJ (395 Cal)

Seafood quiche

PREPARATION TIME: 20 MINUTES + 20 MINUTES REFRIGERATION | TOTAL COOKING TIME: 1 HOUR | SERVES 4–6

2 sheets shortcrust pastry
30 g (1 oz) butter
300 g (10½ oz) mixed raw seafood
90 g (3¼ oz/¾ cup) grated cheddar cheese
3 eggs
1 tablespoon plain (all-purpose) flour
125 ml (4 fl oz/½ cup) cream
125 ml (4 fl oz/½ cup) milk
1 small fennel, finely sliced
1 tablespoon grated parmesan cheese

1 Grease a 23 cm (9 inch) loose-based fluted flan (tart) tin. Lay the pastry sheets so that they slightly overlap and roll out until large enough to fit the tin. Press well into the sides and trim off the excess pastry. Refrigerate for 20 minutes. Preheat the oven to 190°C (375°F/Gas 5).

2 Cover the pastry shell with baking paper and spread with a layer of baking beads or rice. Bake for 15 minutes. Remove the paper and beads and bake for 10 minutes, or until golden. Cool on a wire rack.

3 Heat the butter in a pan and cook the seafood for 2–3 minutes. Leave to cool. Arrange in the pastry shell and sprinkle with the cheddar cheese.

4 In a bowl, beat the eggs together and whisk in the flour, ¼ teaspoon salt, ½ teaspoon freshly ground black pepper, cream and milk. Pour over the seafood filling. Sprinkle the fennel and parmesan cheese over the top. Bake for 30–35 minutes. Leave to cool slightly before serving.

NUTRITION PER SERVE (6)
Protein 20 g; Fat 35 g; Carbohydrate 30 g; Dietary Fibre 1 g; Cholesterol 220 mg; 2190 kJ (520 Cal)

Fit the pastry into the tin, pressing it well into the sides.

Sprinkle the cheddar cheese over the top of the seafood in the pastry shell.

Potato, leek and spinach quiche

PREPARATION TIME: 1 HOUR + 40 MINUTES REFRIGERATION | TOTAL COOKING TIME: 2 HOURS | SERVES 6–8

250 g (9 oz/2 cups) plain (all-purpose) flour
125 g (4½ oz) butter, chilled and cubed
2–3 tablespoons iced water

FILLING
3 potatoes
30 g (1 oz) butter
2 tablespoons oil
2 garlic cloves, crushed
2 leeks, sliced
500 g (1 lb 2 oz) English spinach
125 g (4½ oz/1 cup) grated cheddar cheese
4 eggs
125 ml (4 fl oz/½ cup) cream
125 ml (4 fl oz/½ cup) milk

1 Process the flour and the butter in a food processor for about 15 seconds, or until the mixture is crumbly. Add most of the water and process in short bursts until the mixture just comes together when you squeeze a little between your fingers, adding a little more water if necessary. Turn onto a floured surface and bring together into a ball. Wrap in plastic wrap and refrigerate for at least 30 minutes.

2 Roll out the pastry between two sheets of baking paper until large enough to line a 21 cm (8¼ inch) loose-based fluted deep flan (tart) tin. Place on a baking tray and refrigerate for 20 minutes.

3 To make the filling, peel and thinly slice the potatoes. Melt the butter and oil together in a frying pan; add the garlic and sliced potatoes. Gently turn the potatoes until they are coated, then cover and cook for 5 minutes over low heat. Remove the potatoes with a slotted spoon, drain on paper towel and set aside. Add the leeks to the pan and cook until soft, then remove from the heat.

4 Wash the spinach and put in a saucepan with just the water clinging to the leaves. Cover and cook for 2 minutes, or until just wilted. Allow to cool. Squeeze out the water with your hands, then spread out on paper towel to dry.

5 Preheat the oven to 180°C (350°F/ Gas 4). Cover the pastry shell with baking paper and spread with a layer of baking beads or rice. Bake for 15 minutes. Remove the paper and beads and bake for another 15 minutes.

6 Spread half the cheese over the pastry base, then top with half the potatoes, half the spinach and half the leeks. Repeat these layers again. In a bowl, mix together the eggs, cream and milk and pour over the top. Bake for 1 hour, or until firm. Serve warm or cold.

NOTE: *Spinach can be very gritty, so wash thoroughly in a few changes of water. Squeeze out all the moisture after cooking and dry well on paper towels or a tea towel (dish towel) so that the water does not make the filling too moist.*

NUTRITION PER SERVE (8)
Protein 15 g; Fat 35 g; Carbohydrate 35 g; Dietary Fibre 5 g; Cholesterol 180 mg; 2150 kJ (510 Cal)

Remove the potatoes with a slotted spoon and drain on paper towel.

Cook the spinach for two minutes, or until it has just wilted.

Layer half of the cheese, potato, spinach and leek over the pastry.

Tomato and bacon quiche

PREPARATION TIME: 45 MINUTES + 1 HOUR REFRIGERATION | TOTAL COOKING TIME: 1 HOUR 10 MINUTES | SERVES 6

185 g (6 oz/1½ cups) plain (all-purpose) flour
pinch of cayenne pepper
pinch of mustard powder
125 g (4½ oz) butter, chilled and cubed
40 g (1½ oz/⅓ cup) grated cheddar cheese
1 egg yolk

FILLING
25 g (1 oz) butter
100 g (3½ oz) lean bacon, chopped
1 small onion, finely sliced
3 eggs
185 ml (6 fl oz/¾ cup) cream
½ teaspoon salt
2 tomatoes, peeled, seeded and chopped
    into chunks
90 g (3¼ oz/¾ cup) grated cheddar cheese

1   Process the flour, pepper, mustard and butter together until crumbly. Add the cheese and egg yolk and process in short bursts until the mixture comes together. Add 1–2 tablespoons of cold water if needed. Turn out onto a floured surface and gather into a ball. Wrap in plastic wrap and refrigerate for 30 minutes. Grease a 23 cm (9 inch) loose-based deep flan (tart) tin.

2   To make the filling, melt the butter in a frying pan and cook the bacon for a few minutes until golden. Add the onion and cook until soft. Remove from the heat. In a bowl, lightly beat the eggs, cream and salt together. Add the bacon and onion, then fold in the tomato and cheese.

3   Roll out the pastry on a floured surface until large enough to fit the tin. Trim the excess pastry and refrigerate for 30 minutes. Preheat the oven to 180°C (350°F/Gas 4). Cover the pastry with baking paper and a layer of baking beads or rice. Bake for 10 minutes. Remove the paper and beads and bake for another 10 minutes.

4   Pour the filling into the pastry shell and bake for 35 minutes, or until golden and set.

Cook the bacon in a little butter until golden and then add the onion.

Fold the tomato chunks and cheese into the egg and cream mixture.

NUTRITION PER SERVE
Protein 15 g; Fat 45 g; Carbohydrate 25 g; Dietary Fibre 2 g; Cholesterol 255 mg; 2405 kJ (570 Cal)

Caramelised onion quiche

PREPARATION TIME: 45 MINUTES + 20 MINUTES REFRIGERATION | TOTAL COOKING TIME: 1 HOUR 45 MINUTES | SERVES 6

185 g (6½ oz/1½ cups) plain (all-purpose) flour
125 g (4½ oz) butter, chilled and cubed
1 egg yolk
1–2 tablespoons iced water

FILLING
800 g (1 lb 12 oz) onions, thinly sliced
75 g (2½ oz) butter
1 tablespoon soft brown sugar
185 g (6½ oz/¾ cup) sour cream
2 eggs
40 g (1½ oz) prosciutto, cut into strips
40 g (1½ oz) grated cheddar cheese
2 teaspoons thyme leaves

1 Process the flour and butter in a food processor until crumbly. Add the egg yolk and most of the water. Process in short bursts until the mixture comes together, adding more water if needed. Turn out onto a floured surface and gather into a ball. Wrap in plastic and refrigerate for 20 minutes.

2 Blanch the onion in boiling water for 2 minutes, then drain. Melt the butter in a saucepan and cook the onion over low heat for 25 minutes, or until soft. Stir in the sugar and cook for 15 minutes, stirring occasionally. Preheat the oven to 200°C (400°F/Gas 6). Grease a 23 cm (9 inch) loose-based flan (tart) tin.

3 Roll out the pastry until large enough to fit the tin and trim off the excess. Cover with baking paper and spread with baking beads or rice. Bake for 15 minutes. Remove the paper and beads and bake for 5 minutes.

4 Lightly beat the sour cream and eggs together. Add the prosciutto, cheese and thyme. Stir in the onion and pour the mixture into the pastry shell. Bake for 40 minutes, or until set. If the pastry starts to over-brown, cover with foil.

NUTRITION PER SERVE
Protein 10 g; Fat 45 g; Carbohydrate 30 g; Dietary Fibre 3 g; Cholesterol 230 mg; 2450 kJ (585 Cal)

Add the egg yolk to the crumbly mixture of processed flour and butter.

Stir the soft brown sugar through the softened onion to help it caramelise.

Mushroom quiche with parsley pastry

PREPARATION TIME: 30 MINUTES + 50 MINUTES REFRIGERATION | TOTAL COOKING TIME: 1 HOUR | SERVES 4–6

310 g (11 oz/2½ cups) plain (all-purpose) flour
30 g (1 oz/½ cup) chopped parsley
180 g (6¼ oz) butter, chilled and cubed
2 egg yolks
4 tablespoons iced water

FILLING
30 g (1 oz) butter
1 red onion, chopped
175 g (6 oz) button mushrooms, sliced
1 teaspoon lemon juice
20 g (¾ oz/⅓ cup) chopped parsley
20 g (¾ oz/⅓ cup) chopped chives
2 eggs, lightly beaten
170 ml (5½ oz/⅔ cup) cream

NUTRITION PER SERVE (6)
Protein 6 g; Fat 25 g; Carbohydrate 20 g; Dietary Fibre 2 g; Cholesterol 130 mg; 1350 kJ (320 Cal)

1 Process the flour, parsley and butter in a food processor for 15 seconds, or until crumbly. Add the egg yolk and most of the water. Process in short bursts until the mixture comes together, adding a little more water if needed. Turn out onto a floured surface and gather into a ball. Cover with plastic wrap and refrigerate for at least 30 minutes.

2 Roll out the pastry between two sheets of baking paper until large enough to fit a 35 x 10 cm (14 x 4 inch) loose-based flan (tart) tin. Trim away the excess pastry. Refrigerate for 20 minutes. Preheat the oven to 190°C (375°F/ Gas 5).

3 Cover the pastry with baking paper and spread with a layer of baking beads or rice. Bake for 15 minutes. Remove the paper and beads and bake for another 10 minutes, or until the pastry is dry. Reduce the oven to 180°C (350°F/ Gas 4).

4 Melt the butter in a pan and cook the onion for 2–3 minutes until soft. Add the mushrooms and cook, stirring, for 2–3 minutes until soft. Stir in the lemon juice and herbs. In a bowl, mix the egg and cream together and season.

5 Spread the mushroom filling into the pastry shell and pour over the egg and cream. Bake for 25–30 minutes, or until the filling has set.

Place the flour and parsley in a food processor and add the butter.

The easiest way to line the tin with pastry is to roll the pastry over a rolling pin to lift it.

Pour the combined egg and cream over the mushroom filling.

Green peppercorn and gruyère quiches

PREPARATION TIME: 25 MINUTES + 15 MINUTES REFRIGERATION | TOTAL COOKING TIME: 45 MINUTES | MAKES 4

2 sheets puff pastry
100 g (3½ oz) gruyère cheese, diced
½ small celery stalk, finely chopped
1 teaspoon chopped thyme
2 teaspoons green peppercorns, chopped
1 egg, lightly beaten
60 ml (2 fl oz/¼ cup) cream

1 Lightly grease four deep 8 cm (3¼ inch) loose-based flan (tart) tins. Cut two 14 cm (5½ inch) rounds from each sheet of pastry. Lift the pastry into the tins and press well into the sides. Trim the excess pastry with a sharp knife or by rolling a rolling pin across the top of the tins. Prick the bases with a fork. Refrigerate for at least 15 minutes.

2 Preheat the oven to 220°C (425°F/Gas 7). Bake the pastry shells for about 12 minutes, or until they are browned and puffed. Remove from the oven and, as the pastry is cooling, gently press down the bases if they have puffed too high—this will make room for the filling.

3 Mix together the cheese, celery, thyme and peppercorns and spoon into the pastry cases. Combine the egg and cream and pour over the top. Bake for 25–30 minutes, or until the filling is puffed and set.

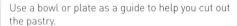

Use a bowl or plate as a guide to help you cut out the pastry.

Gently press down the bases of the pastry shells if they have puffed up too high.

NUTRITION PER QUICHE
Protein 15 g; Fat 35 g; Carbohydrate 30 g; Dietary Fibre 1 g; Cholesterol 115 mg; 2045 kJ (485 Cal)

Oyster and nutmeg quiche

PREPARATION TIME: 20 MINUTES + 20 MINUTES REFRIGERATION | TOTAL COOKING TIME: 1 HOUR | SERVES 4

1 sheet shortcrust pastry

2 eggs

2 teaspoons plain (all-purpose) flour

¼ teaspoon grated nutmeg

2 tablespoons cream

2 tablespoons milk

65 g (2¼ oz/½ cup) grated gruyère cheese

1 dozen fresh oysters, shucked

20 g (¾ oz) parmesan cheese, shaved

1 Line a shallow 19 cm (7½ inch) loose-based flan (tart) tin with the pastry, trimming away the excess. Refrigerate for 20 minutes. Preheat the oven to 180°C (350°F/Gas 4).

2 Cover the pastry shell with baking paper and spread with a layer of baking beads or rice. Bake for 10 minutes. Remove the paper and beads and bake for a further 5 minutes, or until the pastry is lightly golden. Cool on a wire rack.

3 Beat the eggs, then whisk in the flour, nutmeg, cream, milk and a pinch of salt. Stir in the gruyère cheese and pour into the pastry shell.

4 Arrange the oysters in the pastry shell. Sprinkle with the parmesan cheese and bake for 40–45 minutes. Cool slightly before serving.

NUTRITION PER SERVE
Protein 15 g; Fat 25 g; Carbohydrate 15 g; Dietary Fibre 1 g; Cholesterol 155 mg; 1200 kJ (285 Cal)

Cover the pastry shell with baking paper and fill evenly with baking beads.

Whisk the flour, nutmeg, cream, milk and salt into the beaten eggs.

Arrange the shucked oysters in the pastry base and then sprinkle with parmesan cheese.

Fresh herb quiche

PREPARATION TIME: 30 MINUTES + 50 MINUTES REFRIGERATION | TOTAL COOKING TIME: 1 HOUR | SERVES 4–6

185 g (6½ oz/1½ cups) plain (all-purpose) flour
15 g (½ oz/¼ cup) chopped parsley
125 g (4½ oz) butter, chilled and cubed
1 egg yolk
1 tablespoon iced water

FILLING
30 g (1 oz) butter
1 small leek, thinly sliced
1–2 garlic cloves, crushed
4 spring onions (scallions), chopped
15 g (½ oz/¼ cup) chopped parsley
2 tablespoons chopped chives
2 tablespoons chopped dill
2 tablespoons oregano leaves
3 eggs
250 ml (9 fl oz/1 cup) cream
60 ml (2 fl oz/¼ cup) milk
125 g (4½ oz/1 cup) grated cheddar cheese

1 Process the flour, parsley and butter in a food processor for 15 seconds, or until crumbly. Add the egg yolk and most of the water. Process in short bursts until the mixture comes together, adding a little extra water if needed. Turn onto a floured surface and gather into a ball. Wrap in plastic wrap and refrigerate for 30 minutes.

2 Preheat the oven to 190°C (375°F/Gas 5) and grease a 24 cm (9½ inch) loose-based flan (tart) tin. Roll out the pastry, line the tin and trim off any excess. Chill the lined tin for 20 minutes. Cover the pastry with baking paper and spread with a layer of baking beads or rice. Bake for 15 minutes. Remove the paper and beads and bake for a further 10 minutes. Reduce the oven to 180°C (350°F/ Gas 4).

3 Heat the butter in a saucepan and cook the leek, garlic and spring onion for 10 minutes, stirring often. Add the herbs and let cool.

4 In a bowl, beat the eggs, cream and milk and season with freshly ground black pepper. Spread the leek and herb mixture in the pastry base. Pour over the egg mixture and sprinkle with the cheese. Bake for 25–30 minutes, or until golden.

NUTRITION PER SERVE (6)
Protein 15 g; Fat 45 g; Carbohydrate 25 g; Dietary Fibre 2 g; Cholesterol 220 mg; 2300 kJ (545 Cal)

When the mixture is crumbly, add the egg yolk and iced water.

Stir the fresh herbs through the cooked leek.

Pour the mixed egg and cream over the filling and sprinkle with cheddar cheese.

Zucchini and prosciutto quiche

PREPARATION TIME: 35 MINUTES + 20 MINUTES REFRIGERATION I TOTAL COOKING TIME: 1 HOUR 15 MINUTES I SERVES 6

2 sheets shortcrust pastry
2 tablespoons olive oil
100 g (3½ oz) prosciutto
1 onion, chopped
4 zucchini (courgettes), thinly sliced
4 eggs
170 ml (5½ fl oz/⅔ cup) cream
60 ml (2 fl oz/¼ cup) milk
25 g (¾ oz/¼ cup) grated parmesan cheese

1   Place the two sheets of pastry together, slightly overlapping, and roll out until large enough to line a shallow 25 cm (10 inch) loose-based fluted flan (tart) tin. Trim off the excess pastry and refrigerate for 20 minutes. Preheat the oven to 200°C (400°F/Gas 6).

2   Cover the pastry shell with baking paper and spread with a layer of baking beads or rice. Bake for 15 minutes. Remove the paper and beads and bake for another 10 minutes, or until the pastry is lightly golden. Cool on a wire rack.

3   To make the filling, heat the olive oil in a frying pan. Cut the prosciutto into thin strips and cook until it is crisp. Remove from the pan with a slotted spoon and drain on paper towel. Cook the onion until soft and remove from the pan. Cook the zucchini and, when almost cooked, season well. Remove from the heat.

4   In a bowl, mix together the eggs, cream, milk and most of the parmesan cheese.

5   Lay the prosciutto, onion and zucchini in the pastry shell, then pour in the egg and milk mixture. Sprinkle with the remaining parmesan cheese. Bake for 35–40 minutes, until the filling has set and is golden.

Remove the crisp prosciutto from the pan with a slotted spoon.

When almost cooked, season the zucchini with salt and freshly ground black pepper.

NUTRITION PER SERVE
Protein 15 g; Fat 40 g; Carbohydrate 30 g; Dietary Fibre 2 g; Cholesterol 195 mg; 2215 kJ (525 Cal)

Blue cheese and parsnip quiche

PREPARATION TIME: 45 MINUTES + 25 MINUTES REFRIGERATION | TOTAL COOKING TIME: 1 HOUR 10 MINUTES | SERVES 4–6

125 g (4½ oz/1 cup) plain (all-purpose) flour
150 g (5½ oz/1 cup) wholemeal (whole-wheat) flour
100 g (3½ oz) butter, chilled and cubed
1 egg yolk
3 tablespoons iced water

FILLING
½ tablespoon oil
1 small onion, chopped
1 carrot, cut into small cubes
1 parsnip, cut into small cubes
1 teaspoon cumin seeds
1 tablespoon chopped coriander (cilantro) leaves
100 g (3½ oz) mild blue cheese
1 egg, lightly beaten
90 ml (3 fl oz/⅓ cup) cream

1 Process the flours and butter until crumbly. Add the yolk and water. Process in short bursts until the mixture comes together. Add more water if needed. Turn out and gather into a ball. Wrap in plastic and refrigerate for 15 minutes. Preheat the oven to 200°C (400°F/Gas 6) and heat a baking tray. Grease a deep 19 cm (7½ inch) loose-based fluted flan (tart) tin.

2 Roll out the pastry between baking paper. Line the tin and trim. Prick the base with a fork and refrigerate for 10 minutes. Place on the heated tray and bake for 12 minutes, until the pastry is just browned and dry. Leave to cool.

3 Heat the oil in a pan and cook the onion, carrot, parsnip and cumin seeds, stirring, until the onion is translucent. Add the coriander and season well. Remove from heat and cool slightly.

4 Crumble the cheese into the pastry shell and spoon in the filling. Mix together the egg and cream and pour over the filling. Sprinkle with fresh pepper. Bake for 45 minutes, until set.

NUTRITION PER SERVE (6)
Protein 15 g; Fat 45 g; Carbohydrate 40 g; Dietary Fibre 7 g; Cholesterol 210 mg; 2560 kJ (610 Cal)

Blind-bake the pastry shell and then leave on the baking tray to cool.

Spoon the vegetable filling over the cheese in the base of the quiche.

Asparagus and parmesan quiche

PREPARATION TIME: 25 MINUTES + 50 MINUTES REFRIGERATION I TOTAL COOKING TIME: 1 HOUR I SERVES 4–6

185 g (6½ oz/1½ cups) plain (all-purpose) flour
125 g (4½ oz) butter, chilled and cubed
1 egg yolk
2 tablespoons iced water

FILLING
50 g (1¾ oz/½ cup) grated parmesan cheese
30 g (1 oz) butter
1 small red onion, chopped
2 spring onions (scallions), chopped
1 tablespoon chopped dill
1 tablespoon chopped chives
1 egg, lightly beaten
60 g (2 oz/¼ cup) sour cream
60 ml (2 fl oz/¼ cup) cream
400 g (13 oz) tinned asparagus spears, drained

NUTRITION PER SERVE (4)
Protein 15 g; Fat 50 g; Carbohydrate 35 g; Dietary Fibre 4 g; Cholesterol 240 mg; 2800 kJ (665 Cal)

1 Process the flour and butter in a food processor for about 15 seconds until crumbly. Add the egg yolk and most of the water. Process in short bursts until the mixture just comes together. Add a little more water if needed. Turn onto a floured surface and gather into a ball. Wrap in plastic wrap and refrigerate for 30 minutes.

2 Roll out the pastry between two sheets of baking paper until it is large enough to fit a 35 x 10 cm (14 x 4 inch) loose-based flan (tart) tin. Trim away the excess pastry and refrigerate for 20 minutes. Preheat the oven to 190°C (375°F/Gas 5).

3 Cover the pastry with baking paper and spread with a layer of baking beads or rice. Bake for 15 minutes. Remove the paper and beads and bake for another 10 minutes, or until the pastry is dry and golden. Cool slightly, then sprinkle with half the parmesan cheese. Reduce the oven to 180°C (350°F/Gas 4).

4 Melt the butter in a saucepan and cook the onion and spring onion for 2–3 minutes until soft. Stir in the herbs and cool. In a bowl, whisk together the egg, sour cream, cream and remaining parmesan cheese and season well.

5 Spread the onion mixture over the pastry. Lay the asparagus spears over the top and pour over the egg mixture. Bake for 25–30 minutes, or until set.

Trim the excess pastry from the edge of the tin with a sharp knife.

Whisk together the egg, sour cream, cream and remaining parmesan cheese.

Arrange the asparagus decoratively over the onion mixture.

Corn and bacon crustless quiches

PREPARATION TIME: 30 MINUTES | TOTAL COOKING TIME: 35 MINUTES | MAKES 4

4 corn cobs
2 teaspoons olive oil
2 bacon slices, cut into thin strips
1 small onion, finely chopped
3 eggs, lightly beaten
2 tablespoons chopped chives
2 tablespoons chopped parsley
60 g (2½ oz) fresh white breadcrumbs
80 ml (2½ fl oz/⅓ cup) cream

1   Preheat the oven to 180°C (350°F/Gas 4) and lightly grease four 185 ml (6 fl oz/¾ cup) ramekins or dariole moulds.

2   Remove the husks from the corn and, using a coarse grater, grate the corn kernels into a deep bowl—there should be about 1½ cups corn flesh and juice. Heat the oil in a saucepan and cook the bacon and onion for 3–4 minutes, or until the onion softens. Transfer to a bowl. Stir in the corn, egg, chives, parsley, breadcrumbs and cream and season well. Spoon into the ramekins.

3   Put the ramekins in a large baking dish. Add enough hot water to come halfway up the sides of the ramekins. Lay foil loosely over the top. Bake for 25–30 minutes, or until just set.

NUTRITION PER QUICHE
Protein 13 g; Fat 17 g; Carbohydrate 23 g; Dietary Fibre 3 g; Cholesterol 175 mg; 1230 kJ (295 Cal)

Using the coarse side of a grater, grate the corn kernels into a bowl.

Mix together the cooked onion, bacon, corn, eggs, chives, parsley, breadcrumbs and cream.

Cook the quiches in a bain-marie, made by pouring water into a large baking dish.

Smoked salmon and caper quiche

PREPARATION TIME: 25 MINUTES + 40 MINUTES REFRIGERATION | TOTAL COOKING TIME: 1 HOUR 10 MINUTES | SERVES 6–8

185 g (6½ oz/1½ cups) plain (all-purpose) flour
90 g (3¼ oz) butter, chilled and cubed
2 teaspoons cracked black pepper
1 egg yolk
2 tablespoons iced water

FILLING
1 tablespoon olive oil
1 small leek, chopped
½ teaspoon sugar
200 g (7 oz) sliced smoked salmon
50 g (1¾ oz/⅓ cup) frozen peas
2 tablespoons baby capers
75 g (2½ oz) cream cheese
2 eggs
2 teaspoons dijon mustard
185 ml (6 fl oz/¾ cup) cream

1 Process the flour and butter in a food processor for 15 seconds until crumbly. Add the pepper, egg yolk and most of the water. Process in short bursts until the mixture comes together, adding more water if necessary. Turn onto a floured surface and gather into a ball. Cover with plastic wrap and chill for 30 minutes. Preheat the oven to 200°C (400°F/Gas 6). Grease a 17 cm (6½ inch) deep loose-based fluted flan (tart) tin.

2 Lay the pastry in the tin, place on a baking tray and refrigerate for 10 minutes. Prick the base with a fork and bake for 12 minutes.

3 To make the filling, heat the oil in a pan and cook the leek and sugar over low heat for 15 minutes. Cool, then spoon into the pastry. Scrunch up the salmon slices and lay around the edge. Put the peas and capers in the centre.

4 Process the cream cheese, eggs and mustard in a food processor until smooth. Add the cream and pour into the pastry shell. Bake for 40 minutes, or until set.

NUTRITION PER SERVE (8)
Protein 10 g; Fat 25 g; Carbohydrate 20 g; Dietary Fibre 2 g; Cholesterol 150 mg; 1485 kJ (355 Cal)

Prick all over the base of the pastry shell with a fork to prevent it rising up.

Scrunch up the salmon slices and arrange them around the edge of the quiche.

Roasted pumpkin and spinach quiche

PREPARATION TIME: 20 MINUTES | TOTAL COOKING TIME: 1 HOUR 50 MINUTES | SERVES 6

500 g (1 lb 2 oz) butternut pumpkin (squash)
1 red onion, cut into small wedges
2 tablespoons olive oil
1 garlic clove, crushed
1 teaspoon salt
4 eggs
125 ml (4 fl oz/½ cup) cream
125 ml (4 fl oz/½ cup) milk
1 tablespoon chopped parsley
1 tablespoon chopped coriander (cilantro)
  leaves
1 teaspoon wholegrain mustard
6 sheets filo pastry
50 g (1¾ oz) English spinach, blanched
1 tablespoon grated parmesan cheese

NUTRITION PER SERVE
Protein 10 g; Fat 20 g; Carbohydrate 15 g; Dietary
Fibre 2 g; Cholesterol 155 mg; 1200 kJ (285 Cal)

1 Preheat the oven to 190°C (375°F/Gas 5). Cut the pumpkin into 1 cm (½ inch) slices, leaving the skin on. Place the pumpkin, onion, 1 tablespoon of the oil, garlic and salt in a baking dish. Roast for 1 hour, or until lightly golden and cooked.

2 Whisk together the eggs, cream, milk, herbs and mustard. Season with salt and freshly ground black pepper.

3 Grease a 23 cm (9 inch) loose-based fluted flan (tart) tin. Brush each sheet of filo pastry with oil and then line the tin with the six sheets. Fold the sides down, tucking them into the tin to form a crust.

4 Heat a baking tray in the oven for 10 minutes. Place the tart tin on the tray and arrange the vegetables over the base. Pour the egg mixture over the vegetables and sprinkle with the parmesan cheese.

5 Bake for 35–40 minutes, or until the filling is golden brown and set.

Roast the pumpkin and red onion until lightly golden and cooked.

Brush the filo pastry with oil and then arrange in the tin.

Pour the egg and cream mixture over the vegetables in the lined tart tin.

Sweet pies

Pumpkin pie

PREPARATION TIME: 20 MINUTES + 40 MINUTES REFRIGERATION + COOLING | TOTAL COOKING TIME: 1 HOUR 30 MINUTES | SERVES 6–8

150 g (5½ oz/1¼ cups) plain (all-purpose) flour
100 g (3½ oz) unsalted butter, chilled and cubed
2 teaspoons caster (superfine) sugar
4 tablespoons iced water

FILLING
750 g (1 lb 10 oz) butternut pumpkin (squash), peeled, cubed
2 eggs, lightly beaten
185 g (6½ oz/1 cup) soft brown sugar
80 ml (2½ fl oz/⅓ cup) cream
1 tablespoon sweet sherry or brandy
½ teaspoon ground ginger
½ teaspoon ground nutmeg
1 teaspoon ground cinnamon

1 Sift the flour into a large bowl and rub in the butter with your fingertips until the mixture resembles fine breadcrumbs. Mix in the caster sugar. Make a well in the centre, add almost all the water and mix with a flat-bladed knife, using a cutting action, until the mixture comes together in beads, adding more water if needed.

2 Gather the dough together and lift out onto a lightly floured work surface. Press into a disc. Wrap in plastic and refrigerate for 20 minutes.

3 Roll out the pastry between two sheets of baking paper until large enough to line an 18 cm (7 inch) pie dish. Line the dish with pastry, trim away the excess and use to decorate the rim. Cover with plastic wrap and refrigerate for 20 minutes.

4 Preheat the oven to 180°C (350°F/Gas 4). Cook the pumpkin in boiling water until tender. Drain, mash, push through a sieve and leave to cool.

5 Line the pastry shell with baking paper and spread with a layer of baking beads or rice. Bake for 10 minutes, then remove the paper and beads and bake for 10 minutes, or until lightly golden. Set aside to cool.

6 Whisk the eggs and sugar together in a large bowl. Add the cooled pumpkin, cream, sherry and the spices and stir thoroughly. Pour into the pastry shell, smooth the surface and decorate the rim with leftover pastry. Bake for 1 hour, or until set. If the pastry over-browns, cover the edges with foil. Cool before serving.

NUTRITION PER SERVE (8)
Protein 6 g; Fat 16.5 g; Carbohydrate 45 g; Dietary Fibre 2 g; Cholesterol 90 mg; 1470 kJ (350 Cal)

Bake the pastry for 10 minutes, then remove the paper and beads and cook until golden.

Stir the pumpkin, cream, sherry and spices into the egg and sugar mixture.

Raspberry lattice pies

PREPARATION TIME: 50 MINUTES | TOTAL COOKING TIME: 25 MINUTES | MAKES 8

125 g (4½ oz/½ cup) cream cheese
125 g (4½ oz) unsalted butter
185 g (6½ oz/1½ cups) plain (all-purpose)
  flour
1 egg, beaten
1 tablespoon caster (superfine) sugar

FILLING
250 g (9 oz/2 cups) raspberries
70 g (2½ oz) unsalted butter, softened
90 g (3¼ oz/⅓ cup) caster (superfine) sugar
1 egg
70 g (2½ oz/⅔ cup) ground almonds

1 Beat the cream cheese and butter until soft. Stir in the sifted flour with a knife and mix to a dough. Press together to form a ball. Lightly grease eight small pie dishes or eight 125 ml (4 fl oz/½ cup) muffin holes. Roll out the pastry to 3 mm (⅛ inch) thick between two sheets of baking paper. Cut out eight rounds with a 10 cm (4 inch) cutter and ease into the tins.

2 Divide the raspberries among the pastry cases. Cream together the butter and sugar and then beat in the egg. Fold in the almonds and spoon on top of the raspberries.

3 Preheat the oven to 180°C (350°F/Gas 4). Roll out the pastry scraps and cut into 5 mm (¼ inch) wide strips. Weave into a lattice on a board, lightly press down with the palm of your hand and cut into rounds with the 10 cm (4 inch) cutter. Brush the pastry rims of the tartlets with beaten egg, put the lattice rounds on top and gently press down the edges to seal. Re-roll the scraps until all the tartlets are topped. Glaze with beaten egg, sprinkle with caster sugar and bake for 20–25 minutes, or until golden.

Cut out rounds of pastry and then ease into the dishes or tins.

Brush the pastry edges with beaten egg and place the lattice on top.

NUTRITION PER PIE
Protein 10 g; Fat 30 g; Carbohydrate 25 g; Dietary Fibre 4 g; Cholesterol 100 mg; 1677 kJ (400 Cal)

Apple and pecan filo pie

PREPARATION TIME: 25 MINUTES | TOTAL COOKING TIME: 50 MINUTES | SERVES 8

60 g (2¼ oz/½ cup) pecans
50 g (1¾ oz) butter
3 tablespoons caster (superfine) sugar
1 teaspoon finely grated lemon zest
1 egg, lightly beaten
2 tablespoons plain (all-purpose) flour
3 green apples
10 sheets filo pastry
40 g (1½ oz) butter, melted
icing sugar, to dust

1 Preheat the oven to 180°C (350°F/Gas 4). Lightly grease a 35 x 11 cm (14 x 4¼ inch) tin. Spread the pecans in a single layer on an oven tray and bake for 5 minutes to lightly toast. Leave to cool, then chop finely.

2 Beat the butter, sugar, lemon zest and egg with electric beaters until creamy. Stir in the flour and nuts.

3 Peel, core and thinly slice the apples. On a flat surface, layer 10 sheets of the filo pastry, brushing each sheet with melted butter before laying the next sheet on top. Fit the layered pastry loosely into the prepared tin. Spread the nut mixture evenly over the pastry base and lay the apple slices on top.

4 Fold the overhanging pastry over the filling and brush with butter. Trim one side of the pastry lengthways and crumple it over the top of the tart. Bake for 45 minutes, or until brown and crisp. Before serving, dust with icing sugar. Serve hot or cold.

STORAGE: *This tart is best eaten on the day it is made.*

VARIATION: *Thinly sliced pears can be used instead of apples. Walnuts can replace the pecans. Toasting the nuts improves their flavour and makes them a little more crunchy.*

NUTRITION PER SERVE
Protein 4 g; Fat 22 g; Carbohydrate 27 g; Dietary
Fibre 3 g; Cholesterol 51 mg; 1300 kJ (313 Cal)

Lightly toast the pecans in the oven to improve their flavour, before chopping.

Spread the nut mixture into the pastry base and then arrange the sliced apple on top.

Mince pies

PREPARATION TIME: 40 MINUTES + 40 MINUTES REFRIGERATION | TOTAL COOKING TIME: 25 MINUTES | MAKES 12

250 g (9 oz/2 cups) plain (all-purpose) flour
½ teaspoon ground cinnamon
125 g (4½ oz) unsalted butter, chilled and cubed
1 teaspoon finely grated orange zest
30 g (1 oz/¼ cup) icing sugar, sifted
1 egg yolk
3–4 tablespoons iced water

FILLING
60 g (2¼ oz/½ cup) raisins, chopped
60 g (2¼ oz/⅓ cup) soft brown sugar
40 g (1½ oz/⅓ cup) sultanas (golden raisins)
45 g (1½ oz/¼ cup) mixed peel
1 tablespoon currants
1 tablespoon chopped blanched almonds
1 small green apple, grated
1 teaspoon lemon juice
1 teaspoon finely grated lemon zest
1 teaspoon finely grated orange zest
½ teaspoon mixed (pumpkin pie) spice
¼ teaspoon grated ginger
pinch of ground nutmeg
25 g (1 oz) unsalted butter, melted
1 tablespoon brandy
icing (confectioner's) sugar, for dusting

NUTRITION PER PIE
Protein 2 g; Fat 6 g; Carbohydrate 17 g; Dietary
Fibre 1 g; Cholesterol 23 mg; 535 kJ (130 Cal)

1 Sift the flour, cinnamon and ¼ teaspoon salt into a large bowl. Rub the butter into the flour with your fingertips until it resembles fine breadcrumbs. Stir in the orange zest and icing sugar and mix. Make a well in the centre and add the egg yolk and most of the water. Mix with a flat-bladed knife, using a cutting action, until the mixture comes together in beads, adding more water if necessary. Gather together, lift onto a lightly floured work surface and press into a disc, wrap in plastic wrap and refrigerate for 20 minutes. Mix together all the filling ingredients.

2 Preheat the oven to 180°C (350°F/Gas 4). Grease a 12-hole shallow patty pan or mini muffin tin. Roll out two-thirds of the pastry between two sheets of baking paper until 3 mm (⅛ inch) thick. Use an 8 cm (3¼ inch) round biscuit cutter to cut out rounds to line the patty pans.

3 Divide the filling among the patty cases. Roll out the remaining pastry and cut out 12 rounds with a 7 cm (2¾ inch) cutter. Using a 2.5 cm (1 inch) star cutter, cut a star from the centre of each. Use the outside part to top the tarts, pressing the edges together to seal. Refrigerate for 20 minutes.

4 Bake for 25 minutes, or until the pastry is golden. Leave in the pan for 5 minutes before cooling on a wire rack. Dust with icing sugar to serve.

NOTE: *Any extra fruit mince can be stored in a sterilised jar in a cool, dark place for 3 months.*

Mix the pastry using a cutting action until the mixture comes together in beads.

Carefully spoon the fruit mince mixture into the patty cases.

Cut a star shape from the centre of the pastry circles.

Banana cream pie

PREPARATION TIME: 25 MINUTES + 20 MINUTES REFRIGERATION | TOTAL COOKING TIME: 30 MINUTES | SERVES 6–8

375 g (13 oz) shortcrust pastry
90 g (3¼ oz) dark chocolate chips
4 egg yolks
125 g (4½ oz/½ cup) caster (superfine) sugar
½ teaspoon vanilla essence
2 tablespoons custard powder
500 ml (17 fl oz/2 cups) milk
40 g (1½ oz) unsalted butter, softened
1 teaspoon brandy or rum
3 large ripe bananas, thinly sliced, plus extra
    to decorate
60 g (2¼ oz/½ cup) grated dark chocolate

1 Roll out the pastry between two sheets of baking paper to line an 18 cm (7 inch) pie tin, pressing it firmly into the side and trimming away the excess. Refrigerate for 20 minutes.

2 Preheat the oven to 190°C (375°F/Gas 5). Line the pastry with baking paper and spread with baking beads or rice. Bake for 10 minutes, remove the paper and beads and bake for 10–12 minutes, until the pastry is dry and lightly golden.

3 While it is hot, place the chocolate chips in the pastry base. Leave for 5 minutes to melt, then spread over the crust with the back of a spoon.

4 To make the filling, beat the egg yolks, sugar, vanilla and custard powder with electric beaters for 2–3 minutes, or until pale and thick. Bring the milk to boiling point in a small saucepan, then remove from the heat and gradually pour into the egg and sugar mixture, stirring well. Return to the pan and bring to the boil, stirring. Cook for 2 minutes, or until thickened. Remove from the heat and stir in the butter and brandy. Cool completely.

5 Arrange the banana over the chocolate, then pour the custard over the top. Refrigerate until ready to serve. Decorate with banana slices and the grated chocolate.

Beat the egg, sugar, vanilla and custard powder until the mixture is pale and thick.

Arrange the banana over the chocolate, then pour the custard into the pie.

NUTRITION PER SERVE (8)
Protein 8 g; Fat 26 g; Carbohydrate 60 g; Dietary Fibre 2 g; Cholesterol 124 mg; 2060 kJ (490 Cal)

Mango and passionfruit pies

PREPARATION TIME: 25 MINUTES + REFRIGERATION | TOTAL COOKING TIME: 25 MINUTES | MAKES 6

750 g (1 lb 10 oz) sweet shortcrust pastry
3 ripe mangoes, peeled and sliced or chopped,
    or 400 g (14 oz) tin mango slices, drained
60 g (2¼ oz/¼ cup) passionfruit pulp
1 tablespoon custard powder
90 g (3¼ oz/⅓ cup) caster (superfine) sugar
1 egg, lightly beaten
icing sugar, to dust

1   Preheat the oven to 190°C (375°F/Gas 5).
Grease six 8 cm (3¼ inch) fluted flan (tart) tins.
Roll out two-thirds of the pastry between two
sheets of baking paper until 3 mm (⅛ inch) thick.
Cut out six 13 cm (5 inch) circles. Line the tins
with the circles and trim the edges. Refrigerate
while you make the filling.

2   Mix together the mango, passionfruit, custard
powder and sugar.

3   Roll out the remaining pastry between baking
paper to 3 mm (⅛ inch) thick. Cut out six 11 cm
(4¼ inch) circles. Re-roll the trimmings and cut
out small shapes for decorations.

4   Fill the pastry cases with the mango mixture
and brush the edges with egg. Top with the
pastry circles, press the edges to seal and trim.
Decorate with the shapes. Brush the tops with
beaten egg and dust with icing sugar. Bake for
20–25 minutes, or until the pastry is golden.

NUTRITION PER PIE
Protein 11 g; Fat 29 g; Carbohydrate 85 g; Dietary
Fibre 6 g; Cholesterol 114 mg; 2685 kJ (640 Cal)

Line the tins with the pastry circles and trim away
the excess pastry.

Spoon the mango and passionfruit filling into the
pastry cases.

Decorate the tops of the pies with shapes cut from
the pastry trimmings.

Shaker lemon pie

PREPARATION TIME: 20 MINUTES + 20 MINUTES REFRIGERATION | TOTAL COOKING TIME: 50 MINUTES | SERVES 6–8

2 large lemons
60 g (2¼ oz/½ cup) plain (all-purpose) flour
500 g (1 lb 2 oz/2 cups) caster (superfine) sugar
40 g (1½ oz) unsalted butter, melted
4 eggs, lightly beaten
1 egg, extra, lightly beaten, to glaze

PASTRY
375 g (13 oz/3 cups) plain (all-purpose) flour
185 g (6½ oz) unsalted butter, chilled and cubed
2 tablespoons caster (superfine) sugar
4–5 tablespoons iced water

1 Finely grate 1 lemon to give 2 teaspoons of zest. Place the zest in a large bowl. Cut the pith off both lemons and discard. Thinly slice the lemon flesh, discarding the seeds.

2 Sift the flour into the bowl with the zest, then stir in the sugar and a pinch of salt. Add the butter and egg, and stir until smooth. Gently fold in the lemon slices.

3 Preheat the oven to 200°C (400°F/Gas 6) and heat a baking tray. Grease a 20 cm (8 inch) pie dish.

4 To make the pastry, sift the flour and ¼ teaspoon salt into a large bowl and rub in the butter with your fingertips until the mixture resembles fine breadcrumbs. Mix in the caster sugar. Make a well, add almost all the water and mix with a flat-bladed knife, using a cutting action, until the mixture comes together in beads, adding more water if necessary.

5 Gather together on a lightly floured surface and press into a disc. Wrap in plastic wrap and refrigerate for 20 minutes.

6 Roll out two-thirds of the pastry between two sheets of baking paper until large enough to fit the dish. Spoon the lemon filling into the pastry shell.

7 Roll out the remaining pastry until large enough to cover the pie. Using a sharp knife, cut out three small triangles in a row across the centre of the lid. Brush the rim of the pastry base with beaten egg, then press the lid in place. Trim off any excess. Scallop the edges with your fingers, then go around the open scallops and mark with the tines of a narrow fork. Brush the top with egg glaze.

8 Bake on the hot tray for 20 minutes. Reduce the temperature to 180°C (350°F/Gas 4), cover the pie with foil and bake for a further 30 minutes, or until the filling is set and the pastry is golden.

NUTRITION PER SERVE (8)
Protein 9 g; Fat 26 g; Carbohydrate 106 g; Dietary Fibre 2.5 g; Cholesterol 161 mg; 2880 kJ (690 Cal)

Use a small sharp knife to remove all of the skin and pith from the lemons.

Gently fold the lemon slices into the butter and egg mixture.

Farmhouse rhubarb pie

PREPARATION TIME: 40 MINUTES + REFRIGERATION I TOTAL COOKING TIME: 50 MINUTES I SERVES 6

185 g (6½ oz/1½ cups) plain (all-purpose) flour, sifted
125 g (4½ oz) unsalted butter, chilled and cubed
2 tablespoons icing sugar
1 egg yolk
1 tablespoon iced water

FILLING
250 g (9 oz/1 cup) sugar
750 g (1 lb 10 oz) chopped rhubarb
2 large apples, peeled, cored and chopped
2 teaspoons grated lemon zest
3 pieces preserved ginger, sliced
2 teaspoons sugar
sprinkle of ground cinnamon

1   Mix the flour, butter and icing sugar in a food processor until crumbly. Add the yolk and water and process until the dough comes togcthcr. Wrap in plastic wrap and rcfrigcratc for 15 minutes.

2   Preheat the oven to 190°C (375°F/Gas 5). Roll out the pastry to a rough 35 cm (14 inch) circle and line a greased 20 cm (8 inch) pie plate, leaving the extra pastry to hang over the edge. Refrigerate while you prepare the filling.

3   Heat the sugar and 125 ml (4 fl oz/½ cup) water in a pan for 4–5 minutes or until syrupy. Add the rhubarb, apple, lemon zest and ginger. Cover and simmer for 5 minutes, until the rhubarb is cooked but still holds its shape.

4   Drain off the liquid and cool the rhubarb. Spoon into the pastry base and sprinkle with the sugar and cinnamon. Fold the overhanging pastry roughly over the fruit and bake for 40 minutes, or until golden.

Simmer until the rhubarb is tender but still holds its shape.

Fold the overhanging pastry roughly over the fruit so that there is an open area in the middle.

NUTRITION PER SERVE
Protein 6 g; Fat 20 g; Carbohydrate 82 g; Dietary Fibre 6 g; Cholesterol 83 mg; 2145 kJ (513 Cal)

Nutty fig pie

PREPARATION TIME: 40 MINUTES + 20 MINUTES REFRIGERATION | TOTAL COOKING TIME: 1 HOUR | SERVES 8

375 g (13 oz) sweet shortcrust pastry
200 g (7 oz) hazelnuts
100 g (3½ oz/ ⅔ cup) pine nuts
100 g (3½ oz) flaked almonds
100 g (3½ oz) blanched almonds
150 ml (5 fl oz) cream
60 g (2¼ oz) unsalted butter
90 g (3¼ oz/¼ cup) honey
95 g (3¼ oz/½ cup) soft brown sugar
150 g (5½ oz) dessert figs, quartered

1 Preheat the oven to 200°C (400°F/Gas 6) and grease a 20 cm (8 inch) pie tin. Roll the pastry out between two sheets of baking paper until large enough to line the tin, trimming away the excess. Use a fork to prick the base several times and score the edge. Refrigerate for 20 minutes, then bake for 15 minutes, or until dry and lightly golden. Allow to cool.

2 Meanwhile, bake the hazelnuts on a baking tray for 8 minutes, or until the skins start to peel away. Tip into a tea towel (dish towel) and rub to remove the skins. Place the pine nuts, flaked almonds and blanched almonds on a baking tray and bake for 5–6 minutes, or until lightly golden.

3 Place the cream, butter, honey and sugar in a saucepan and stir over medium heat until the sugar dissolves and the butter melts. Remove from the heat and stir in the nuts and figs. Spoon into the pastry case and bake for 30 minutes, or until the pastry is golden and the filling is set. Remove and cool before slicing.

Roll out the pastry until large enough to line the pie tin, letting the excess hang over the edge.

Spoon the nut and fig filling into the pastry-lined pie tin.

NUTRITION PER SERVE
Protein 11 g; Fat 57 g; Carbohydrate 44 g; Dietary Fibre 5.5 g; Cholesterol 57 mg; 3030 kJ (725 Cal)

Pear and pecan pie

PREPARATION TIME: 25 MINUTES + 40 MINUTES REFRIGERATION + COOLING | TOTAL COOKING TIME: 50 MINUTES | SERVES 6

250 g (9 oz/2 cups) plain (all-purpose) flour
100 g (3½ oz) unsalted butter, chilled and cubed
65 g (2¼ oz) white vegetable shortening, chilled and cubed
2 teaspoons caster (superfine) sugar
3–4 tablespoons iced water

FILLING
40 g (1½ oz) unsalted butter
180 g (6¼ oz/½ cup) golden syrup (or use half honey and half dark corn syrup)
2 tablespoons cornflour (cornstarch)
¼ teaspoon ground ginger
½ teaspoon grated lemon zest
½ teaspoon mixed (pumpkin pie) spice
4 pears, peeled, cored and thinly sliced
100 g (3½ oz/1 cup) pecans, chopped
1 tablespoon caster (superfine) sugar
1 tablespoon ground pecans
1 tablespoon sugar
1 egg, lightly beaten

1 To make the pastry, sift the flour and ¼ teaspoon salt into a large bowl and rub in the butter and shortening with your fingertips until the mixture resembles fine breadcrumbs. Mix in the sugar. Make a well in the centre, add almost all the water and mix with a flat-bladed knife, using a cutting action, until the mixture comes together in beads, adding more water if necessary.

2 Gather the dough together and lift onto a lightly floured work surface. Press into a ball and flatten slightly into a disc. Cover in plastic wrap and refrigerate for 20 minutes.

3 Preheat the oven to 200°C (400°F/Gas 6) and heat a baking tray. Grease an 18 cm (7 inch) pie dish. Roll out two-thirds of the pastry between two sheets of baking paper and line the dish, trimming away the excess. Cover in plastic wrap and refrigerate for 20 minutes.

4 For the filling, gently heat the butter and golden syrup in a saucepan over medium heat and quickly add the cornflour, ginger, lemon zest and mixed spice and stir until smooth. Add the pears, then stir in half the chopped pecans and cook for 5 minutes, or until the pear is tender. Cool completely.

5 Combine the caster sugar and remaining chopped pecans and scatter over the pastry base. Add the filling.

6 Combine the ground pecans and sugar. Roll out the remaining pastry to form a pie lid. Brush with beaten egg. Cut long wide strips of baking paper and arrange over the pie lid in straight lines with wide gaps between. Scatter the nut and sugar mixture over the exposed pastry and roll lightly with the rolling pin to embed them. Lift off the paper strips, then position the lid on the pie, pinching the edges down to seal. Trim the rim.

7 Bake on the hot tray in the centre of the oven for 20 minutes. Reduce the oven to 180°C (350°F/Gas 4), cover the top with foil and bake for another 20 minutes. Cool in the tin. Serve warm or cold.

NUTRITION PER SERVE
Protein 7 g; Fat 34 g; Carbohydrate 69 g; Dietary Fibre 5 g; Cholesterol 62 mg; 2485 kJ (595 Cal)

Add the cornflour, ginger, lemon zest and mixed spice and stir until smooth.

Scatter the nut and sugar mixture over the pastry top, so that it forms stripes.

Carefully remove the paper strips from the pastry top without dislodging the nut topping.

Peach pie

PREPARATION TIME: 35 MINUTES + 20 MINUTES REFRIGERATION | TOTAL COOKING TIME: 1 HOUR | SERVES 6–8

500 g (1 lb 2 oz) sweet shortcrust pastry
2 x 825 g (1 lb 13 oz) tins peach slices, drained
125 g (4½ oz/½ cup) caster (superfine) sugar
30 g (1 oz/¼ cup) cornflour (cornstarch)
¼ teaspoon almond essence
20 g (¾ oz) unsalted butter, chopped
1 tablespoon milk
1 egg, lightly beaten
1 tablespoon caster (superfine) sugar, extra,
    to sprinkle

1 Roll out two-thirds of the dough between two sheets of baking paper until large enough to line an 18 cm (7 inch) pie tin, pressing it firmly into the side and trimming away the excess. Refrigerate for 20 minutes.

2 Preheat the oven to 200°C (400°F/Gas 6). Line the pastry with baking paper and spread with a layer of baking beads or rice. Bake for 10 minutes, remove the paper and beads and return to the oven for 5 minutes, or until the base is dry and lightly golden. Allow to cool.

3 Mix the peaches, caster sugar, cornflour and almond essence and spoon into the pastry shell. Dot with butter and moisten the edge with milk.

4 Roll out the remaining dough to a 25 cm (10 inch) square. Using a fluted pastry cutter, cut the pastry into ten strips, each 2.5 cm (1 inch) wide. Lay the strips in a lattice pattern over the filling. Press firmly on the edges and trim. Brush the lattice with egg and sprinkle with the extra sugar. Bake for 10 minutes, reduce the oven to 180°C (350°F/Gas 4) and bake for another 30 minutes, or until the top is golden.

Combine the peaches with the caster sugar, cornflour and almond extract.

Lay the pastry strips in a lattice pattern over the top of the filling.

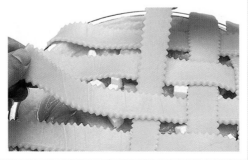

NUTRITION PER SERVE
Protein 7 g; Fat 25 g; Carbohydrate 70 g; Dietary Fibre 3 g; Cholesterol 62 mg; 2195 kJ (525 Cal)

Chocolate and peanut butter pie

PREPARATION TIME: 30 MINUTES + 4 HOURS 15 MINUTES REFRIGERATION | TOTAL COOKING TIME: 5 MINUTES | SERVES 10–12

200 g (7 oz) chocolate biscuits with cream
   centre, crushed
60 g (2¼ oz) unsalted butter, melted
250 g (9 oz/1 cup) cream cheese
90 g (3¼ oz/¾ cup) icing sugar, sifted
125 g (4½ oz/½ cup) smooth peanut butter
1 teaspoon vanilla essence
300 ml (10½ fl oz) cream, whipped
60 ml (2 fl oz/¼ cup) cream, extra
3 teaspoons unsalted butter, extra
100 g (3½ oz) dark chocolate, grated
honey-roasted chopped nuts, to garnish

1 Mix the biscuit crumbs with the melted
butter and press the mixture into a deep 18 cm
(7 inch) pie dish. Refrigerate for 15 minutes.

2 Beat the cream cheese and icing sugar with
electric beaters until smooth. Add the peanut
butter and vanilla essence and beat together well.
Stir in a little of the whipped cream until the
mixture is smooth, then very gently fold in the
remaining whipped cream.

3 Pour two-thirds of the filling into the pie
shell and smooth the top. Refrigerate the pie and
the remaining filling for 2 hours, or until firm.

4 Put the extra cream and butter in a small
saucepan and stir over medium heat until the
butter is melted and the cream just comes to
a simmer. Remove from the heat and add the
grated chocolate. Stir until smooth and silky.
Cool to room temperature, then pour over the
top of the pie, smoothing if necessary with a
spatula dipped in hot water. Refrigerate for
2 hours, or until the topping is firm. Remove the
extra filling from the fridge about 30 minutes
before you serve.

5 Fill a piping (icing) bag with the softened
filling and pipe rosettes around the edge of the
pie. Scatter the nuts around the outer edge. Serve
in thin wedges as this pie is rich.

NUTRITION PER SERVE (10)
Protein 7 g; Fat 35 g; Carbohydrate 25 g; Dietary
Fibre 1.5 g; Cholesterol 76 mg; 1820 kJ (435 Cal)

Gently fold the whipped cream into the loosened
peanut butter filling.

Pour the cooled chocolate over the top of the pie
and smooth with a spatula.

Walnut pie with caramel sauce

PREPARATION TIME: 40 MINUTES + REFRIGERATION | TOTAL COOKING TIME: 40 MINUTES | SERVES 8

250 g (9 oz/2 cups) plain (all-purpose) flour

180 g (6¼ oz) unsalted butter, chilled and cubed

40 g (1½ oz/⅓ cup) icing sugar

1 egg yolk

3–4 tablespoons iced water

1 egg yolk, lightly beaten, to glaze

icing sugar and walnuts, to garnish

FILLING

2 eggs

210 g (7½ oz) caster (superfine) sugar

150 g (5½ oz) walnuts, finely chopped

CARAMEL SAUCE

20 g (¾ oz) unsalted butter

140 g (5 oz/¾ cup) soft brown sugar

1 teaspoon vanilla essence

100 ml (3½ fl oz) cream

1 Sift the flour and ½ teaspoon salt into a large bowl and rub in the butter with your fingertips until the mixture resembles fine breadcrumbs. Mix in the icing sugar. Make a well in the centre, add the egg yolk and almost all the water and mix with a flat-bladed knife, using a cutting action, until the mixture comes together in beads, adding more water if necessary.

2 Gather the dough together and lift onto a lightly floured work surface. Press together into a ball and flatten slightly into a disc. Wrap in plastic wrap and refrigerate for 20 minutes.

3 Preheat the oven to 180°C (350°F/Gas 4). Grease a fluted 35 x 11 cm (14 x 4¼ inch) flan (tart) tin. Beat the eggs and caster sugar with a spoon or whisk for 2 minutes. Stir in the walnuts.

4 Divide the dough into two portions, with one slightly larger than the other. Roll the larger portion out between two sheets of baking paper until large enough to line the base and sides of the tin. Refrigerate, covered in plastic wrap, and roll out the remaining portion of pastry until it is large enough to cover the top of the tin.

5 Pour the walnut filling into the pastry case, brush the rim with the egg yolk and position the lid in place, pressing the edges to seal. Trim the edge. Make a steam hole in the top. Brush with egg yolk and bake for 30–35 minutes. Leave to cool for at least 1 hour (do not refrigerate).

6 To make the caramel sauce, place the butter, brown sugar, vanilla and cream in a saucepan and cook, stirring, for 5 minutes, or until the sauce is thick. Dust the pie with the icing sugar and sprinkle with walnuts. Drizzle with the caramel sauce to serve.

NUTRITION PER SERVE
Protein 9 g; Fat 50 g; Carbohydrate 84 g; Dietary Fibre 2.5 g; Cholesterol 193 mg; 3345 kJ (800 Cal)

Pour the walnut filling into the pastry case and brush the rim with beaten egg yolk.

To make the caramel sauce, stir the butter, sugar, vanilla and cream over heat until thick.

Key lime pie

PREPARATION TIME: 25 MINUTES + 2 HOURS REFRIGERATION | TOTAL COOKING TIME: 25 MINUTES | SERVES 8

125 g (4½ oz) sweet wheatmeal biscuits
90 g (3¼ oz) butter, melted
4 egg yolks
400 g (14 oz) tin condensed milk
125 ml (4 fl oz/½ cup) lime juice
2 teaspoons finely grated lime zest
250 ml (9 fl oz/1 cup) cream, to serve

1   Finely crush the biscuits in a food processor for 30 seconds. Transfer to a bowl, add the butter and mix thoroughly. Press into a 23 cm (9 inch) pie dish and refrigerate until firm. Preheat the oven to 180°C (350°F/Gas 4).

2   Beat the egg yolks, condensed milk, lime juice and zest with electric beaters for 1 minute. Pour into the crust and smooth the surface. Bake for 20–25 minutes, or until set.

3   Refrigerate the pie for 2 hours or until well chilled. Serve with cream.

NUTRITION PER SERVE
Protein 9 g; Fat 19 g; Carbohydrate 47 g; Dietary Fibre 1 g; Cholesterol 120 mg; 1615 kJ (385 Cal)

Process the wheatmeal biscuits in a food processor until finely crushed.

Press the crumb base into a 23 cm (9 inch) diameter pie dish.

Beat the egg yolks, condensed milk, lime juice and zest until well combined.

Freeform blueberry pie

PREPARATION TIME: 30 MINUTES + 20 MINUTES REFRIGERATION I TOTAL COOKING TIME: 30 MINUTES I SERVES 6–8

185 g (6½ oz/1½ cups) plain (all-purpose) flour

100 g (3½ oz) unsalted butter, chilled and cubed

2 teaspoons grated orange zest

1 tablespoon caster (superfine) sugar

2–3 tablespoons iced water

FILLING

40 g (1½ oz/⅓ cup) crushed amaretti biscuits or almond bread

60 g (2¼ oz/½ cup) plain (all-purpose) flour

1 teaspoon ground cinnamon

90 g (3¼ oz/⅓ cup) caster (superfine) sugar

500 g (1 lb 2 oz/3¼ cups) blueberries

milk, for brushing

1 Sift the flour into a large bowl and rub in the butter with your fingertips until the mixture resembles fine breadcrumbs. Stir in the orange zest and sugar. Make a well in the centre, add almost all the water and mix with a flat-bladed knife, using a cutting action, until the mixture comes together in beads. Add more water if necessary to bring the dough together. Turn out onto a lightly floured surface and gather into a ball. Wrap in plastic wrap and refrigerate for 20 minutes.

2 Preheat the oven to 200°C (400°F/Gas 6). For the filling, combine the crushed biscuit, flour, cinnamon and 1½ tablespoons sugar. Roll the pastry out to a 36 cm (14 inch) circle and sprinkle with the biscuit mixture, leaving a 4 cm (1½ inch) border. Arrange the blueberries evenly over the biscuit base, then bring up the edges of the pastry to make a crust.

3 Brush the side of the pie with the milk. Sprinkle with the remaining sugar and bake for 30 minutes, or until the sides are crisp and brown. Serve at room temperature.

NUTRITION PER SERVE (8)
Protein 4 g; Fat 13 g; Carbohydrate 51 g; Dietary Fibre 3 g; Cholesterol 33 mg; 1370 kJ (325 Cal)

Sprinkle the crushed biscuit mixture over the pastry circle, leaving a border.

Arrange the blueberries over the biscuit mixture, then bring up the edges of the pie.

Quince pie with sticky syrup

PREPARATION TIME: 50 MINUTES + 20 MINUTES REFRIGERATION | TOTAL COOKING TIME: 3 HOURS | SERVES 6–8

440 g (15½ oz/2 cups) raw (demerara) sugar

1 vanilla bean, split in half

6 cardamom pods, bruised

2 star anise

1 cinnamon stick

2 kg (4 lb 8 oz) quinces, peeled, cored and cut into large wedges

PASTRY

100 g (3½ oz) plain (all-purpose) flour

100 g (3½ oz) self-raising flour

100 g (3½ oz) lard, chilled and grated

1–2 tablespoons iced water

2 tablespoons milk

¼ teaspoon ground cinnamon

2 teaspoons caster (superfine) sugar

1 Place the sugar, vanilla bean, cardamom pods, star anise and cinnamon stick in a stockpot or very large saucepan with 1 litre (35 fl oz/4 cups) water and stir over low heat until the sugar dissolves. Add the quinces and bring to the boil, then reduce the heat and simmer for 2 hours, or until orange and tender.

2 Remove the quinces with a slotted spoon and set aside. Strain the syrup into a bowl, then return it to the pan and boil for 10 minutes, or until reduced, thick and sticky.

3 Preheat the oven to 200°C (400°F/Gas 6). For the pastry, sift the flours and a little salt into a large bowl, add the lard and rub with your fingertips until the mixture resembles fine breadcrumbs. Make a well in the centre, add most of the water and mix with a flat-bladed knife, using a cutting action, until the mixture comes together in beads, adding more water if needed.

4 Gently gather the dough together and lift onto a lightly floured surface. Press together into a ball and flatten slightly into a disc. Wrap in plastic wrap and refrigerate for 20 minutes.

5 Spoon the quinces into a 20 cm (8 inch) pie plate and mix in 125 ml (4 fl oz/½ cup) of the reserved syrup. Roll out the dough between two sheets of baking paper until large enough to cover the pie, allowing any excess to hang over, and pinch the edges to seal. Trim away the excess pastry. Cut steam holes in the top and decorate with pastry trimmings. Brush the pastry with milk and sprinkle the combined cinnamon and sugar over the pie. Place on a baking tray and bake for 35–40 minutes, or until crisp and golden. Warm the remaining syrup and serve with the pie.

NUTRITION PER SERVE (8)
Protein 4 g; Fat 13 g; Carbohydrate 67 g; Dietary Fibre 12 g; Cholesterol 13 mg; 1645 kJ (395 Cal)

Pour a small amount of syrup over the quinces in the pie plate.

Cover the filling with the dough and pinch the edges firmly to seal.

Cherry pie

PREPARATION TIME: 25 MINUTES + 15 MINUTES REFRIGERATION | TOTAL COOKING TIME: 40 MINUTES | SERVES 6–8

150 g (5½ oz/1¼ cups) plain (all-purpose) flour

30 g (1 oz/¼ cup) icing sugar

60 g (2¼ oz) ground almonds

100 g (3½ oz) unsalted butter, chilled and cubed

3 tablespoons iced water

2 x 700 g (1 lb 9 oz) tins pitted morello cherries, drained

1 egg, lightly beaten

caster (superfine) sugar, to sprinkle

1 Sift the flour and icing sugar into a bowl and then stir in the ground almonds. Add the butter and rub in with your fingertips until the mixture resembles fine breadcrumbs. Add almost all the water and cut into the flour mixture with a flat-bladed knife until the mixture forms beads, adding the remaining water if necessary.

2 Turn the dough out onto a lightly floured surface and press together until smooth. Roll out the dough to a 25 cm (10 inch) circle. Cover with plastic and refrigerate for about 15 minutes.

3 Preheat the oven to 200°C (400°F/Gas 6). Spoon the cherries into a 23 cm (9 inch) round pie dish. Cover the pie dish with the pastry top and trim away the excess. Roll out the trimmings to make decorations. Brush the pastry top with beaten egg to secure the decorations and sprinkle lightly with caster sugar. Place the pie dish on baking tray and bake for 35–40 minutes, or until golden.

Rub the butter into the flour, using your fingertips until the mixture is fine and crumbly.

Brush the beaten egg all over the top of the pastry, using a pastry brush.

NUTRITION PER SERVE (8)
Protein 5 g; Fat 14 g; Carbohydrate 37 g; Dietary Fibre 4 g; Cholesterol 54 mg; 1233 kJ (295 Cal)

Apple strudel

PREPARATION TIME: 20 MINUTES | TOTAL COOKING TIME: 30 MINUTES | SERVES 8–10

4 green cooking apples

30 g (1 oz) butter

2 tablespoons orange juice

1 tablespoon honey

3 tablespoons sugar

90 g (3 oz/¾ cup) sultanas (golden raisins)

2 sheets puff pastry

3 tablespoons ground almonds

1 egg, lightly beaten

2 tablespoons soft brown sugar

1 teaspoon ground cinnamon

1   Preheat the oven to 220°C (425°F/Gas 7). Lightly grease two oven trays. Peel, core and thinly slice the apples. Heat the butter in a pan and cook the apples for 2 minutes until lightly golden. Add the orange juice, honey, sugar and sultanas and stir until the sugar dissolves and the apples are just tender. Leave to cool completely.

2   Place a sheet of pastry on a flat work surface. Fold in half and make small cuts in the folded edge at 2 cm (¾ inch) intervals. Open out the pastry and sprinkle with half of the ground almonds. Drain the cooked apple and place half of the apple in the centre of the pastry. Brush the edges with egg and fold together, pressing firmly.

3   Place the strudel on one of the oven trays, seam side down. Brush with egg and sprinkle with half of the combined sugar and cinnamon. Make another strudel with the other sheet of pastry and remaining apple filling. Bake for 20–25 minutes, or until the pastry is golden and crisp.

VARIATION: *Many types of fresh or tinned fruit, such as pears, cherries and apricots, can be used for strudel.*

NUTRITION PER SERVE (8)
Protein 5 g; Fat 18 g; Carbohydrate 45 g; Dietary Fibre 4 g; Cholesterol 42 mg; 1412 kJ (337 Cal)

Make small cuts in the folded edge of the pastry at intervals.

Put the strudel on the oven tray and sprinkle with the combined sugar and cinnamon.

Rhubarb pie

PREPARATION TIME: 40 MINUTES + 30 MINUTES REFRIGERATION + COOLING | TOTAL COOKING TIME: 1 HOUR | SERVES 6

335 g (11¾ oz/2⅔ cups) plain (all-purpose) flour
40 g (1½ oz) unsalted butter, chilled and cubed
85 g (3 oz) white vegetable shortening, chilled and cubed
2 tablespoons icing sugar
150 ml (5 fl oz) iced water

FILLING
1.5 kg (3 lb 5 oz) rhubarb, trimmed and chopped
250 g (9 oz/1 cup) caster (superfine) sugar
½ teaspoon ground cinnamon
2½ tablespoons cornflour (cornstarch)
30 g (1 oz) unsalted butter, cubed
1 egg, lightly beaten
icing sugar, to dust

1 Grease a 20 cm (8 inch) ceramic pie dish. Sift the flour and ½ teaspoon salt into a large bowl and rub in the butter and shortening until the mixture resembles fine breadcrumbs. Stir in the icing sugar. Make a well, add almost all the water and mix with a flat-bladed knife, using a cutting action, until it comes together in beads. Add more water if necessary.

2 Gently gather the dough together and lift onto a lightly floured work surface. Press into a ball, flatten into a disc, wrap in plastic wrap and refrigerate for 30 minutes.

3 For the filling, put the rhubarb, sugar, cinnamon and 2 tablespoons water in a saucepan and stir over low heat until the sugar is dissolved. Cover and simmer for 5–8 minutes, stirring occasionally, until the rhubarb is tender. Mix the cornflour with 60 ml (2 fl oz/¼ cup) water and add to the pan. Bring to the boil, stirring until thickened. Allow to cool.

4 Preheat the oven to 180°C (350°F/Gas 4) and heat a baking tray. Roll out two-thirds of the dough to a 30 cm (12 inch) circle to line the pie dish. Spoon the rhubarb into the dish and dot with butter.

5 Roll out the remaining pastry to form a lid. Moisten the pie rim with egg and press the top in place. Trim the edges and make a slit in the top. Decorate with pastry trimmings. Brush with egg and bake on the hot tray for 35–40 minutes, or until golden. Dust with icing sugar to serve.

NUTRITION PER SERVE
Protein 7.5 g; Fat 22 g; Carbohydrate 82 g; Dietary Fibre 6 g; Cholesterol 55 mg; 2290 kJ (545 Cal)

Simmer the rhubarb filling, stirring occasionally, until tender.

Moisten the rim of the pastry with egg and press the pastry top into place.

Almond pies

PREPARATION TIME: 20 MINUTES | TOTAL COOKING TIME: 25 MINUTES | MAKES 8

30 g (1 oz) flaked almonds
60 g (2 oz) unsalted butter, softened
60 g (2 oz/½ cup) icing sugar
60 g (2 oz/¾ cup) ground almonds
30 g (1 oz/¼ cup) plain (all-purpose) flour
1 egg
½ tablespoon rum or brandy
¼ teaspoon vanilla essence
4 sheets puff pastry
1 egg, lightly beaten
1 tablespoon sugar, to sprinkle

1 Preheat the oven to 200°C (400°F/Gas 6). Toast the flaked almonds on a baking tray for 2–3 minutes, or until just golden. Remove the almonds and return the tray to the oven to keep it hot.

2 Beat together the butter, icing sugar, ground almonds, flour, eggs, rum and vanilla with electric beaters for 2–3 minutes, until smooth and combined. Fold in the flaked almonds.

3 Cut out eight 10 cm (4 inch) rounds and eight 11 cm (4¼ inch) rounds from the puff pastry. Spread the smaller rounds with the filling, leaving a small border. Brush the borders with beaten egg and cover with the tops. Seal the edges with a fork. Pierce the tops to make steam holes. Brush with egg and sprinkle with sugar. Bake on the hot tray for 15–20 minutes, or until the pastry is puffed and golden.

Divide the almond filling equally between the eight puff pastry bases.

Seal the top pastry to the bottom by crimping the edges with a fork.

NUTRITION PER PIE
Protein 12 g; Fat 46 g; Carbohydrate 50 g; Dietary Fibre 3 g; Cholesterol 128 mg; 2750 kJ (655 Cal)

Plum cobbler

PREPARATION TIME: 25 MINUTES I TOTAL COOKING TIME: 40 MINUTES I SERVES 6

750 g (1 lb 10 oz) plums
90 g (3¼ oz/⅓ cup) sugar
1 teaspoon vanilla essence

TOPPING
125 g (4½ oz/1 cup) self-raising flour
60 g (2¼ oz) unsalted butter, chilled and
    cubed
60 g (2¼ oz/⅓ cup) soft brown sugar
60 ml (2 fl oz/¼ cup) milk
1 tablespoon caster (superfine) sugar

1 Preheat the oven to 200°C (400°F/Gas 6).
Cut the plums into quarters and remove the
stones. Put the plums, sugar and 2 tablespoons
water in a saucepan and bring to the boil,
stirring, until the sugar dissolves.

2 Reduce the heat, then cover and simmer for
5 minutes, or until the plums are tender. Remove
the skins if you prefer. Add the vanilla and
spoon the mixture into a 750 ml (26 fl oz/3 cup)
ovenproof dish.

3 To make the topping, sift the flour into a
large bowl and add the butter. Rub in the butter
with your fingertips until the mixture resembles
fine breadcrumbs. Stir in the brown sugar and
2 tablespoons of the milk. Stir with a knife to
form a soft dough, adding more milk if necessary.

4 Turn out onto a lightly floured surface and
gather together to form a smooth dough. Roll
out until 1 cm (½ inch) thick and cut into rounds
with a 4 cm (1½ inch) cutter.

5 Overlap the rounds around the inside edge of
the dish over the filling. Lightly brush with milk
and sprinkle with sugar. Bake on a tray for
30 minutes, or until the topping is golden and
cooked through.

Sift the flour into a bowl, then rub in the butter with
your fingertips.

Roll out the dough to a thickness of 1 cm (½ cm),
then cut into rounds.

NUTRITION PER SERVE
Protein 3 g; Fat 9 g; Carbohydrate 50 g; Dietary
Fibre 3.5 g; Cholesterol 25 mg; 1245 kJ (295 Cal)

Lemon meringue pie

PREPARATION TIME: 30 MINUTES + 20 MINUTES REFRIGERATION | TOTAL COOKING TIME: 1 HOUR | SERVES 6–8

375 g (13 oz) sweet shortcrust pastry
30 g (1 oz/¼ cup) plain (all-purpose) flour
30 g (1 oz/¼ cup) cornflour (cornstarch)
230 g (8 oz/1 cup) caster (superfine) sugar
185 ml (6 fl oz/¾ cup) lemon juice
1 tablespoon grated lemon zest
50 g (1¾ oz) unsalted butter, chopped
6 egg yolks

MERINGUE
4 egg whites
345 g (12 oz/1 cup) caster (superfine) sugar
pinch of cream of tartar

1   Lightly grease an 18 cm (7 inch) pie plate. Roll out the pastry between two sheets of baking paper into a 30 cm (12 inch) circle to line the pie plate, and trim away the excess. Press a teaspoon into the pastry rim to make a decorative edge. Prick all over the base with a fork. Cover and refrigerate for 20 minutes. Preheat the oven to 180°C (350°F/Gas 4).

2   Line the pastry with baking paper and spread with a layer of baking beads or rice. Bake for 15 minutes, then remove the paper and beads and bake for 15–20 minutes, or until the pastry is dry. Leave to cool. Increase the oven to 200°C (400°F/Gas 6).

3   To make the lemon filling, put the flours, sugar, lemon juice and zest in a saucepan. Gradually add 310 ml (10¾ fl oz/1¼ cups) water and whisk over medium heat until smooth. Cook, stirring, for another 2 minutes, or until thickened. Remove from the heat and vigorously whisk in the butter and egg yolks. Return to low heat and stir for 2 minutes, or until the filling is very thick.

4   To make the meringue, in a clean, dry bowl beat the egg whites, sugar and cream of tartar with electric beaters for 10 minutes, until thick and glossy.

5   Spread the lemon filling over the cooled pastry base, then spread the meringue over the top, piling it high in the centre. Use a knife to form peaks in the meringue. Bake for 12–15 minutes, or until lightly browned.

NUTRITION PER SERVE (6)
Protein 11 g; Fat 28 g; Carbohydrate 133 g; Dietary Fibre 1.5 g; Cholesterol 217 mg; 3385 kJ (810 Cal)

Trim away the excess pastry and press a teaspoon around the rim to create a decorative edge.

Spread the meringue over the pie and then form into peaks with a knife.

Bramble pie

PREPARATION TIME: 30 MINUTES + 30 MINUTES REFRIGERATION | TOTAL COOKING TIME: 40 MINUTES | SERVES 4–6

125 g (4½ oz/1 cup) self-raising flour
125 g (4½ oz/1 cup) plain (all-purpose) flour
125 g (4½ oz) unsalted butter, chilled and cubed
2 tablespoons caster (superfine) sugar
1 egg, lightly beaten
3–4 tablespoons milk

FILLING
2 tablespoons cornflour (cornstarch)
2–4 tablespoons caster (superfine) sugar, to taste
1 teaspoon grated orange zest
1 tablespoon orange juice
600 g (1 lb 5 oz) brambles (see NOTE)
1 egg yolk, mixed with 1 teaspoon water

1 Mix the flours, butter and sugar in a food processor for 30 seconds or until the mixture is fine and crumbly. Add the egg and almost all the milk; process for another 15 seconds or until the mixture comes together, adding more milk if needed. Turn onto a lightly floured surface and gather into a ball. Refrigerate for 30 minutes.

2 Put the cornflour, sugar, orange zest and juice in a saucepan and mix well. Add half the brambles and stir over low heat for 5 minutes until the mixture boils and thickens. Cool, then add the remaining brambles. Pour into a 750 ml (26 fl oz/3 cup) pie dish.

3 Preheat the oven to 180°C (350°F/ Gas 4). Divide the dough in half and roll out one half large enough to cover the dish. Trim away the excess. Roll out the other half and use cutters of various sizes to cut out enough hearts to cover the top. Brush the pie top with egg glaze. Bake for 35 minutes or until golden brown.

NOTE: *Brambles include any creeping stem berries, such as boysenberries, blackberries, loganberries and youngberries. Use one variety or a combination.*

When the mixture has thickened, add the remaining brambles to the pan and stir.

Use various-sized heart-shaped cutters to make shapes to decorate the top of the pie.

NUTRITION PER SERVE (6)
Protein 8 g; Fat 20 g; Carbohydrate 65 g; Dietary Fibre 7 g; Cholesterol 115 mg; 1960 kJ (470 Cal)

Pear and apple crumble pie

PREPARATION TIME: 20 MINUTES + 20 MINUTES REFRIGERATION | TOTAL COOKING TIME: 1 HOUR 10 MINUTES | SERVES 8

375 g (13 oz) shortcrust pastry
3 pears
4 green apples
60 g (2½ oz/¼ cup) caster (superfine) sugar
2 teaspoons grated orange zest
90 g (3¼ oz/¾ cup) raisins
60 g (2¼ oz/¼ cup) plain (all-purpose) flour
60 g (2¼ oz/¼ cup) soft brown sugar
½ teaspoon ground ginger
60 g (2¼ oz) unsalted butter

1 Roll out the pastry between two sheets of baking paper until large enough to line an 18 cm (7 inch) pie dish, trimming away the excess. Wrap in plastic wrap and refrigerate for 20 minutes.

2 Meanwhile, peel, core and slice the pears and apples and place in a large saucepan. Add the sugar, orange zest and 2 tablespoons water and cook over low heat, stirring occasionally for 20 minutes, or until the fruit is tender but still holding its shape. Remove from the heat, add the raisins and a pinch of salt, mix and leave to cool completely. Spoon into the pie dish.

3 Preheat the oven to 200°C (400°F/Gas 6) and preheat a baking tray. To make the topping, put the flour, brown sugar and ginger in a bowl and rub in the butter with your fingertips until the mixture resembles coarse breadcrumbs. Sprinkle over the fruit.

4 Put the dish on the hot baking tray and bake for 10 minutes, then reduce the oven temperature to 180°C (350°F/Gas 4) and bake for another 40 minutes, or until browned. Check the pie after 20 minutes and cover with foil if the topping is over-browning.

NUTRITION PER SERVE
Protein 5 g; Fat 22 g; Carbohydrate 72 g; Dietary Fibre 5 g; Cholesterol 42 mg; 2055 kJ (490 Cal)

Cook the pear and apple pieces, stirring occasionally, until tender.

Sprinkle the crumble mixture over the pear and apple filling.

Deep-dish apple pie

PREPARATION TIME: 40 MINUTES + 20 MINUTES REFRIGERATION | TOTAL COOKING TIME: 50 MINUTES | SERVES 6–8

2 teaspoons semolina
185 g (6½ oz/1½ cups) plain (all-purpose) flour
60 g (2¼ oz/½ cup) self-raising flour
125 g (4½ oz) unsalted butter, chilled and cubed
60 g (2¼ oz/¼ cup) caster sugar
1 egg
3–4 tablespoons iced water

FILLING
875 g (1 lb 15 oz) apples, peeled, cored, halved and thinly sliced
60 g (2¼ oz/¼ cup) caster (superfine) sugar
½ teaspoon ground cinnamon
¼ teaspoon ground mixed (pumpkin pie) spice
1 egg, separated
raw (demerara) sugar, to sprinkle

NUTRITION PER SERVE (8)
Protein 5.5 g; Fat 15 g; Carbohydrate 51 g; Dietary Fibre 3.5 g; Cholesterol 84.5 mg; 1470 kJ (350 Cal)

1 Grease a deep 19 cm (7½ inch) pie dish, then sprinkle it with semolina. Sift the flours and ¼ teaspoon salt into a large bowl. Rub in the butter with your fingertips until the mixture resembles fine breadcrumbs. Mix in the sugar. Make a well in the centre, add the egg and most of the water and mix with a flat-bladed knife, using a cutting action, until the mixture comes together in beads, adding a little more water if necessary.

2 Turn out the dough onto a lightly floured work surface and gather into a smooth disc. Wrap in plastic and refrigerate for 20 minutes. Preheat the oven to 200°C (400°F/Gas 6).

3 Combine the apple, sugar, cinnamon and mixed spice in a large bowl.

4 Roll out the dough between two sheets of baking paper to a rough 40 cm (16 inch) circle and line the dish, leaving the excess pastry hanging over the rim. Brush the base with egg yolk and then pile the apple filling in the centre.

5 Bring the pastry edges up and over the filling, leaving a gap in the centre. Tuck and fold the pastry as necessary. Brush the pastry with egg white and sprinkle with the raw sugar. Bake for 20 minutes, then reduce the heat to 180°C (350°F/Gas 4). Bake for another 30 minutes, or until the pastry is crisp and golden. Check the pie and cover with foil if the pastry is over-browning. Serve hot or at room temperature, and dust lightly with icing sugar.

Peel the apples, remove the cores and cut each in half, then slice thinly.

Brush the pastry with egg white and sprinkle with the raw sugar.

Plum pie

PREPARATION TIME: 15 MINUTES + 20 MINUTES REFRIGERATION I TOTAL COOKING TIME: 55 MINUTES I SERVES 8

600 g (1 lb 5 oz) sweet shortcrust pastry
14 large plums, halved, stoned and roughly
    chopped, or 2 x 825 g (1 lb 13 oz) tins
    plums, drained
95 g (3¼ oz/½ cup) soft brown sugar
1 teaspoon grated lemon zest
1 teaspoon grated orange zest
30 g (1 oz) unsalted butter, softened
2 tablespoons plain (all-purpose) flour
½ teaspoon ground cinnamon
1 egg, lightly beaten
caster (superfine) sugar, for sprinkling

1   Preheat the oven to 180°C (350°F/Gas 4).
Grease a 23 cm (9 inch) pie tin.

2   Roll out two-thirds of the pastry between
two sheets of baking paper and line the pie tin.
Trim away the excess pastry. Refrigerate with the
remaining pastry for 20 minutes.

3   Combine the plums, brown sugar, citrus zest
and butter in a large bowl. Sift the flour and
cinnamon together over the plums mixture and
fold through. Place in the pie tin. Roll out the
remaining pastry to cover the pie and trim the
edge. Pinch the edges and cut a small steam hole
in the centre. Brush the pastry with egg and bake
for 55 minutes, or until the pastry is golden.
Sprinkle with caster sugar before serving.

Fold the sifted flour and cinnamon through the plum mixture.

Cover the pie with the pastry lid, trim the edges and pinch to seal.

NUTRITION PER SERVE
Protein 7 g; Fat 23 g; Carbohydrate 54 g; Dietary
Fibre 5 g; Cholesterol 53 mg; 1870 kJ (445 Cal)

Pecan pie

PREPARATION TIME: 30 MINUTES + 20 MINUTES REFRIGERATION | TOTAL COOKING TIME: 1 HOUR 10 MINUTES | SERVES 6

185 g (6½ oz/1½ cups) plain (all-purpose) flour
125 g (4½ oz) unsalted butter, chilled and cubed
2–3 tablespoons iced water

FILLING
200 g (7 oz/12 cups) pecans
3 eggs, lightly beaten
50 g (1¾ oz) unsalted butter, melted and cooled
140 g (5 oz/¾ cup) soft brown sugar
170 ml (5½ fl oz/⅔ cup) light corn syrup
1 teaspoon vanilla essence
icing (confectioner's) sugar, for dusting

1 Mix the flour and butter in a food processor for 20 seconds or until fine and crumbly. Add almost all the water and process briefly until the mixture comes together, adding more water if necessary. Turn out onto a lightly floured surface and gather into a ball.

2 Roll the pastry out to a large rectangle and line a fluted 35 x 11 cm (14 x 4¼ inch) flan (tart) tin. Refrigerate for 20 minutes.

3 Preheat the oven to 180°C (350°F/Gas 4). Cover the pastry with baking paper and spread with a layer of baking beads or rice. Bake for 15 minutes. Remove the paper and rice and bake for another 10 minutes, or until dry and golden. Cool completely.

4 Spread pecans over the pastry base. Whisk together the egg, butter, sugar, corn syrup, vanilla and a pinch of salt, then pour carefully over the nuts. Decorate with pastry trimmings, then put the tin on an oven tray and bake for 45 minutes. Lightly dust with icing sugar and allow to cool before serving at room temperature.

NUTRITION PER SERVE
Protein 10 g; Fat 53 g; Carbohydrate 42 g; Dietary Fibre 5 g; Cholesterol 125 mg; 2850 kJ (676 Cal)

Line the tin with the pastry and trim off any excess before refrigerating.

After baking for 15 minutes, discard the paper and baking beads or rice.

Apple pie

PREPARATION TIME: 45 MINUTES + 20 MINUTES REFRIGERATION | TOTAL COOKING TIME: 1 HOUR | SERVES 6–8

6 large green apples, peeled, cored and cut into wedges
2 tablespoons caster (superfine) sugar
1 teaspoon finely grated lemon zest
pinch of ground cloves
2 tablespoons apricot jam
1 egg, lightly beaten
1 tablespoon sugar

PASTRY
310 g (11 oz/2½ cups) plain (all-purpose) flour
4 tablespoons self-raising flour
185 g (6½ oz) butter, chilled and cubed
2½ tablespoons caster (superfine) sugar
6–7 tablespoons iced water

1 Put the apples in a large heavy-based saucepan with the sugar, lemon zest, cloves and 2 tablespoons water. Cover and simmer for 8 minutes, or until just tender, shaking the pan occasionally. Drain and cool.

2 To make the pastry, sift the flours into a bowl. Rub the butter into the flour with your fingertips until the mixture resembles fine breadcrumbs. Add the sugar, mix well and make a well in the centre. Add most of the water and mix with a flat-bladed knife, using a cutting action, until the mixture comes together in beads, adding water if needed. Gather the pastry together on a floured surface. Divide into two, making one half a little bigger. Wrap in plastic and refrigerate for 20 minutes.

3 Preheat the oven to 200°C (400°F/Gas 6). Roll out the larger piece of pastry between two sheets of baking paper and line a 23 cm (9 inch) pie plate, trimming away the excess pastry. Brush the jam over the base and spoon in the apple filling. Roll out the remaining piece of pastry between two sheets of baking paper until large enough to cover the pie. Brush a little water around the rim to secure the top. Trim off the excess pastry, pinch the edges together and cut steam holes in the top.

4 Roll out the trimmings to make leaves to decorate the pie. Brush the top lightly with egg and sprinkle with sugar. Bake for 20 minutes, then reduce the oven temperature to 180°C (350°F/Gas 4) and bake for 30–35 minutes, or until golden brown.

NUTRITION PER SERVE (6)
Protein 7 g; Fat 20 g; Carbohydrate 60 g; Dietary Fibre 4 g; Cholesterol 95 mg; 1955 kJ (465 Cal)

Roll out the pastry between two sheets of baking paper to prevent sticking.

Invert the pastry into the pie dish and peel off the baking paper.

Sweet tarts

Citrus tart

PREPARATION TIME: 1 HOUR + 30 MINUTES REFRIGERATION | TOTAL COOKING TIME: 1 HOUR 45 MINUTES | SERVES 8

125 g (4½ oz/1 cup) plain (all-purpose) flour
75 g (2½ oz) unsalted butter, softened
1 egg yolk
2 tablespoons icing sugar, sifted

FILLING
3 eggs
2 egg yolks
185 g (6½ oz/¾ cup) caster (superfine) sugar
125 ml (4 fl oz/½ cup) cream
185 ml (6 fl oz/¾ cup) lemon juice
1½ tablespoons finely grated lemon zest
2 small lemons
140 g (5 oz/⅔ cup) sugar

1 To make the pastry, sift the flour and a pinch of salt into a large bowl. Make a well in the centre and add the butter, egg yolk and icing sugar. Work together the butter, yolk and sugar with your fingertips, then slowly incorporate the flour. Bring together into a ball—you may need to add a few drops of iced water. Flatten the ball slightly, wrap in plastic wrap and refrigerate for 20 minutes.

2 Preheat the oven to 200°C (400°F/Gas 6). Lightly grease a shallow 20 cm (8 inch) loose-based flan (tart) tin.

3 Roll the pastry out between two sheets of baking paper to about 3 mm (⅛ inch) thick to fit the tin. Trim away the excess pastry and refrigerate for 10 minutes. Line the pastry with baking paper, spread with a layer of baking beads or rice and bake for 10 minutes, or until cooked. Remove the paper and beads and bake for 6–8 minutes, or until the pastry is lightly golden and dry. Leave to cool.

4 Reduce the oven to 150°C (300°F/ Gas 2). Whisk together the eggs, egg yolks and sugar, add the cream and lemon juice and mix well. Strain into a bowl and add the zest. Place the tin on a baking sheet on the middle shelf of the oven and carefully pour in the filling. Bake for 40 minutes, or until just set—the filling will wobble in the middle when the tin is firmly tapped. Cool before removing from the tin.

5 Wash and scrub the lemons well. Slice very thinly. Combine the sugar and 200 ml (7 fl oz) water in a small frying pan and stir over low heat until the sugar has dissolved. Add the lemon slices and simmer over low heat for 40 minutes, or until the peel is very tender and the pith looks transparent. Lift out of the syrup and drain on baking paper. Arrange over the top of the tart.

NUTRITION PER SERVE
Protein 6 g; Fat 18 g; Carbohydrate 60 g; Dietary Fibre 1 g; Cholesterol 180 mg; 1766 kJ (422 Cal)

Work the butter, yolk and sugar together, then slowly incorporate the flour.

Bake the tart until the citrus filling is just set—it should still wobble when you tap the tin.

Simmer the lemon slices until they are very tender and the pith is transparent.

Banoffie pie

PREPARATION TIME: 35 MINUTES + 1 HOUR 15 MINUTES REFRIGERATION | TOTAL COOKING TIME: 40 MINUTES | SERVES 8

150 g (5½ oz/1¼ cups) plain (all-purpose) flour
2 tablespoons icing sugar
90 g (3¼ oz) ground walnuts
80 g (2¾ oz) unsalted butter, chilled and cubed
2–3 tablespoons iced water

FILLING
400 g (14 oz) tin condensed milk
30 g (1 oz) unsalted butter
1 tablespoon golden syrup (if unavailable, use half honey and half dark corn syrup)
4 bananas, sliced
375 ml (13 fl oz/1½ cups) cream

1 Sift the flour and icing sugar into a large bowl. Add the walnuts. Rub in the butter until the mixture resembles fine breadcrumbs. Add the water, mixing with a knife until the dough just comes together. Turn out onto a lightly floured surface and press together into a ball. Wrap in plastic wrap and refrigerate for 15 minutes. Roll out until large enough to line a 23 cm (9 inch) fluted flan (tart) tin, trimming away the excess. Refrigerate for 20 minutes.

2 Preheat the oven to 180°C (350°F/Gas 4). Cover the pastry with baking paper and spread with a layer of baking beads or rice. Bake for 15 minutes, then remove the paper and beads. Bake the pastry for another 20 minutes, or until dry and lightly golden. Leave to cool completely.

3 Heat the condensed milk, butter and golden syrup in a small saucepan for 5 minutes, stirring constantly until it boils, thickens and turns a light caramel colour. Cool slightly. Arrange half the banana over the pastry and pour the caramel over the top. Refrigerate for 30 minutes.

4 Whip the cream and spoon over the caramel. Top with more banana before serving.

Stir the condensed milk, butter and syrup over the heat until it boils, thickens and turns caramel.

Whip the cream and then spoon over the caramel, before topping with banana slices.

NUTRITION PER SERVE
Protein 10 g; Fat 45 g; Carbohydrate 66 g; Dietary Fibre 3 g; Cholesterol 116 mg; 2940 kJ (700 Cal)

Chocolate-almond tarts

PREPARATION TIME: 40 MINUTES + 20 MINUTES REFRIGERATION I TOTAL COOKING TIME: 15 MINUTES I MAKES 18 TARTS

125 g (4½ oz/1 cup) plain (all-purpose) flour
60 g (2¼ oz) unsalted butter, chilled and
    cubed
1 tablespoon icing sugar
1 tablespoon lemon juice

FILLING
1 egg
90 g (3¼ oz/⅓ cup) caster (superfine) sugar
2 tablespoons cocoa powder
90 g (3¼ oz/½ cup) ground almonds
3 tablespoons cream
3 tablespoons apricot jam
18 blanched almonds
icing (confectioner's) sugar, to serve

1 Preheat the oven to 180°C (350°F/Gas 4). Lightly grease two 12-cup shallow patty pans or mini muffin tins. Mix the flour, butter and icing sugar in a food processor for 10 seconds, or until fine and crumbly. Add the juice and process until the dough forms a ball.

2 Roll out the dough between two sheets of baking paper to 6 mm (¼ inch) thick. Cut rounds with a 7 cm (2¾ inch) fluted cutter to line the tins and refrigerate for 20 minutes.

3 Beat the egg and sugar with electric beaters until thick and pale. Sift the cocoa over the top. With a flat-bladed knife, stir in the ground almonds and cream.

4 Place a dab of jam in the centre of each pastry base. Spoon the filling over the jam and place an almond in the centre of each one. Bake for 15 minutes, or until puffed and set on top. Leave in the tins for 5 minutes, then cool on a wire rack. Sprinkle with icing sugar to serve.

Use a flat-bladed knife to stir the ground almonds and cream into the filling.

Spoon the filling into the pastry cases and then place a blanched almond on top of each one.

NUTRITION PER TART
Protein 2 g; Fat 8 g; Carbohydrate 15 g; Dietary Fibre 1 g; Cholesterol 23 mg; 560 kJ (135 Cal)

Honey and pine nut tart

PREPARATION TIME: 25 MINUTES + 15 MINUTES REFRIGERATION | TOTAL COOKING TIME: 1 HOUR | SERVES 6

250 g (9 oz/2 cups) plain (all-purpose) flour
1½ tablespoons icing sugar
115 g (4 oz) unsalted butter, chilled and
    cubed
1 egg, lightly beaten
2 tablespoons iced water

FILLING
235 g (8½ oz/1½ cups) pine nuts
180 g (6¼ oz/½ cup) honey
115 g (4 oz) unsalted butter, softened
125 g (4½ oz/½ cup) caster (superfine) sugar
3 eggs, lightly beaten
¼ teaspoon vanilla essence
1 tablespoon almond liqueur
1 teaspoon finely grated lemon zest
1 tablespoon lemon juice
icing sugar, for dusting

1 Preheat the oven to 190°C (375°F/Gas 5) and place a baking tray on the middle shelf. Lightly grease a 23 x 3.5 cm (9 x 1½ inch) deep loose-based flan (tart) tin. Sift the flour and icing sugar into a large bowl and rub in the butter with your fingertips until the mixture resembles fine breadcrumbs. Make a well in the centre and add the egg and water. Mix with a flat-bladed knife, using a cutting action, until the dough comes together in beads.

2 Turn out onto a lightly floured work surface and press together into a ball. Roll out to a circle 3 mm (⅛ inch) thick to line the tin and trim away any excess pastry. Prick the base all over with a fork and chill for 15 minutes. Cut out leaves from the trimmings for decoration. Cover and chill.

3 Line the pastry with baking paper and spread with a layer of baking beads or rice. Bake on the heated tray for 10 minutes, then remove.

4 Reduce the oven to 180°C (350°F/Gas 4). Spread the pine nuts on a baking tray and roast in the oven for 3 minutes, or until golden. Heat the honey in a small saucepan until runny. Beat the butter and sugar in a bowl until smooth and pale. Gradually add the egg, a little at a time, beating well after each addition. Mix in the honey, vanilla, liqueur, lemon zest and juice and a pinch of salt. Stir in the pine nuts, spoon into the pastry case and smooth the surface. Arrange the pastry leaves in the centre.

5 Place on the hot tray and bake for 40 minutes, or until golden and set. Cover the top with foil after 25 minutes. Serve warm, dusted with icing sugar, perhaps with crème fraîche or mascarpone cheese.

NUTRITION PER SERVE
Protein 14 g; Fat 63 g; Carbohydrate 83 g; Dietary Fibre 3.5 g; Cholesterol 217 mg; 3936 kJ (940 Cal)

Use a small ball of pastry to press the pastry into the base and side of the tin.

Arrange the pastry leaves over the smoothed pine nut filling.

Berry ricotta cream tartlets

PREPARATION TIME: 1 HOUR + 1 HOUR REFRIGERATION | TOTAL COOKING TIME: 40 MINUTES | SERVES 6

185 g (6½ oz/1½ cups) plain (all-purpose) flour
90 g (3¼ oz/½ cup) ground almonds
40 g (1½ oz/⅓ cup) icing sugar
125 g (4½ oz) unsalted butter, chilled and cubed
1 egg, lightly beaten

FILLING
200 g (7 oz) ricotta cheese
1 teaspoon vanilla essence
2 eggs
160 g (5¾ oz/⅔ cup) caster (superfine) sugar
125 ml (4 fl oz/½ cup) cream
60 g (2¼ oz/½ cup) raspberries
80 g (2¾ oz/½ cup) blueberries
icing sugar, to dust

1   Sift the flour into a large bowl, then add the ground almonds and icing sugar. Rub in the butter with your fingertips until it resembles fine breadcrumbs. Make a well in the centre, add the egg and mix with a flat-bladed knife, using a cutting action, until the mixture comes together in beads. Turn onto a lightly floured work surface and gather into a ball. Wrap in plastic wrap and refrigerate for 30 minutes.

2   Grease six 8 cm (3¼ inch) deep loose-based flan (tart) tins. Roll out the pastry between two sheets of baking paper to fit the base and side of the tins, trimming away the excess. Prick the bases with a fork, then refrigerate for 30 minutes. Preheat the oven to 180°C (350°F/Gas 4).

3   Line the pastry bases with baking paper and cover with baking beads or rice. Bake for 8–10 minutes, then remove the paper and beads. Mix the ricotta cheese, vanilla, eggs, sugar and cream in a food processor until smooth. Divide the berries among the tarts and pour over the filling. Bake for 25–30 minutes, or until just set—the top should be soft but not too wobbly. Cool. Dust with icing sugar to serve.

Gently gather the dough together and press into a ball. Wrap in plastic wrap and refrigerate.

Divide the berries among the pastry cases and then pour the filling over the top.

NUTRITION PER SERVE
Protein 14 g; Fat 42 g; Carbohydrate 62 g; Dietary Fibre 3.5 g; Cholesterol 187 mg; 2780 kJ (665 Cal)

Tarte tatin

PREPARATION TIME: **15** MINUTES | TOTAL COOKING TIME: **1** HOUR **10** MINUTES | SERVES **6**

100 g (3½ oz) unsalted butter
185 g (6½ oz/¾ cup) sugar
6 large pink lady or fuji apples, peeled, cored
    and quartered (see NOTE)
1 sheet puff pastry

1 Preheat the oven to 220°C (425°F/Gas 7).
Lightly grease a 23 cm (9 inch) shallow cake tin.
Melt the butter in a frying pan, add the sugar
and cook, stirring, over medium heat for
4–5 minutes, or until the sugar starts to
caramelise and turn brown. Continue to cook,
stirring, until the caramel turns golden brown.

2 Add the apple to the pan and cook over low
heat for 20–25 minutes, or until it starts to turn
golden brown. Carefully turn the apple over and
cook the other side until evenly coloured. If a
lot of liquid comes out of the apple, increase the
heat until it has evaporated—the caramel should
be sticky rather than runny. Remove from the
heat. Using tongs, arrange the hot apple in circles
in the tin and pour the sauce over the top.

3 Place the pastry over the apple, tucking the
edge down firmly with the end of a spoon. Bake
for 30–35 minutes, or until the pastry is cooked.
Leave for 15 minutes before inverting onto a
serving plate.

NOTE: *The moisture content of apples varies
quite a lot, which affects the cooking time. Golden
delicious, pink lady or fuji apples are good to use
because they don't break down during cooking.*

Cook the butter and sugar until the caramel is golden brown.

Arrange the pastry over the top of the apple in the tin, to cover it completely, tucking down the edge.

NUTRITION PER SERVE
Protein 2 g; Fat 20 g; Carbohydrate 47 g; Dietary
Fibre 1.5 g; Cholesterol 50 mg; 1544 kJ (370 Cal)

Prune and almond custard tart

PREPARATION TIME: 2 HOURS + 1 HOUR SOAKING + 2 HOURS 30 MINUTES REFRIGERATION | TOTAL COOKING TIME: 50 MINUTES | SERVES 8–10

375 g (13 oz) pitted prunes
170 ml (5½ fl oz/⅔ cup) muscat or sweet
  sherry
4 tablespoons redcurrant jelly

ALMOND SHORTCRUST PASTRY
185 g (6½ oz/1½ cups) plain (all-purpose)
  flour
60 g (2¼ oz/½ cup) ground almonds
60 g (2¼ oz/¼ cup) caster (superfine) sugar
125 g (4½ oz) unsalted butter, chilled and
  cubed
1 egg yolk
2–3 tablespoons iced water
60 g (2¼ oz) marzipan, grated

CUSTARD CREAM
3 tablespoons custard powder
420 ml (14½ fl oz/1⅔ cups) milk
125 g (4½ oz/½ cup) sour cream
1 tablespoon caster (superfine) sugar
2 teaspoons vanilla essence

1 Put the prunes in a saucepan with the muscat or sherry and leave to soak for 1 hour. Simmer over very low heat for 10 minutes, or until the prunes are tender but not mushy. Remove the prunes from the liquid with a slotted spoon and leave to cool. Add the redcurrant jelly to the pan and stir over low heat until dissolved. Cover and set aside.

2 To make the pastry, mix the flour, ground almonds and sugar in a food processor for 15 seconds. Add the butter and process for 15 seconds until crumbly. Add the egg yolk and enough water to make the dough just come together. Add more water if needed. Turn out onto a lightly floured surface and gather into a ball. Refrigerate for 15 minutes. Preheat the oven to 180°C (350°F/Gas 4) and heat a baking tray.

3 Roll out the pastry between two sheets of baking paper until large enough to line a lightly greased 23 cm (9 inch) loose-based flan (tart) tin, trimming away the excess. If the pastry is too soft, it may need to be refrigerated for another 10 minutes.

4 Cover the pastry with baking paper and spread with a layer of baking beads or rice. Chill for 15 minutes and then bake on the heated baking tray for 15 minutes.

Remove the beads and paper, reduce the oven to 160°C (315°F/Gas 2–3) and bake for another 5 minutes. Sprinkle the marzipan over the pastry base and bake for a further 5–10 minutes, or until golden. Leave in the tin to cool.

5 To make the custard cream, blend the custard powder with a little of the milk until smooth. Transfer to a saucepan and add the remaining milk, sour cream and sugar. Stir over medium heat for 5–7 minutes, or until thickened. Stir in the vanilla. (If you aren't using the custard cream immediately, lay plastic wrap on the surface to prevent a skin forming.)

6 Spread the warm custard cream evenly over the pastry pase. Arrange the prunes over the custard. Warm the redcurrant and muscat mixture and carefully spoon over the tart to cover it completely. Refrigerate for at least 2 hours to let the custard firm up before serving.

STORAGE: *This tart is best assembled on the same day as serving.*

NUTRITION PER SERVE (8)
Protein 7 g; Fat 25 g; Carbohydrate 60 g; Dietary Fibre 5 g; Cholesterol 88 mg; 2060 kJ (490 Cal)

Cook the prunes over low heat until they are tender but not mushy.

Add only enough iced water to make the dough come together.

Spread the warm custard cream evenly over the pastry base.

Low-fat banana and blueberry tart

PREPARATION TIME: 30 MINUTES | TOTAL COOKING TIME: 25 MINUTES | SERVES 6–8

125 g (4½ oz/1 cup) plain (all-purpose) flour
60 g (2¼ oz/½ cup) self-raising flour
1 teaspoon cinnamon
1 teaspoon ground ginger
40 g (1½ oz) unsalted butter, chilled and
    cubed
95 g (3¼ oz ½ cup) soft brown sugar
125 ml (4 fl oz/½ cup) buttermilk
200 g (7 oz/1¼ cups) blueberries
2 bananas
2 teaspoons lemon juice
1 tablespoon raw (demerara) sugar
icing (confectioner's) sugar, to serve

1 Preheat the oven to 200°C (400°F/Gas 6).
Lightly grease a baking tray or pizza tray. Sift the
flours and spices into a bowl. Add the butter and
sugar and rub in until the mixture resembles fine
breadcrumbs. Make a well in the centre and add
enough buttermilk to mix to a soft dough.

2 Roll the dough on a lightly floured surface
into a 23 cm (9 inch) circle. Place on the tray and
roll the edge into a lip to hold in the fruit.

3 Spread the blueberries over the dough. Slice
the bananas, toss them in the lemon juice, and
arrange over the top. Sprinkle with the sugar, and
bake for 25 minutes, until the base is browned.
Dust with icing sugar and serve immediately.

Rub the butter into the flour with your fingertips
until the mixture resembles fine breadcrumbs.

Put the circle of dough on the tray and roll the edge
to form a lip.

NUTRITION PER SERVE (6)
Protein 5 g; Fat 6 g; Carbohydrate 55 g; Dietary
Fibre 3 g; Cholesterol 20 mg; 1215 kJ (290 Cal)

Filo peach tartlets

PREPARATION TIME: 40 MINUTES | TOTAL COOKING TIME: 25 MINUTES | MAKES 8

6 sheets filo pastry
60 g (2¼ oz) unsalted butter, melted
90 g (3¼ oz/¾ cup) slivered almonds
1½ teaspoons ground cinnamon
90 g (3¼ oz/½ cup) soft brown sugar
185 ml (6 fl oz/¾ cup) orange juice, strained
4 peaches

1   Preheat the oven to 180°C (350°F/Gas 4). Cut each sheet of pastry into eight squares. Line eight large muffin holes with three layers of filo pastry, brushing between layers with melted butter and overlapping the sheets at angles.

2   Mix together the almonds, cinnamon and half the sugar. Sprinkle into the pastry cases, then cover with three final squares of filo brushed with butter. Bake for 10–15 minutes.

3   Meanwhile, dissolve the remaining sugar in the orange juice in a saucepan, bring to the boil, reduce the heat and simmer. Halve the peaches and slice thinly. Add to the syrup and stir gently to coat the fruit. Simmer for 2–3 minutes then lift from the pan with a slotted spoon. Arrange the peaches on the pastries and serve.

VARIATION: *You can use tinned peaches if fresh are not available.*

NUTRITION PER TARTLET
Protein 2 g; Fat 7 g; Carbohydrate 27 g; Dietary Fibre 1 g; Cholesterol 20 mg; 750 kJ (180 Cal)

Brush the filo squares with melted butter and use three to line each tin.

Sprinkle the combined almonds, cinnamon and half the sugar over the pastry bases.

Remove the peaches from the syrup with a slotted spoon.

Strawberry and mascarpone tart

PREPARATION TIME: 45 MINUTES + 45 MINUTES REFRIGERATION | TOTAL COOKING TIME: 35 MINUTES | SERVES 6

185 g (6½ oz/1½ cups) plain (all-purpose) flour
125 g (4½ oz) unsalted butter, chilled and cubed
80 ml (2½ fl oz/⅓ cup) iced water

FILLING
500 g (1 lb 2 oz) strawberries, hulled and halved
2 teaspoons vanilla essence
50 ml (1¾ fl oz) Drambuie (whiskey liqueur)
60 g (2¼ oz/⅓ cup) soft brown sugar
250 g (9 oz) mascarpone cheese
300 ml (10½ fl oz) whipping cream
2 teaspoons finely grated orange zest

NUTRITION PER SERVE
Protein 9.5 g; Fat 53 g; Carbohydrate 37 g; Dietary Fibre 3 g; Cholesterol 162 mg; 2729 kJ (652 Cal)

1   Sift the flour into a large bowl and rub the butter into the flour with your fingertips until it resembles fine breadcrumbs. Make a well in the centre, add almost all the water and mix with a flat-bladed knife, using a cutting action, until the mixture comes together in beads, adding the remaining water if needed. Gently gather the dough together and lift out onto a lightly floured surface.

2   Roll out the dough between two sheets of baking paper until large enough to line a lightly greased 23 cm (9 inch) loose-based flan (tart) tin. Trim away the excess pastry then refrigerate for 15 minutes. Preheat the oven to 200°C (400°F/Gas 6) and heat up a baking tray.

3   Line the pastry with baking paper and spread with a layer of baking beads or rice. Bake on the tray for 15 minutes. Remove the paper and beads and bake for 15–20 minutes, or until dry and golden. Cool completely.

4   Mix together the strawberries, vanilla, Drambuie and 1 tablespoon of the sugar in a bowl. In another bowl, mix the mascarpone, cream, orange zest and remaining sugar. Cover both bowls and refrigerate for 30 minutes, tossing the strawberries once or twice.

5   Whip two-thirds of the mascarpone mixture until firm, then evenly spoon it into the tart shell. Drain the strawberries, reserving the liquid. Pile the strawberries onto the tart. Serve slices of tart with a drizzle of the reserved strawberry liquid and the remaining mascarpone mixture.

Mix the flour, butter and water with a flat-bladed knife until the dough comes together in beads.

Remove the paper and baking beads from the pastry shell.

Portuguese custard tarts

PREPARATION TIME: 40 MINUTES | TOTAL COOKING TIME: 40 MINUTES | MAKES 12

150 g (5½ oz/1¼ cups) plain (all-purpose)
  flour
25 g (1 oz) white vegetable shortening,
  softened
30 g (1 oz) unsalted butter, softened
250 g (9 oz/1 cup) sugar
500 ml (17 fl oz/2 cups) milk
3 tablespoons cornflour (cornstarch)
1 tablespoon custard powder
4 egg yolks
1 teaspoon vanilla essence

1 Sift the flour into a large bowl and add about
185 ml (6 fl oz/¾ cup) water, or enough to form
a soft dough. Gather together, then roll out on
baking paper into a 24 x 30 cm (9½ x 12 inch)
rectangle. Spread with the vegetable shortening.
Roll up from the short edge to form a log.

2 Roll the dough out into a rectangle once
again, and spread with the butter. Roll up into a
log and slice into 12 even-sized pieces. Working
from the centre, use your fingertips to press out
each round until large enough to line twelve
80 ml (2½ fl oz/⅓ cup) muffin holes.
Refrigerate tins.

3 Put the sugar and 80 ml (2½ fl oz/⅓ cup)
water in a saucepan and stir over low heat until
the sugar dissolves.

4 Mix a little of the milk with the cornflour
and custard powder to form a smooth paste, and
add to the sugar syrup with the remaining milk,
egg yolks and vanilla. Stir over low heat until
thickened. Place in a bowl, then cover and cool.

5 Preheat the oven to 220°C (425°F/Gas 7).
Divide the filling among the bases and bake for
25–30 minutes, or until the custard is set and
the tops have browned. Cool in the tins, then
transfer to a wire rack.

Slice the roll of dough into 12 even-sized pieces
with a sharp knife.

With your fingertips press each round out to a
circle and press into the tin.

NUTRITION PER TART
Protein 3.5 g; Fat 7 g; Carbohydrate 35 g; Dietary
Fibre 0.5 g; Cholesterol 75 mg; 892 kJ (215 Cal)

Lime and blueberry tart

PREPARATION TIME: 30 MINUTES + 20 MINUTES REFRIGERATION | TOTAL COOKING TIME: 1 HOUR | SERVES 8

375 g (13 oz) sweet shortcrust pastry
3 eggs
125 g (4½ oz/½ cup) caster (superfine) sugar
60 ml (2 fl oz/¼ cup) buttermilk
1 tablespoon lime juice
2 teaspoons finely grated lime zest
2 tablespoons custard powder
250 g (9 oz) blueberries
icing (confectioner's) sugar, to serve

1 Roll out the pastry between two sheets of baking paper to line a 23 cm (9 inch) pie tin, trimming away the excess pastry. Refrigerate for 20 minutes. Preheat the oven to 200°C (400°F/Gas 6).

2 Line the pastry with baking paper and spread with baking beads or rice. Bake for 10 minutes, remove the paper and beads and bake for 4–5 minutes, until the pastry is dry. Cool slightly. Reduce the oven to 180°C (350°F/Gas 4).

3 To make the filling, beat the eggs and sugar with electric beaters until thick and pale. Add the buttermilk, lime juice and zest, and sifted custard powder. Stir together, then spoon into the pastry shell. Bake for 15 minutes, then reduce the oven to 160°C (315°F/Gas 2–3) and cook for another 20–25 minutes, or until the filling has coloured slightly and is set. Leave to cool (it will sink a little), then top with the blueberries. Serve sprinkled with icing sugar.

Bake the pastry, then remove the paper and beads and bake for another 5 minutes.

Stir the buttermilk, lime juice and zest and custard powder into the egg mixture.

NUTRITION PER SERVE
Protein 5.5 g; Fat 14 g; Carbohydrate 38.5 g; Dietary Fibre 1 g; Cholesterol 81.5 mg; 1240 kJ (295 Cal)

Passionfruit tart

PREPARATION TIME: 30 MINUTES + 20 MINUTES REFRIGERATION | TOTAL COOKING TIME: 45 MINUTES | SERVES 8

125 g (4½ oz/1 cup) plain (all-purpose) flour
45 g (1½ oz/¼ cup) ground almonds
60 g (2¼ oz/¼ cup) caster (superfine) sugar
60 g (2¼ oz) unsalted butter, chilled and cubed
2–3 tablespoons iced water

FILLING
6 egg yolks
125 g (4½ oz/½ cup) caster (superfine) sugar
185 g (6½ oz/¾ cup) fresh passionfruit pulp
75 g (2½ oz) unsalted butter
1½ teaspoons gelatine
125 ml (4 fl oz/½ cup) whipping cream

1   Preheat the oven to 180°C (350°F/Gas 4). Mix the flour, ground almonds, sugar and butter in a food processor for 30 seconds or until fine and crumbly. Add almost all the water and process for another 30 seconds or until the dough just comes together (add more water if necessary). Turn out onto a lightly floured surface and press together into a smooth ball.

2   Roll out the pastry to fit a 23 cm (9 inch) fluted flan (tart) tin, trimming away the excess. Refrigerate for 20 minutes. Cover with baking paper and spread with a layer of baking beads or rice. Bake for 15 minutes, then discard the paper and beads. Bake for another 15 minutes, or until the pastry is lightly golden and dry. Cool completely.

3   Whisk the yolks and sugar in a heatproof bowl for 1 minute or until slightly thickened and pale. Stir in the passionfruit pulp. Stand the bowl over a pan of simmering water and stir gently but constantly for 15 minutes, adding the butter gradually until the mixture thickens. Remove from the heat and cool slightly.

4   Put the gelatine in a small bowl with 1 tablespoon water. Leave until spongy, then stir until dissolved. Stir thoroughly into the passionfruit filling. Cool to room temperature, stirring occasionally. Fold in the whipped cream. Spread into the pastry shell and smooth the surface. Keep chilled until ready to serve.

STORAGE: *Keep the tart refrigerated until you are ready to serve.*

NUTRITION PER SERVE
Protein 7 g; Fat 40 g; Carbohydrate 40 g; Dietary Fibre 3 g; Cholesterol 240 mg; 2257 kJ (540 Cal)

Add almost all the iced water and mix until the dough just starts to come together.

Whisk the egg yolks and sugar until thickened and pale, then stir in the passionfruit pulp.

Dissolve the gelatine in a little water and then stir into the passionfruit filling.

Low-fat fruit tarts

PREPARATION TIME: 25 MINUTES + 30 MINUTES REFRIGERATION | TOTAL COOKING TIME: 20 MINUTES | MAKES 6

125 g (4½ oz/1 cup) plain (all-purpose) flour
30 g (1 oz/¼ cup) custard powder
30 g (1 oz/¼ cup) icing sugar
40 g (1½ oz) unsalted butter
2 tablespoons skim milk
2 x 125 g (4½ oz) tubs low-fat fromage frais
100 g (3½ oz) ricotta cheese
strawberries, hulled and halved; blueberries;
    and kiwi fruit, peeled and sliced
3–4 tablespoons redcurrant jelly

1 Lightly grease six 7 cm (2¾ inch) shallow
loose-based flan (tart) tins. Process the flour,
custard powder, icing sugar and butter in a food
processor until the mixture forms fine crumbs,
then add enough skim milk to form a soft dough.
Gather the dough together into a ball, wrap
in plastic wrap and refrigerate for 30 minutes.
Preheat the oven to 200°C (400°F/Gas 6).

2 Divide the dough into six portions and roll
out to fit the tins. Cover with baking paper and
spread with a layer of baking beads or rice. Bake
for 10 minutes, remove the paper and beads and
bake for another 10 minutes, or until golden.
Allow to cool before removing from the tins.

3 Mix the fromage frais and ricotta until
smooth. Spread over the pastry bases and top
with the fruit. Heat the redcurrant jelly until
liquid in a small saucepan and brush over
the fruit.

Cover the pastry with baking paper and fill with a
layer of baking beads or uncooked rice.

Remove the rice or beads and paper and return the
pastry to the oven until golden.

NUTRITION PER TART
Protein 3.5 g; Fat 8 g; Carbohydrate 20 g; Dietary
Fibre 1 g; Cholesterol 20 mg; 690 kJ (165 Cal)

Golden pine nut tarts

PREPARATION TIME: 25 MINUTES | TOTAL COOKING TIME: 20 MINUTES | MAKES 24

60 g (2¼ oz/½ cup) plain (all-purpose) flour
60 g (2¼ oz) unsalted butter, chilled and
    cubed
3 tablespoons pine nuts
20 g (¾ oz) unsalted butter, melted
180 g (6¼ oz/½ cup) golden syrup (if
    unavailable, substitute with half honey and
    half dark corn syrup)
2 tablespoons brown sugar

1 Preheat the oven to 180°C (350°F/Gas 4) and brush two 12-hole patty pans or mini muffin tins with melted butter.

2 Mix the flour and butter in a food processor for 20–30 seconds or until the mixture comes together. Turn out onto a lightly floured surface and press into a smooth ball. Roll out to a thickness of 3 mm (⅛ inch). Cut out rounds with a 5 cm (2 inch) fluted scone cutter. Lift rounds gently with a flat-bladed knife and line each muffin hole. Spread the pine nuts on a baking tray and toast in the oven for 1–2 minutes, until just golden. Cool a little, then divide among the pastry cases.

3 Whisk together the melted butter, syrup and sugar. Pour over the pine nuts. Bake for 15 minutes, until golden. Leave the tarts in the trays for 5 minutes before cooling on a wire rack.

NUTRITION PER TART
Protein 0.5 g; Fat 4 g; Carbohydrate 9 g; Dietary
Fibre 0 g; Cholesterol 9 mg; 297 kJ (71 Cal)

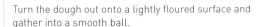
Turn the dough out onto a lightly floured surface and gather into a smooth ball.

Toast the pine nuts until lightly golden and then divide among the pastry cases.

Whisk together the butter, syrup and sugar and pour over the pine nuts.

Raspberry shortcake

PREPARATION TIME: 30 MINUTES + 50 MINUTES REFRIGERATION | TOTAL COOKING TIME: 25 MINUTES | SERVES 8

125 g (4½ oz/1 cup) plain (all-purpose) flour
4 tablespoons icing sugar
90 g (3¼ oz) unsalted butter, chilled and cubed
1 egg yolk
½ teaspoon vanilla essence

TOPPING
750 g (1 lb 10 oz) fresh raspberries
3–4 tablespoons icing sugar, to taste
4 tablespoons redcurrant jelly

NUTRITION PER SERVE (8)
Protein 4 g; Fat 10 g; Carbohydrate 34 g; Dietary
Fibre 6 g; Cholesterol 50 mg; 1026 kJ (245 Cal)

1 Put the flour and icing sugar in a food processor. Add the butter and process for 15 seconds, or until the mixture is crumbly. Process for 10 seconds, adding the egg yolk, vanilla and enough cold water (about ½–1 tablespoon) to make the dough just come together. Turn out onto a lightly floured surface and gather together into a ball. Wrap in plastic wrap and refrigerate for 30 minutes.

2 Preheat the oven to 180°C (350°F/Gas 4). Roll out the pastry to fit a fluted 20 cm (8 inch) loose-based flan (tart) tin and trim the edges. Prick all over with a fork and chill for 20 minutes. Bake for 15–20 minutes, or until golden. Cool on a wire rack.

3 To make the topping, set aside 500 g (1 lb 2 oz) of the best raspberries and mash the rest with the icing sugar. Spread the mashed raspberries over the shortcake just before serving. Cover with the whole raspberries.

4 Heat the redcurrant jelly until liquid in a small saucepan and brush over the raspberries with a soft brush. Slice and serve.

VARIATION: *You can use 800 g (1 lb 12 oz) frozen raspberries. Thaw in the packet overnight in the fridge and only use when ready to serve.*

Remove any excess pastry by rolling across the top of the tin.

Mash the icing sugar into the raspberries to make the filling.

Use a soft pastry brush to heavily coat the raspberries with warm glaze.

Pear and almond flan

PREPARATION TIME: 15 MINUTES + 2 HOURS 30 MINUTES REFRIGERATION | TOTAL COOKING TIME: 1 HOUR 10 MINUTES | SERVES 8

150 g (5 oz/1¼ cups) plain (all-purpose) flour
90 g (3¼ oz) butter, chilled and cubed
60 g (2¼ oz/¼ cup) caster (superfine) sugar
2 egg yolks
1 tablespoon iced water

FILLING
165 g (5¾ oz) unsalted butter, softened
160 g (5¾ oz/⅔ cup) caster (superfine) sugar
3 eggs
230 g (8¼ oz/2¼ cups) ground almonds
1½ tablespoons plain (all-purpose) flour
2 ripe pears

1 Grease a shallow 24 cm (9½ inch) loose-based flan (tart) tin. Place the flour, butter and sugar in a food processor and process until the mixture resembles breadcrumbs. Add the egg yolks and water and mix until the dough just comes together. Turn out onto a lightly floured surface and gather into a ball. Wrap in plastic wrap and refrigerate for 30 minutes. Preheat the oven to 180°C (350°F/Gas 4).

2 Roll the pastry between baking paper until large enough to line the tin, trimming any excess. Sparsely prick the base with a fork. Line with baking paper and a layer of baking beads or rice and bake for 10 minutes. Remove the paper and beads and bake for another 10 minutes.

3 Mix the butter and sugar with electric beaters for 30 seconds (do not cream the mixture). Add the eggs one at a time, beating after each addition. Fold in the ground almonds and flour and spread smoothly over the cooled pastry base.

4 Peel and halve the pears lengthways and remove the cores. Cut them crossways into 3 mm (⅛ inch) slices. Separate the slices slightly, then place each half on top of the tart to form a cross. Bake for 50 minutes, or until the filling has set (the middle may still be soft). Cool in the tin and refrigerate for at least 2 hours before serving.

Fold in the ground almonds and flour and mix until well combined.

Halve each pear lengthways and carefully remove the core.

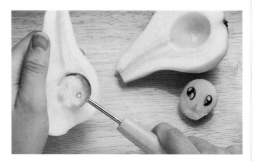

NUTRITION PER SERVE
Protein 7 g; Fat 30 g; Carbohydrate 48 g; Dietary Fibre 2 g; Cholesterol 165 mg; 2085 kJ (500 Cal)

Chocolate tarts

PREPARATION TIME: 30 MINUTES + 20 MINUTES REFRIGERATION | TOTAL COOKING TIME: 15 MINUTES | MAKES 24

250 g (9 oz/2 cups) plain (all-purpose) flour
2 tablespoons custard powder
125 g (4½ oz) unsalted butter, chilled and
    cubed
1 egg yolk
2–3 tablespoons iced water

FILLING
250 g (9 oz/1 cup) cream cheese, at room
    temperature
125 g (4½ oz/½ cup) caster (superfine) sugar
1 egg
125 g (4½ oz) dark chocolate, melted
3 tablespoons ground almonds
100 g (3½ oz) white chocolate, melted

1 Preheat the oven to 180°C (350°F/ Gas 4).
Lightly grease two 12-cup shallow patty pans or
mini muffin tins. Mix the flour, custard powder
and butter in a food processor for 30 seconds,
or until fine and crumbly. Add the egg yolk and
almost all of the water and process for
20 seconds or until the mixture just comes
together, adding the rest of the water if necessary.
Turn out onto a lightly floured surface and gather
into a smooth ball. Wrap in plastic wrap and
refrigerate for 20 minutes.

2 Divide the dough in half, re-wrap one portion
and set aside. Roll the other half between two
sheets of baking paper until 3 mm (⅛ inch) thick.
Cut out rounds with a 7 cm (2¾ inch) fluted
cutter to line the tins. Repeat with the other
portion of pastry. Refrigerate both trays while
preparing the filling.

3 Beat the cream cheese and sugar until light
and creamy. Add the egg and cooled melted dark
chocolate. Beat until there are no streaks visible.
Stir in the ground almonds. Spoon the mixture
into the pastry cases and bake for 15 minutes, or
until just beginning to firm (the filling will set on
standing.) Cool on a wire rack. Drizzle with the
melted white chocolate and leave to set.

NUTRITION PER TART
Protein 3 g; Fat 12 g; Carbohydrate 20 g; Dietary
Fibre 1 g; Cholesterol 40 mg; 827 kJ (200 Cal)

Cut out pastry rounds with a fluted pastry cutter and use to line the patty pans.

Spoon the chocolate filling into the pastry bases and then bake until just firm.

Date and mascarpone tart

PREPARATION TIME: 50 MINUTES + 25 MINUTES REFRIGERATION | TOTAL COOKING TIME: 45 MINUTES | SERVES 6–8

90 g (3¼ oz/½ cup) rice flour
60 g (2¼ oz/½ cup) plain (all-purpose) flour
2 tablespoons icing sugar
25 g (1 oz/¼ cup) desiccated coconut
100 g (3½ oz) marzipan, chopped
100 g (3½ oz) unsalted butter, chilled and
    cubed

FILLING
200 g (7 oz) fresh dates, stones removed
2 eggs
2 teaspoons custard powder
125 g (4 oz) mascarpone cheese
2 tablespoons caster (superfine) sugar
80 ml (2½ fl oz/⅓ cup) cream
2 tablespoons flaked almonds
icing (confectioner's) sugar, to serve

NUTRITION PER SERVE (8)
Protein 7 g; Fat 27 g; Carbohydrate 50 g; Dietary
Fibre 4 g; Cholesterol 106 mg; 1890 kJ (450 Cal)

1 Preheat the oven to 180°C (350°F/Gas 4) and grease a shallow 35 x 10 cm (14 x 4 inch) fluted loose-based flan (tart) tin.

2 Mix the flours, icing sugar, coconut and marzipan in a food processor for 10 seconds. Add the butter and mix for 10–20 seconds, or until the dough just comes together when squeezed. (Do not over-process.) Turn out onto a lightly floured surface and gather into a ball. Wrap in plastic and refrigerate for 15 minutes.

3 Cut the dates into quarters lengthways. Roll out the pastry between two sheets of baking paper until large enough to line the tin, trimming away the excess. Refrigerate for another 5–10 minutes. Cover the pastry-lined tin with baking paper and spread with a layer of baking beads or rice. Place the tin on an oven tray and bake for 10 minutes. Remove from the oven and discard the paper and beads. Return to the oven and bake for another 5 minutes or until just golden. Leave to cool.

4 Arrange the dates over the pastry base. Whisk together the eggs, custard powder, mascarpone, sugar and cream until smooth. Pour over the dates and sprinkle with flaked almonds. Bake for 25–30 minutes, or until golden and just set. Dust with icing sugar and serve immediately, while still hot from the oven.

Process the mixture until the dough will just come together when squeezed.

Ease the pastry into the tin and then trim away the excess with a knife or rolling pin.

Arrange the dates in the pastry case and then pour the custard filling over the top.

Little lemon tarts

PREPARATION TIME: 40 MINUTES + 10 MINUTES REFRIGERATION I TOTAL COOKING TIME: 20 MINUTES I MAKES 24

250 g (9 oz/2 cups) plain (all-purpose) flour
125 g (4 oz) unsalted butter, chilled and cubed
2 teaspoons caster (superfine) sugar
1 teaspoon finely grated lemon zest
1 egg yolk
2–3 tablespoons iced water

FILLING
125 g (4½ oz/½ cup) cream cheese, softened
125 g (4½ oz/½ cup) caster (superfine) sugar
2 egg yolks
2 tablespoons lemon juice
125 ml (4 fl oz/½ cup sweetened condensed milk
icing (confectioner's) sugar, for dusting

1 Preheat the oven to 180°C (350°F/Gas 4) and lightly oil two 12-hole patty pans or mini muffin tins.

2 Sift the flour into a bowl. Rub in the butter until the mixture resembles fine breadcrumbs. Add the sugar, lemon zest, egg yolk and water and mix with a flat-bladed knife, using a cutting action, until the mixture forms beads. Turn out onto a lightly floured surface and gently gather into a smooth ball. Wrap in plastic wrap and refrigerate for 10 minutes.

3 Beat the cream cheese, sugar and egg yolks until smooth and thickened. Add the lemon juice and condensed milk and beat together well.

4 Roll out the dough between two sheets of baking paper to 3 mm (⅛ inch) thick. Cut into rounds with a 7 cm (2¾ inch) fluted cutter and line the patty pans. Lightly prick each base several times with a fork and bake for 10 minutes, or until just starting to turn golden. Spoon 2 teaspoons of filling into each case and bake for another 8–10 minutes, or until the filling has set. Cool slightly before removing from the tins. Dust with the icing sugar to serve.

Rub the butter into the flour with your fingertips until the mixture resembles fine breadcrumbs.

Lightly prick each pastry case three times with a fork to prevent the pastry rising.

NUTRITION PER TART
Protein 3 g; Fat 7 g; Carbohydrate 18 g; Dietary Fibre 0.5 g; Cholesterol 41 mg; 611 kJ (146 Cal)

Orange macadamia tarts

PREPARATION TIME: 40 MINUTES + 15 MINUTES REFRIGERATION | TOTAL COOKING TIME: 55 MINUTES | MAKES 6

185 g (6½ oz/1½ cups) plain (all-purpose)
   flour
100 g (3½ oz) unsalted butter
3–4 tablespoons iced water

FILLING
240 g (8 oz/1½ cups) macadamia nuts
3 tablespoons brown sugar
2 tablespoons light corn syrup
20 g (¾ oz) unsalted butter, melted
1 egg, lightly beaten
2 teaspoons finely grated orange zest
icing (confectioner's) sugar, to serve

1   Preheat the oven to 180°C (350°F/Gas 4).
Spread the nuts on an oven tray and bake for
8 minutes, or until lightly golden. Leave to cool.

2   Mix the flour and butter in a food processor
for 15 seconds, or until fine and crumbly. Add
almost all the water and process briefly until the
dough just comes together, adding more water if
necessary. Turn out onto a lightly floured surface
and press together into a smooth ball. Divide
into six portions and roll out to line six 8 cm
(3¼ inch) fluted flan (tart) tins. Refrigerate the
lined tins for 15 minutes.

3   Line the tins with baking paper and spread
with a layer of baking beads or rice. Bake for
15 minutes, then discard the paper and beads.
Bake for another 10 minutes, or until the pastry
is dry and lightly golden. Cool completely.

4   Divide the nuts among the tarts. Use a wire
whisk to beat together the sugar, corn syrup,
butter, egg, orange zest and a pinch of salt. Pour
over the nuts and bake for 20 minutes, until set
and lightly browned. Sprinkle with icing sugar to
serve.

NUTRITION PER TART
Protein 7 g; Fat 43 g; Carbohydrate 40 g; Dietary
Fibre 3 g; Cholesterol 80 mg; 2360 kJ (560 Cal)

Spread the macadamia nuts on an oven tray and roast until lightly golden.

Divide the nuts among the pastry cases and then pour the filling over the top.

Summer berry tart

PREPARATION TIME: 35 MINUTES + 20 MINUTES REFRIGERATION I TOTAL COOKING TIME: 35 MINUTES I SERVES 4–6

125 g (4½ oz/1 cup) plain (all-purpose) flour
90 g (3 oz) unsalted butter, chilled and cubed
2 tablespoons icing sugar
1–2 tablespoons iced water

FILLING
3 egg yolks
2 tablespoons caster (superfine) sugar
2 tablespoons cornflour (cornstarch)
250 ml (9 oz/1 cup) milk
1 teaspoon vanilla essence
250 g (9 oz) strawberries, hulled and halved
125 g (4½ oz) blueberries
125 g (4½ oz) raspberries
1–2 tablespoons redcurrant jelly

1 Mix the flour, butter and icing sugar in a food processor for 15 seconds, or until fine and crumbly. Add enough of the water to make the dough just come together. Turn onto a lightly floured surface and shape into a ball. Roll out to line a 20 cm (8 inch) fluted flan (tart) tin, trimming away the excess. Refrigerate for 20 minutes. Preheat oven to 180°C (350°F/Gas 4).

2 Line the tin with baking paper and a layer of baking beads or rice and bake for 15 minutes. Remove the paper and beads and bake for another 15 minutes, until dry and lightly golden.

3 Whisk the egg yolks, sugar and cornflour until pale. Heat the milk in a small pan to almost boiling, then pour gradually into the egg mixture, beating constantly. Strain back into the pan. Stir over low heat for 3 minutes or until the custard boils and thickens. Remove from the heat and add the vanilla. Transfer to a bowl, lay plastic wrap directly on the surface to prevent a skin forming, and leave to cool.

4 Spread the custard in the pastry shell and top with the strawberries, blueberries and raspberries. Heat the redcurrant jelly until liquid and brush over the fruit.

Press plastic wrap onto the surface of the custard to prevent a skin forming.

Warm the redcurrant jelly in a small saucepan until it is liquid and brush over the fruit.

NUTRITION PER SERVE (6)
Protein 6 g; Fat 17 g; Carbohydrate 36 g; Dietary Fibre 2 g; Cholesterol 133 mg; 1317 kJ (315 Cal)

Low-fat passionfruit tart

PREPARATION TIME: 25 MINUTES + 30 MINUTES REFRIGERATION | TOTAL COOKING TIME: 1 HOUR | SERVES 8

90 g (3¼ oz/¾ cup) plain (all-purpose) flour
2 tablespoons icing sugar
2 tablespoons custard powder
30 g (1 oz) unsalted butter, chilled and cubed
3 tablespoons light evaporated milk

FILLING
125 g (4½ oz/½ cup) ricotta cheese
1 teaspoon vanilla essence
30 g (1 oz/¼ cup) icing sugar
2 eggs, lightly beaten
4 tablespoons passionfruit pulp (about
    8 passionfruit)
185 ml (6 fl oz/¾ cup) light evaporated milk
icing (confectioner's) sugar, to serve

1   Preheat the oven to 200°C (400°F/Gas 6) and lightly grease a 23 cm (9 inch) loose-based flan (tart) tin.

2   Sift the flour, icing sugar and custard powder into a bowl and rub in the butter until the mixture resembles fine breadcrumbs. Add enough evaporated milk to form a soft dough. Bring together on a lightly floured surface until just smooth. Gather into a ball, wrap in plastic wrap and refrigerate for 15 minutes.

3   Roll the pastry out on a floured surface, to fit the tin, and trim the excess. Refrigerate for 15 minutes. Cover with baking paper and a layer of baking beads or rice. Bake for 10 minutes, remove the beads and paper and bake for another 5–8 minutes, until golden. Allow to cool. Reduce the oven to 160°C (315°F/Gas 2–3).

4   Beat the ricotta cheese with the vanilla and icing sugar until smooth. Add the egg, passionfruit pulp and evaporated milk, and beat well. Put the tin on a baking tray and gently pour in the mixture. Bake for 40 minutes, or until set. Allow to cool in the tin. Dust with icing sugar to serve.

NUTRITION PER SERVE
Protein 8 g; Fat 6.5 g; Carbohydrate 25 g; Dietary Fibre 3 g; Cholesterol 65 mg; 750 kJ (180 Cal)

When the ricotta mixture is smooth, add the eggs, passionfruit pulp and milk.

Put the tin on a baking tray to catch any drips and gently pour in the filling.

Basics

Perfect pastry

What does 'rub in the butter' mean? How do you 'line the tin with pastry'? Why are some pastry cases baked blind before they are filled? These are some of the questions that can vex newcomers to pastry-making. Take a little time to read the following hints and all will be clear.

Which pastry?

For most of the recipes in this book, you can make your own pastry or buy ready-made. If we specify a home-made pastry it is because the taste is better in that particular pie. We have used only a few types of pastry throughout this book. Beginners should probably choose recipes using the easiest pastries, such as shortcrust or quick flaky. Puff pastry requires a lot more rolling and chilling and is a little less predictable when baked. Instead of, or as well as, butter, some pastries use olive oil and others lard. Some shortcrusts have sugar or an egg added—you could use bought shortcrust, but the pastry won't be quite as rich. Plain shortcrust can be used for sweet pies but sweet pastry is most commonly used.

Ingredients

Pastry at its simplest is flour mixed with half its weight in some form of fat, then bound with water.

Flour Plain white (all-purpose) flour is the one most commonly used for pastry. For a slightly different texture, a combination of wholemeal (whole-wheat) plain and plain white flour can be used. Store your flour in an airtight container.

Fat Butter is the most commonly used fat for making pastry and gives a wonderful colour to the pastry. Use real butter, not margarine or softened butter blends. Sometimes a mixture of butter and lard is used, sometimes all lard. Lard gives a good flaky texture. Butter and lard are usually chilled and cut into cubes to make it easier to incorporate them into the flour, keeping the pastry cooler and more manageable. Generally, unsalted butter should be used for sweet and salted butter for savoury recipes. Olive oil is sometimes used to give pastries a different texture, for example in a traditional spinach pie.

Salt Salt can be added to both sweet and savoury pastry to add flavour.

Sugar Caster (superfine) sugar is used in sweet shortcrust pastry as its fine texture ensures that it blends well.

Liquid The usual binding liquid in pastry-making is iced water, but sometimes an egg or an egg yolk will be used to enrich the dough. You will find that most pastry recipes only give an approximate liquid measure because the amount will vary according to the flour, the temperature, the altitude and the humidity. Add a little at a time and work it in until the pastry 'starts to come together' in clumps that can then be pressed together.

Tools of the trade

Food processor While not essential, a food processor can make pastry-making easy. Pastry should be kept cool and a processor means you don't need to touch the dough as you mix. If you prefer, you can use the processor just to combine the butter and flour before continuing to mix by hand.

Marble pastry board Although not strictly necessary, marble boards are favoured by pastry-makers for their cool and hygienic surface. If you don't have one, place a roasting tin full of iced water on your work surface for a while to cool the surface before rolling your pastry.

Rolling pins An essential tool in pastry-making. They are now available in traditional wood, marble, plastic and stainless steel. Lightly sprinkle your rolling pin with flour to prevent the pastry sticking. You can also use the rolling pin to lift the pastry into the tin and then trim away the excess pastry by rolling over the top.

Baking paper Very useful when rolling out pastry. The dough is rolled out between two sheets of paper, the top sheet is removed and the pastry is inverted into the tin before removing the other sheet. A crumpled sheet of baking paper is also used to line pastry shells when blind baking.

Baking beads Reusable baking beads are spread in a layer over baking paper to weigh down pastry during blind baking. They are available in kitchenware shops and department stores. Dried beans or uncooked rice can also be used and stored in a jar for re-use.

Cutters Available in all shapes and sizes. They are used to cut bases and tops for small pies and to cut out pieces of dough to decorate pies. Cutters may need to be dusted lightly with flour to prevent them from sticking to the pastry. If you don't have a pastry cutter, a fine-rimmed glass, turned upside down, is a good substitute.

Pie tins and dishes Available in many styles. While testing the pies for this book we baked with metal, glass and ceramic pie dishes. We found the crispest base crusts were achieved in the metal tins.

Pastry brushes Used for glazing. A glaze gives the pastry crispness and colour. Pastry can also be sealed and joined by brushing the edges with milk or beaten egg. Use only a small amount of liquid or your pastry may become soggy.

Pastry-makers' tips

1 Dough must be kept cool. Work in a cool kitchen if possible. If you are baking in summer, chill your work surface by leaving a tin of iced water on it before you start rolling or shaping. Make sure all the ingredients are as cool as possible and that they stay cool during the preparation.

2 Because your hands are warm, try to handle the pastry as little as possible. Cool your hands under cold water. Good pastry-makers work quickly—too much handling will cause the cooked pastry to toughen and shrink.

3 Flours vary in their moisture content. Because of this variation, the liquid (usually iced water) is not added all at once. Test the dough by pinching a little piece together. If it holds together and doesn't crumble, you don't need more liquid. If the pastry is too dry, it will be difficult to put into tins; if too wet it will shrink when cooked.

4 Pastry should be wrapped in plastic wrap and put in the fridge for 20–30 minutes before rolling or shaping. In hot weather, refrigerate the pastry for at least 30 minutes.

5 For ease of rolling, roll out dough between two sheets of baking paper.

6 Pies with a bottom crust benefit from being cooked on a heated metal baking tray. Put the tray in the oven as the oven warms up.

7 Pastry can be stored in the fridge for 2 days or frozen for up to 3 months. Ensure that it is well sealed in plastic wrap and clearly labelled and dated. Thaw on a wire rack to let the air circulate.

8 Pastry should always be cooked in a preheated oven, never one that is still warming up. It is a good idea to use an oven thermometer.

9 Pies can be frozen as long as the filling is suitable (don't freeze creamy, egg fillings) and the pastry has not already been frozen. For best results, a frozen pie should be reheated in a slow oven.

10 To test if a pie is cooked, poke a metal skewer into the centre. If the skewer comes out cold, the pie needs to be baked for longer.

Ready-made pastry

For busy cooks, there is a large range of ready-made frozen or refrigerated pastries available at supermarkets. Standard puff and shortcrust pastries are available in blocks, and puff, butter puff and shortcrust pastries also come as ready-rolled sheets. The recipe will simply say '2 sheets puff pastry' or '250 g shortcrust pastry' and these should be thawed. Thaw frozen block pastry for 2 hours before using. Sheets take only 5–10 minutes to thaw at room temperature.

Lining the tin

Roll out the dough between two sheets of baking paper, or on a lightly floured surface. Always roll from the centre outwards, rotating the dough, rather than rolling backwards and forwards. Reduce the pressure towards the edges of the dough. If you used baking paper, remove the top sheet and invert the pastry over the tin, then peel away the other sheet. Centre the pastry as it can't be moved once in place. Quickly lift up the sides so they don't break over the edges of the tin. Use a small ball of dough to press the pastry into the side of the tin. Trim away the excess pastry with a small, sharp knife or by rolling the rolling pin over the top. However gently you handle the dough it is bound to shrink slightly, so let it sit a little higher above the side of the tin. Chill the pastry in the tin for 20 minutes to relax it and minimise shrinkage.

Blind baking

If a pie or tart is to have a liquid filling, the pastry usually requires blind baking to partially cook it before filling. This prevents the base becoming soggy.

When blind baking, the pastry needs to be weighted down to prevent it rising. Cover the base and side with a crumpled piece of baking paper or greaseproof paper. Pour in a layer of baking beads (also called pie weights), dried beans or uncooked rice and spread out over the paper to cover the pastry base. Bake for the recommended time (usually about 10 minutes), then remove the paper and beads. The beads are re-usable and dried beans or rice can also be kept in a separate jar for re-use for blind baking (but they are not now suitable for eating). Return the pastry to the oven for 10–15 minutes, or as specified in the recipe, until the base is dry with no greasy patches. Let the pastry cool completely.

The filling should also be completely cooled before filling the shell—filling a cold shell with a hot mixture can also cause the pastry to become soggy.

Index

Index

Published by Bay Books, an imprint of Murdoch Books Pty Limited.

Murdoch Books Australia
Pier 8/9, 23 Hickson Road
Millers Point NSW 2000
Phone: + 61 (0) 2 8220 2000
Fax: + 61 (0) 2 8220 2558
www.murdochbooks.com.au

Chief Executive: Juliet Rogers
Publishing Director: Kay Scarlett

Project manager: Kristin Buesing
Editor: Glenda Downing
Design concept: Heather Menzies
Design: Heather Menzies and Jacqueline Richards
Photographer: Valerie Martin
Stylist: Mary Harris
Food preparation: Jo Glynn
Introduction text: Leanne Kitchen
Production: Liz Malcolm

National Library of Australia Cataloguing-in-Publication Data
Homestyle Pies and Tarts. Includes index.
ISBN 978 1 74196 164 5 (pbk).
Pies. Pastry. 641.865

A catalogue record for this book is available from the British Library.

Colour separation by Splitting Image in Clayton, Victoria, Australia.
Printed by i-Book Printing Ltd. in 2009. PRINTED IN CHINA.

IMPORTANT: Those who might be at risk from the effects of salmonella poisoning
(the elderly, pregnant women, young children and those suffering from immune deficiency diseases)
should consult their doctor with any concerns about eating raw eggs.

CONVERSION GUIDE: You may find cooking times vary depending on the oven
you are using. For fan-forced ovens, as a general rule, set the oven temperature
to 20°C (35°F) lower than indicated in the recipe.